Anyone who's seen Tim Seelig the soul of a musician, the sass standup comic. You'll find all c heart-breaking memoir about one man's journey towards the light.

Armistead Maupin
Best-selling author of *Tales of the City* series

No life is easy, and Tim Seelig's amazing life has had more than its share of vicissitudes and tragedies, as well as triumphs. All are recounted here with humor and insight. Tim is someone I feel fortunate to know and proud to have worked with."

Stephen Schwartz
Broadway composer

Tim Seelig reminds us, in this heartfelt book, that it's never too late to be who you are. He reminds us that in this discovery there is only the truth of real happiness. As Tim discovers who he is, we begin to celebrate who we truly are.

Sheila Nevins
MTV Documentaries

This book is funny because Tim is funny. It's interesting because Tim is interesting. But what surprises, much like Tim himself, is how quickly it grabs your heart. He turns words into music, music into memory, and memoir into magic. Simply put: I was deeply moved.

Andrew Lippa
Broadway Composer

Tim Seelig has written an inspiring, sometimes heartbreaking and often very funny account of his remarkable journey from conservative Texas Baptist roots to visionary artist and leader of the LGBTQ community. Spanning seven decades, his story is a powerful account of personal struggle, complicated love and spiritual liberation.

Cleve Jones
Author, *When We Rise: My Life in the Movement*, and AIDS activist

OMG! This book is a must read. Tim is not only an incredible man, but his story is one that speaks to many of us who have lived his life, well, similar lives. Tim offers hope and insight to us all. Yes, many lifetimes wrapped into one incredible journey that continues on to do even more extravagant and wonderful things to the benefit of the world.

Reverend Dr. Neil G. Thomas
Senior Pastor, Cathedral of Hope, UCC

Wickedly funny, poignant, tragic, deeply human and celebrative earth, this memoir of Tim Seelig demonstrates resilience and grace. The arc of the narrative from exclusion to welcoming the true self offers a vision of hope. Sharing his ecclesiological DNA of origin and friendship since college allows me to witness a life of liberative resolve that continues to make an impact.

Molly Marshall
Retired President and Professor of Theology and Spiritual Formation
Central Baptist Theological Seminary

Tim has taught us that a good concert should result in laughter, tears and chill bumps. If the same criteria apply to memoirs he has a hit! In telling his truth Tim has encouraged us all to reflect on our lives and examine the places where we are not yet living our authentic selves. Bravo!

Robin Godfrey
Executive Director—GALA Choruses
Gay and Lesbian Choruses

Every great story reveals a transformative moment in someone's life. Tim's story has a revealing transformation on every page. Two extraordinary tales in one epic saga—much like the Old and New Testaments, but different and with more glitter.

David Charles Rodrigues
Award-winning Filmmaker, *Gay Chorus Deep South*

This book has Tim Seelig's singular voice in full display—irreverent, deeply felt, the God's honest truth. As I read each chapter, I was inspired by Tim's courage and perseverance as he faced each new challenge. This book is, as Tim writes, a hymn of hope. It is also a love story to all the people and all the angels in his life.

Rev. David Cowell
UCC Minister, Board Certified Chaplain

This inspiring memoir is an honest, funny, sometimes raw exploration of what it looks like to influence men and women by discovering your truly authentic self—and sharing it openly with the world. If you're anything like me, you'll find insights into your own journey as you follow Tim on the course of his more-than-ordinary life.

Gary Rifkin, CSP
Chief Learning Officer—CoreClarity, Inc.

TALE OF TWO TIMS

BIG OL' BAPTIST, BIG OL' GAY

Tim

TIM SEELIG

© 2020

Published in the United States by Nurturing Faith Inc., Macon GA,
www.nurturingfaith.net.

Library of Congress Cataloging-in-Publication Data is available.

ISBN: 978-1-63528-106-4

You may forget what I wrote.

I hope you will never forget how it made you feel.

Dedication

This book is lovingly dedicated to my brightest light,
Corianna Seelig Gustafson.

Contents

Foreword

By Jim Dant

Fear is an intrinsic motivator that has the ironic capacity to both keep us alive and keep us from living.

In spring 2017 I was contacted by a representative of the San Francisco Gay Men's Chorus (SFGMC). They had heard through the grapevine that First Baptist Church, Greenville, South Carolina, would be willing to serve as a concert venue for the Lavender Pen Tour. As senior minister I verified the legitimacy of the offer. In the days that followed, I received a series of emails from Dr. Tim Seelig, artistic director of the SFGMC. The emails were tentative at best, suspicious at worst. I suggested we dispense with emails and speak by telephone.

In the earliest moments of our discourse, we agreed to be completely honest with each other. In that honesty, we both shared our fears. Tim feared another chapter of abuse at the hands of the Baptists. He feared the shunning and shaming his beloved chorus might receive. He feared the disingenuous handshakes that so many ministers and congregations had given in the past. He feared violence in all its many forms. I feared repercussions. I feared logistics. I feared a further distancing. I feared a label. I feared an entity I did not know. We candidly spoke these fears to one another. Then we had to decide: Were these fears keeping us alive or keeping us from living? We landed on the latter.

We laid our fears aside, and the rest is history. There is now an atypical, holy bond between the 2,200-member First Baptist Church of Greenville, South Carolina and the 300-plus singers and staff of the SFGMC. Since the conclusion of the Lavender Pen Tour, we have celebrated life together and grieved together. Dr. Tim Seelig has returned to First Baptist Greenville as a vocalist, conductor, and friend. The SFGMC has returned to Greenville for an encore performance at our downtown performing arts venue, the Peace Center. I've been privileged to walk alongside Tim and other chorus members during subsequent chapters of their lives. In short, fear might have kept us apart and kept us from living, but we set our fears aside. We chose life.

Tim has done it again. He has set fear aside and chosen life. With his signature mix of class and sarcastic crass, he shares the stories of his life. He fearlessly falls into the mess and invites us to laugh with him, cry with him, hope with him, get angry with him, doubt with him, and curse with him. His greatest invitation, however, is tucked between all these lines. Tim invites us to open our lives to the grace life has to offer—even when we can't see it or are convinced we don't want it or need it. What Tim does not invite us to do is to be afraid. Because while fear can sometimes keep you alive, it most often keeps you from living. And this book is all about life.

Acknowledgments

This has been the most difficult section to write. Undoubtedly, I have left someone out. Here goes.

First and foremost, thank you to my friends who helped with creating, pruning, and editing the book prior to turning it over to the wonderful folks at Nurturing Faith.

Jennifer Viegas, co-publisher, co-editor of the *San Francisco Bay Times*, gave me invaluable insight in how to write in the first place. She has been editing my monthly column for four years. Some of the stories come from those articles. Dan England edited most of the first drafts, and then Jennifer—along with her co-partner in all things, Betty Sullivan—completed the task as they went to print.

Elliot Simon helped fix the little details I couldn't be bothered with or actually didn't know. He helped cut my exclamation marks and all caps down a great deal, as well as my favorite—the ellipsis.

Bobby Jo Valentine assisted me pretty much 24/7 throughout the months I was writing and on crutches. I was not a pleasant human. He was/is a dream. And he is love.

Dan England, best ex-husband a man could ever have. He knows me too well, and I could not have written this book without him. He remembered stories I had long buried.

Michael Tate, the man who hired me at the San Francisco Gay Men's Chorus and the dearest friend and supporter ever. He is brilliant—and not just for hiring me!

Justin Taylor, wisdom personified, coached me on the book and my life. He guides from a distance—the best kind of guide.

Paul Saccone, one of my San Francisco rocks. He helps me with all things, including the audiobook. A bestie.

Jim Dant, my Mother Confessor in all things.

Many friends may not have actually touched the book but certainly touched my life.

Chris Verdugo, my work-husband, who supports me in my vocation every day.

Mitch Galli, my associate artistic director, who cleans up all my messes, sometimes before I make them.

Gary Rifkin and Michael Renquist, who led me through dark days in Dallas.

John Alecca and Phill Barber, friends from Dallas to San Francisco. There at my side always.

Michael Sullivan, who had the blind faith to hire me at the Turtle Creek Chorale in 1987.

As I got in touch with some of the darker family chapters of my life, that very family stood by me bravely to help tell our stories. I can't thank Judson, Corianna, Clay, and Juliana enough. Your unconditional love of Bop Bop gives me joy every single day.

Barbara Bamberg, former associate accompanist at First Baptist Houston and my studio accompanist at Houston Baptist University, who stood by my side and "loved me through it all."

These lifelong friends: Robert Steele, Bryan Stuart, Craig Gregory, Kenn McBryde, Reed Hoke, Robin Godfrey, Michael Piazza, Steve Gallagher, Glenn DeSandre, Danette Kong, James Eakin, David Cowell, Peter Ohm.

All the people I wrote about in the book, and countless others, who helped make me the man I am today. They guided, loved, and shook their heads often!

I also want to thank all the people who taught me, by vivid example, who I most definitely did not want to become! Without them, I may have never had the guts to tell the truth and seek a better world.

To those of you who, upon learning that I was writing this, have come up and asked, "Am I in your book?" You'll find out by the end, and thank you for purchasing it in your search.

Introduction

"When I go to bed at night, I count blessings instead of sheep."—John Bucchino.

The decision to write my life story began as an exercise to make sense out of it all. But it moved quickly to being a tool that would help me put it all in order.

My life has been punctuated by some pretty dramatic events. I wanted to recall stories that had been forgotten or buried. I wanted it all out there.

In 2018 I was having dinner with my dear friend, composer Stephen Schwartz. As a young artist and student at Carnegie Mellon University, Stephen had sought the assistance of a therapist, Dr. Doris Hunter. Stephen was a natural-born entertainer and storyteller, and Dr. Hunter would listen patiently to his comic monologue about what was going on in his life. Occasionally, smiling or even chuckling, she would reach over and put her hand on his arm and say, "Stephen, we both know it isn't really funny."

I have always used humor to cover some of the deepest pain; we all do that, of course. I honed the skill. Yet I wanted to make sure my story is authentically Tim. Most of all, it absolutely had to bring joy to the reader.

At the urging of friend and publisher Greg Gilpin, I wrote a book in 2003 published by Shawnee Press. After five printings, *The Perfect Blend* is now in its second edition. That led to four more books about singing and the choral art. That is definitely what I *do*, but it is far from who I *am*.

These earlier published works share the professional side of what many decades taught me, but nothing of the personal side and the lessons learned there. This is the book I *needed* to write now.

Some years ago, my career was taking me in many wonderful directions: singing, conducting, writing, and making lists for everyone and anyone in my vicinity. I was already speaking from the stage in concerts and in front of classrooms and convention halls.

A close friend from the National Speakers Association, Gary Rifkin, connected me with one of the nation's finest speaking coaches, Juanelle Teague. Our work over several months culminated in an entire weekend locked in a room with the coach and a scribe as she unraveled my life into many little pieces and Post-its on the floor.

The scribe, working quietly in the corner, wrote down every word as my innards were spilled all over the lovely Berber carpet. She continued "scribing" through gales of laughter and pangs of pain.

I gathered those innards up in my murse (man-purse), though I needed a steamer trunk, then went my merry way, wondering if perhaps this experienced coach had finally met someone who was actually helpless. Well, that was not the case.

In a few weeks, she called back with the message that she had discovered the "core essence" of my life experiences. It was "liberating change." I would have never thought of that, but she nailed it.

For some, the adage "Change is the only thing constant in life" may relate primarily to the weather or one's outfit. Those have not been my changes, although I do worry about both. Joys and tragedies have steered my direction. These have certainly been big changes—some that I asked for, most I did not.

During the coaching process, one exercise was to write about a significant event from each year of my life. This sounded impossible, but I started with a vague memory at age three—something about playing dress-up with my little friends and declaring myself the most beautiful.

I began filling in the years: age eighteen, high school graduation; twenty-two, first marriage; sixty-four, second marriage. Along the way, of course, were clothing changes, tire changes, job changes, hair changes (okay, hair losses).

There were spectacular mountaintops and deep valleys to balance them out. One highlight for each year fell into place. My coach then pointed me to the three that had been most pivotal in forming who I am today. Each had to do with a dramatic change. Each had to do with life delivering a blow and me getting up from it and moving forward, never wallowing in self-pity but incorporating the pain or loss or failure into my life experiences to make me a better man. I didn't even know it was happening while in the middle of it.

The theme "liberating change" rang true and authentic. As difficult as these experiences were when going through them, each turned out to be a blessing or a launching pad to greater things. It also had the world to do with what no one could ever take away: music, humor, truth.

That's why I wanted to write a book about me. By sharing my roller coaster journey, perhaps others' twists and turns, ups and downs may seem a little tamer or at least conquerable. So take this ride with me; I promise it won't be boring! At the end, I hope you are smiling.

ACT ONE

Chapter 1

My Life:
Grand Opera in Two Acts

A baby was born, wrapped in swaddling clothes, lying in Fort Worth, Texas. The father seemed happy about the birth. The mother was extra happy, thanks to the C-section. Big brother, not so much. But, alas, something was wrong. The lighting? The outfit? The big brother who probably taunted the precious baby when the parents turned their heads? Perhaps the baby boy sensed the disappointment that he was not "Katy," the hoped-for girl who was to have been named for the maternal grandmother.

Regardless of the reason, the newborn cried for two years. Perhaps he was a tiny, red-faced soothsayer seeing a glimpse of the future, the grand opera that, in two thirty-five-year-each acts, was just beginning. It was the start of a wild life full of "you can't make this up" moments, just like opera.

I set my sail toward opera land, with a good dose of Opryland thrown in. The decision was made for me by some opera director in the sky. He/she also decided what kind of opera it would be and what role I would play. My voice, temperament, and body type suited the lighter opera buffa, or comic operas, specifically Mozart. There's lots of tomfoolery, fun, and even some gender-bending roles. How delightful! Yes, please.

But no, the regisseur (the "big cheese") ignored opera buffa and chose verismo for the libretto of my life.

Verismo marks a period when opera composers started getting real, writing about daily life. The stories got gritty and dramatic—and explicit. Most are in four acts. That's a lot of Tim. That's the hand I was dealt. No Mozart for me (although that is what I eventually moved to Switzerland to sing).

Opera buffa focuses on gods, mythological figures, or kings and queens. It is all kind of "pretty": little ballet numbers, beautiful costumes (I absolutely love the latest fashion from 1750). Verismo was going to be the story of my life.

Verismo focuses on the average contemporary man and woman and their problems. Check. Generally, that means of a sexual, romantic, or violent nature. In my case, I'd use two out of these three. There was always a terminal illness. Check. Sadly, this included an uber-dramatic tenor running around the room with tales of woe (enter Tim's real life). The baritone, me, would be a priest, a general fix-it guy, a soothsayer, or just someone who stirs the pot. I have my own stirrer. The props master need not provide that.

Let's look closer at how that pertains to my plot.

- Yes to god(s). Lots of them. "It's complicated."
- Yes to queens. Lots of those. "More, please."
- Yes to sex and romance. "It's complicated, delicious, and disastrous."
- Yes to terminal illnesses. "It's my life since age thirty-six."
- No to mythological figures, kings, and violence. At least no violence.

Operas have very clear villains and heroes. In creating the plot, we must decide how many acts and how many scenes. *The Guinness Book of World Records* says it's *Die Meistersinger von Nürnberg* by Richard Wagner, which boasts five hours and fifteen minutes of music. I have a lot more music than that.

For my opera, we are going with a much simpler two-act affair. Each will cover about thirty-five years. There will be a long intermission (with a two-drink minimum). The scene changes dramatically between Acts I and II. The stage crew has to change the scenery completely. When we told the costume designers about the "look" of the first act, they almost walked out. When we told them about Act II, they decided to stay! There will be two completely different casts, except for perhaps five people who appear in both. There will be no crossover until the dream sequence for the finale, when both casts come together and actually get along.

There you have it. The baby boy prepared himself by crying for the first two years, and then the fun began. There has been a great deal of crying and unspeakable amounts of joy as well.

The fat lady will sing. It might be my mother. She was on a diet for her entire life. I am not in charge of casting the roles.

Curtain up on *Tim: The Opera*.

Chapter 2

The Glamour and the Grit

The movie *The Glamour and the Grit* is a story of the haves and have-nots, the princess and the pauper, even the Hatfields and the McCoys upon occasion. My family tree has them all.

My maternal grandfather was known as "Judge Garrett," even though he later became a U.S. congressman. I bear his name as my middle name. He was larger than life and funny. With his big, booming voice, everyone knew when he entered a room. He held court wherever he went.

He was an oil baron during the boom-and-bust days in West Texas. It was during the boom when he was elected to Congress. He gathered up his wife and five kids, had all new clothes tailor-made for them, and told them to get the hay out of their hair and the poop off their boots. Away they went from their farm outside Eastland, Texas, to Washington, D.C. The Clampetts hit the nation's capital and took to it so that, soon, it fit like a glove.

His wife, Sallie Day Garrett, was the most wonderful West Texas woman: feisty, funny, and warm all around. She was very active in the suffrage movement and women's rights from the beginning. She would have been dubbed a "feminist" if that word had existed.

No one messed with Sallie. She had the final word—even with Congressman "Judge" Garrett. Sallie lived a wonderful life, loving her five children and their children. She was famous for never making a decision, instead saying, "We'll see." Her house smelled like johnnycakes made with cornmeal and hot water.

I never knew my paternal grandfather, who tragically died in a car accident in 1932. My grandmother was left with three small children with only her hands and drive to eke out a living during the Great Depression. Her first language was German, and the work ethic was in full bloom. She rolled up her sleeves and did the things she knew. She took in sewing, but that wasn't enough.

She knew how to cook, so she rented a tiny building on the corner of the Fredericksburg, Texas, high school playground. She would get up at four o'clock every morning to cook amazing lunches at "The Stand." Her children were required to help. She kept her cash profit in an old Calumet Baking Soda can, yet she instilled dignity in all three kids. We loved her house, which smelled like the famous stuffed noodles she made at The Stand every day.

She had thirteen grandchildren and was adamant about equal treatment. At Christmas, she would buy gifts for them all. Since each gift didn't cost the same, she taped pennies or nickels to the package so that everyone was treated equally.

My mom, Virginia Garrett, was as grand as it gets. She was Texas Baptist royalty. She dressed it, lived it, and loved it. And she paid her loyal subjects back with the most gracious smile, stunning singing voice, and a moment of feeling special, because that's the way she made them feel. She walked through life on a pedestal. She was her father's girl. This just might repeat itself two generations later. Virginia was always a colorful one, even as a young girl. It has to be where I got it.

Every Sunday morning, the whole family loaded in the car and headed the five miles or so to the First Baptist Church. One morning, Mom, Virginia Nell, was running behind. Everyone else was in the car—and it was hot. Judge Garrett was dressed to the nines—he was, after all, a county judge. He walked halfway to the house and hollered out for Virginia Nell to get on out to the car. From inside the house, the girl with a huge voice hollered back, "By George, I'm powdering my face!"

That was the worst cussing possible at that time. Apparently, her father gave her a good whoopin' and she headed to the car. They rode quietly to church. Judge Garrett and the family unfolded themselves proudly from the car, dusted themselves off, only to find several chickens and a rooster still on the top of the car. The Garretts were horrified. The church folk were delighted. By George, no one noticed Virginia Nell's freshly powdered face. She had sweated it off in the car!

My mother had found her calling. From that moment on, she was Queen of Everything. In high school, she and Margaret Truman would board the train in Washington, D.C., and travel together to take voice lessons with a world-renowned teacher at Westminster Choir College in Princeton, New Jersey. Mom was invited to all the swell events.

When it came time for college, she decided to go back to Judge Garrett's congressional district. She was offered a vocal music scholarship to Baptist-related Hardin-Simmons University. She showed up in a limo with a driver, two weeks late! The diva had arrived. Her house, for my entire life, smelled like L'air Du Temps, the only fragrance she would wear. And she didn't cook!

John Earl's story could not have been any more different if you were making stuff up. Growing up in a German-speaking household, dirt poor and with no father, he was wound tighter than a Swiss clock. He grew up as one of God's frozen people: Lutheran. He excelled in academics and, when not working at "The Stand," managed to be the drum major of the marching band.

That came in handy, as he was offered a full scholarship to Hardin-Simmons in Abilene, Texas, and to be the drum major of the world-famous Cowboy Band. He otherwise had nothing, although his mother had done her best. On the day he left for college, he had only five dollars and a suitcase. He hitchhiked the 400 miles. It was 1942.

He arrived to find that the band had disbanded because of the war. He was not allowed in the Army because of flat feet, so he stayed in school, working two or three jobs through his college career. He was also "saved" from the Lutherans and fully indoctrinated into the Baptist life.

The first big argument around my parents' marriage was that Dad and the Lutherans wanted beer and barbeque at the wedding reception. The Baptist contingent was horrified. The Baptists won, of course. No alcohol—just "Baptist punch" (ginger ale and lime sherbet, which we pronounced *sherbert*) and petit fours.

Judge Garrett and Sallie came to visit the young couple in their first apartment. The judge noticed my mother using a broom. He stormed into the room and said, "I did not raise my daughter to sweep floors." Mom didn't do "wifely" chores for the next sixty years.

So now, the cast of "The Glamour and the Grit," in order of appearance:

- Judge Garrett. Powerful center of attention who spent his life in service to others.
- Sallie Garrett. Activist, feminist, sweet glue of the family.
- Katy Seelig. Survivor. Workaholic. Frugal.
- Dr. John Earl Seelig. Overachiever. Driven. Distant. Gave his life to the Baptists.
- Virginia Seelig. Star of the show. Grand. Funny. Charismatic. Could wow an audience.

The proverbial acorn did not fall far from those trees. "Put 'em all together and what'a you got?" You already know. Who needs Myers-Briggs?

Lights, camera, action! A little glamour and a little grit.

Chapter 3

Confused Stork

Sometimes you get an absentminded stork—my luck of the draw. He flies around and drops baby packages on various houses without really reading the labels. Well, Mr. Stork did a number in 1951 when he dropped a nameless baby (who the stork thought was Katy) into a small group of misfits—Mom, Dad, and two-year-old Steve—already clinging by a thread.

Steve was so damn cute, the apple of everyone's eye. Tim was red-faced and looked like something from *The Howling*. You think I'm making this up? Steve's baby pictures fill books. He was that adorable—in diapers, first tooth, hundreds of photos. There is literally one picture of Tim from birth to about three. There is one "professional" (Sears) portrait. It looks as if the photographer waited until poor Tim was filling his diaper—and it was not an easy poop. That's the shot. That's what you get.

Steve tried to keep his "favored" spot for the rest of his life. When I stopped crying, I came on pretty strong as a contender. Steve and I enjoyed some amazing successes professionally. We shared charisma and humor, but we were from different planets in every other respect.

Even so, we shared a room for our entire childhood until Steve left for college. We had three bedrooms, but Mom and Dad each had their own—for lots of reasons. The situation, however, seemed strange for a young, dynamic couple in their thirties. Friends would always ask about it and got the same lame excuses that Mom and Dad tried out on us: Dad snored. Dad got up early. Mom had to sing tomorrow. They actually never said, "Because we don't really like each other."

As for my own living arrangement with Steve, it was a small room for growing boys: twin beds too close together, separated by school desks and dressers. It is a wonder we did not kill each other.

Act I introduces the brothers. That is always fodder for opera.

- I was uptight. He was loose as a goose.
- I was uber-disciplined. He was not.
- I was the ugly duckling. He was voted "Most Handsome" in his senior class of 1,000.

- I buried myself in music and math. Steve dabbled in sports, cars, girls, and a little shoplifting.
- Truth be told, I am certain there was a modicum of envy on my part in the easy way that he—with his charm, poise, and those eyes—got whatever he wanted.
- It seemed nothing came easy for me. I worked hard for everything.
- I worked and worked to make money and save money. When our house burned down, it included a stack of IOUs for money borrowed by Steve from the little banker, me. All was lost. Steve got off scot-free, to be repeated many times.

The two years' difference meant I followed him in elementary, junior high, and high school after he had established the Seelig "force field." He was not happy to have me coming along trying to plant my own small flag in the corner of the high school playing field. So I didn't. I just steered clear with my thirty pounds overweight, glasses, braces, and lovely acne just to top off the look like sprinkles on an ice cream cone. On the other hand, I dove into schoolwork. The German work ethic from my dad kicked in from the beginning. Like my mom, who skated through life as a congressman's daughter, to a large extent Steve skated on the Seelig brand.

We shared a lot of activities—because being a Seelig meant church, church choir, church youth group—but we never bonded. Through the years, we provided some pretty fabulous props in Mom and Dad's press photos.

The four of us never took a vacation, so we didn't have to pretend to be some happy family piling into our 1955 Ford Country Squire station wagon, wood trimming and all, driving from Fort Worth to Disneyland with a water cooler and sandwich supplies. That never happened. I still long for such a family trip—a bit, a very small bit.

"Vacation" for us was either tagging along with Mom or Dad to their respective duties at Southern Baptist Convention meetings or back and forth to the two Baptist summer encampments: Glorieta, New Mexico; and Ridgecrest, North Carolina. There, we played with other children of professional Baptists while Mom and Dad worked. I believe we even got to try fishing once in a river in New Mexico.

Steve was a born leader, a master manipulator, and funny, funny, funny. He mastered physical comedy and wild histrionics. A green bean up his nose to make people laugh was not unusual. Food fights were his favorite.

I don't blame the stork. He was just doing his job the best he could. Had I been consulted, I would have pointed another house where little Tim was supposed to go and instructed him to drop Katy with the Seeligs.

Chapter 4

Baptist Womb to Tomb

Baptist born,
Baptist bred,
And when I die,
I'll be Baptist dead.

I was no more than six weeks old when I was first dragged to church on a Sunday morning and enrolled in the "Cradle Roll." Attendance records started that day. Only later did I learn that some of my friends who grew up in other traditions actually got really pretty lace dresses—even the boys—and got sprinkled.

Getting sprinkled at six weeks or even six months was totally confusing to me. There is no way a baby can know it's a full-blown sinner at that point. That comes around the age of five. No, six-week-old baptism is a waste of good lace and a tablespoon of water if you ask me. And what's a baby doing wearing a full-length gown with a hat and little ballet slippers to match? (Jealous much? Yes.)

The Baptists waited 'til we were just old enough to have the bejesus scared out of us so we could invite Jesus in. That was the "age of accountability," when you knew deep down inside that some of the sins you were committing (at six) were mortal sins. This was the moment it dawned on you that you needed to get baptized. No sprinkles for the Baptists.

Believing if you were hit by a car between the knowing and the dunking that you were going straight to hell is why Church of Christ folks keep their dunking pool filled *all the time*. Baptists usually fill 'er up as needed. The rest of the time it serves as a terrarium for plastic plants and silk flowers.

Life Lessons at Four:
- My place was on the front pew Sunday mornings and evenings and Wednesdays.
- Steve's place was next to me on the front pew at church.
- Dad's place was seated on the platform.
- Mom's place was on the platform in the choir or singing the "special music."
- Mom and Dad could keep their eye on us from their vantage points.
- I learned the meaning of a raised eyebrow: "Don't even think about it!"

- I learned to sit perfectly still.
- I learned to be a "big boy."
- I learned that it was very important what people thought about the Seelig brand.
- I learned we dressed up; appearances were everything.
- I learned we absolutely do not share problems with others outside the family.
- I learned that we did things *really* big. It was never a small church or event.
- I learned that earning approval entailed a very specific set of requirements.
- I learned lots and lots of hymns about blood and torture devices like the cross.
- I learned about all the sins church members should not be doing.
- I learned about matching church hats, gloves, and purses. Mom left hers in my care.
- I learned I had a Jesus-shaped hole in my heart.
- I learned about the narrow way.

Small is the gate and narrow the way that leads to life, and only a few find it. Wide is the gate and broad is the way that leads to destruction [and lots find that one!] (Matt 7:14).

My own revelation came at six years old. My parents and I were sitting in the living room. The plastic cover, designed to keep the riffraff off between the nice people's visits, had been removed and the sofa pillows fluffed. Everything was perfect, except it was hot. I was clear what was about to happen. Mr. Blackstone was coming to visit.

It was a Sunday afternoon—a good time for such things. He rang the bell, greeted my parents, and we sat down awkwardly, everyone with posture never used in normal life. Mr. Blackstone was the pastor of Lake Highlands Baptist Church, where we were members. Dad was already a bigwig with the Baptist administration in downtown Dallas, so I'm pretty sure some of Mr. Blackstone's sweat was the pressure of "What if I mess this up in front of Dr. Seelig?"

We had a short conversation about the heat lingering on into September or something equally mundane. Then we launched into why we were really there. Mr. Blackstone had it down: This wasn't his first time to convince a six-year-old that he or she was going straight to hell if the conversation didn't go well. He asked if I knew I was a sinner. I had already been schooled on my personal sins.

He then asked if I knew how to change my course to one headed for heaven, where my Mom and Dad would be and where I would have a glorified body to strut around with on the streets of gold. Well, that was no decision at all. If I accepted Jesus, I got a new made-to-order body and lots of gold. I was in. When I said yes, there was crying all around. They were all so proud that my name was written in the Lamb's Book of Life.

But I was assured God would not be sitting there the rest of my life with a big eraser. Baptists don't really believe "once saved, always saved." It takes a lot of work conforming to stay in good graces with the church folk. And even if God didn't have an eraser, they sure did. If you started backsliding, as if you were on a Slip 'N Slide, they were happy to provide the extra water to get you to the bottom.

So I got baptized.

When we got dunked, we moved to our membership in the "Sunbeams," a little fraternity/sorority for five- to six-year-old boys and girls singing, "A sunbeam, a sunbeam, Jesus wants me for a sunbeam. I'll be a sunbeam for him." (That last word is multisyllabic. Drag it out. Here we go: "I'll be a sunbeam for heeeeeyum." Perfect.)

By the age of seven, most of us were now aware of our mortal sinship, so we needed to be separated by gender. After all, girls and boys like different things by this point. Boys went to Royal Ambassadors while the girls joined Girls' Auxiliary.

The girls began at the lowest rank and advanced as they memorized Bible verses and did good deeds. Best part? There were pageants! A "good" Baptist girl wouldn't be in a beauty pageant or be a debutante, so we made our own. They were lavish affairs. All levels were required to wear a white gown.

The steps for the Girls' Auxiliary were:
- Maiden
- Lady in Waiting
- Lady
- Princess
- Queen
- Regal Queen
- Imperial Queen
- Superior Queen
- Sovereign Queen

Oh, goodness. I was in heaven, climbing the stair steps to Sovereign Queen in the privacy of my own home and using a plunger for my scepter and a bath towel for my cape, practicing and practicing the Texas Dip. Did you just think, "What the hell?"

For this I will go to the media as proof: "Often considered the most extreme of all bows, the Texas Dip sets Lone Star State debs apart. The debutante lunges, stacks her knees, lowers herself all the way to the ground, and folds her body over her gown, arms outstretched, while smiling at the audience under a spotlight." I was good at it.

Royal Ambassadors had titles and ranks too, just more butch:

- Junior Royal Ambassador
- Intern
- Intermediate Royal Ambassador
- Envoy
- Special Envoy
- Dean
- Senior Royal Ambassador
- Ambassador Extraordinary
- Ambassador Plenipotentiary

The RA manual (available online!) lists their activities:

- Nature study;
- Collection of insects, butterflies, special leaves, and small animals;
- Identification of animals, birds, snakes, and trees.

Hobbies may include:

- Carving of wood;
- Collection of stamps;
- Crafts learning and practicing;
- Making of brooms, cage (animal trap), basket weaving.

And here are the approved games for the boys to play when not making animal traps or identifying snakes: Scrabble, Ludo, Chess, Whot, and Checkers.

Sounds terrible.

Oh, God, please let me be in the Girls' Auxiliary!

Chapter 5

From Sofa to *Romper Room*

Oh, little Tim.

I was precocious, overachieving, people-pleasing, and usually dressed up. They credit my big voice to those two years of incessant vocalizing! "I'm not getting my way, and you people are obviously not listening or trying hard enough."

My first public performances, much like many of yours, were standing on the piano bench singing for captive guests and family. My parents were so proud. I was a little one with a big voice. Where was *America's Got Talent* then, huh?

My mother was a professional singer and voice teacher. When I was young, she taught lessons in our home. I wanted to be part of those lessons—mostly to be near her. I didn't want to have to stay in the other room, so I discovered a sneaky way of crawling into the room when the student's back was turned. I hid behind the sofa in the living room, where the lessons were taught. I'm sure my mother thought I was in the other room watching more of Miss Debbie and *Romper Room*.

I could remain unnoticed for hours, soaking up the pearls of wisdom, the steady progress of the singing students, and learning all *24 Italian Songs and Arias*. I missed much of the kids' songs. I knew the previously referenced classical pieces and most of the songs in *The Baptist Hymnal*. That is wildly foretelling.

Upon one occasion, however, I apparently could take it no more. The student was simply not "getting it." My mother was being very patient, coaxing, encouraging, accepting the much-needed payment. But my patience no longer matched that of the teacher.

At one egregious turn of phrase, one more failed attempt at *"Caro Mio Ben,"* for heaven's sake, I simply had to assist. I let out what must have been a horrific "Ewwwwww," as if having smelled something long dead. From that time on, I was banished to the other room to exercise my heightened sense of criticism from afar.

Sitting behind the sofa, or under the piano on a palette when there was no student, was the closest I ever felt to my mother. She was not a hugger or a holder or a toucher. But lying there on the floor, listening to her magnificent mezzosoprano voice—some even called her a contralto—I felt safe. I felt she was being vulnerable to practice in front of me.

The rich warmth of her voice resonated off the hardwood floor. The vibrations went through my body. I pretended that I was being held by her. I never wanted to leave. Today, when I listen to her recordings, I feel the same way. Her voice conveys a love she was never able to express in any other way. But I have the recordings!

Romper Room TV debut

In 1956 there were only three channels on television, and those were in black and white. *Romper Room* had the corner on the market from 1953 to 1994—long before *Sesame Street* or a big purple dinosaur took over the airwaves.

I had assumed it was a national program, but I found out later it was regional. Miss Nancy was actually Miss Betty or Miss Cathy in other markets. In fact, my own Miss Debbie may have been famous only where I lived in Texas. But she was the most glamorous preschool teacher in the world, leading a group of real children through a morning of games and fun.

Looking through her magic mirror straight into the camera, she listed the names of the children she saw out there in television land, and every one of us just knew she would call our names—because she could see us! Parents weren't all that creative in naming their children back then. There were only about ten for each gender, so it wasn't that hard. It would never work today. I see Christie, Kristi, Christy, and Kristi. And then, of course, there's Krysty. But I digress.

I had developed my lungs the first two years, and my artistry had been honed by listening to my mother teach voice lessons. And because I was something of a ham at a very early age, my mother dressed me up and took me to the open casting call for *Romper Room* with the divine Miss Debbie. The audition went great. It was pretty nonthreatening. Lo and behold, I was selected. Oh, the rejoicing was glorious.

When the day to begin filming rolled around, my mother dressed me in my brand-new short pants, socks, and Buster Brown shoes. I was ready for my national television debut. She bought a fabulous new dress and a Sunday "go-to-meeting" hat, so I guess we were both ready for *our* debut—after posing for pictures next to our very fancy DeSoto Adventurer before we left our house! I gotta say, for middle-class people, we had some pretty fabulous cars. Not Dad's choice. Mom loved cars for some reason. Maybe she needed a really nice car to help with her scars from having arrived at the First Baptist with chickens on the roof.

This was my first step toward the ultimate—becoming a Mouseketeer! We arrived at the studio and were told to wait in the outer room. I had not yet met Miss Debbie in person since some underling conducted the auditions. I could not wait.

They opened the door to the elaborate set, and after all these years we still can't figure out exactly what was not to my liking. But something set me off. I don't know if I didn't like my outfit or I realized I was going to have to share the stage with other children. Perhaps I was just insulted at having to wait ten minutes past the call time for my close-up, or maybe I didn't like the lighting on the set. Most likely, I realized it was "regional." But for whatever reason, two-year-old Tim returned and began to cry.

I was not to be consoled. The producer spoke with my mother and, not being able to curb my sobs, thanked us for our trouble and sent us away. Even if I had gotten control of myself, my face would have been so blotched from the weeping that it would have rendered me unfit for even the small, grainy screen. Home we went.

Actions have consequences. I had ruined my entire future in television because of my actions.

It was a very long ride home. This very day would come back to haunt me exactly twenty years later in Salzburg, Austria. And now, sixty years after the *Romper Room* debacle, I've been on the big screen and I'm going to be on the small screen! Not regional. Who's crying now?

I still "failed" *Romper Room*. I'm pretty sure I went home, took off my new clothes and Buster Brown shoes, and went out to play with my blond cocker spaniel, Honey Boy. He was the first of many wonderful canines who accompanied me throughout my life. If a dog is a boy's best friend, I have had the joy of many best friends over these six decades. I think more than anything, I was sad that I disappointed my mom, because she seemed really excited.

I just continued doing what I was doing before the life-changing opportunity came my way. There would be others. I had no idea then, of course, that getting up, dusting myself off, and moving on to something positive would be the throughline of my life.

Lesson learned: Actions have consequences, and I would not go down that path again—until Linz, Austria.

Chapter 6

Life's Volume Knob

The exuberance of my childhood brought me such joy. It was all a wonder. Each new melody, rhythm, and hand movement (no movement below the waist—that's dancing) thrilled me to no end.

At the ages of three and five, my brother and I were stars. From the "stage" of the piano bench in the living room, we sometimes escaped to play with other children. We skipped and played and ran around like crazy children. Every activity was done *fortissississimo*. There was nothing we did that was *pianissississimo*.

Although expressed in the narrow confines of church, the music and joy I found there would last unabated and untarnished the rest of my musical life. Once I got too big to stand on the piano bench, however, things changed. Someone was telling me to tone it down. The same people who put me on that piano bench and encouraged me to sing out were putting their fingers to their lips and saying, "Shhhhh."

I was taught the right way to sing, the right time to sing, and the right volume to sing. Layer upon layer of insecurity was added. My beautiful and unique song began its process of conforming. Could I risk going against the tide and remaining unique and true to myself? I could not.

The big box that had once held us and encouraged us to sing out, to use big gestures, and to perform with reckless abandon began getting smaller. Then the death knell of all questions entered my mind and my soul—a question that would alter my life completely: "What will people think?"

My outrageous, creative, and unique expression began a slow death. It took me back to four-year-old Tim on the front pew. People liked that Tim who sat completely still like a little guard at Buckingham Palace.

The "refinement" continued. It wasn't just singing or dancing. Our gestures went from huge and expressive to small and intimidated, with elbows stuck inextricably to our sides.

We were told to:
- Walk a certain way.
- Hold our books a certain way.
- Talk a certain way.
- Stand a certain way.

- Cross our legs a certain way.
- Lower our voice and never be "flamboyant."

It continued in school. I spent years with people beating out our individualism, creativity, and uniqueness. We wanted to fit in more than anything in the world.

I was told to:

- Line up—single file.
- Color inside the lines.
- Not veer from the norm.
- Color leaves green and flowers red.
- Wear a uniform or robe in choir.
- Use a black folder.
- Stand in the crook of the piano when singing a solo.
- Don't move. Don't gesture.
- For heaven's sake, don't look like you are having fun!
- Conform—at all costs.

My own creativity suffered from those strictures. My "creative volume knob" was being turned down, seemingly daily. Remember: *Small is the gate and narrow the way that leads to life.*

Time would tell if I could stay the course, paint within the lines. This would be my song, "What I Want," from *Serenade of Life*, written with my friend James Eakin:

Tim:	The World:
I want to sing.	*"There's no money in that."*
I want to dance.	*"Good girls don't dance."*
I want to be pretty.	*"Pretty is as pretty does."*
I want to paint.	*"Fine, but stay within the lines."*
I want to be like Fred Astaire or maybe Yul Brynner.	*"You have too much hair."*
I want to be like Sylvester Stallone. No, I'm not, I'm just big boned.	*"You're too fat."*
I want ice cream.	*"It'll go straight to your hips."*
I want a puppy.	*"I'm busy; talk to your mother."*

I want to have children and get married.

"*Not in that order.*"

I want world peace.

"*Thank you, Miss America.*"

I want to be like G.I. Joe or Bernadette Peters.

"*You're a boy; G.I. Joe for you.*"

I want to be like Neil Armstrong and land on the moon while singing a song about Barbie and hiking trips.

"*No Barbie. And absolutely no Ken.*"

Someday I'll be the king of the world a song about Barbie and hiking trips.

"*Yes, you will.*"

And I won't clean my room.

"*Yes, you will.*"

Or take out the trash.

"*No allowance for you.*"

And I'll sleep until noon.

"*Don't you use that tone with me.*"

I'm gonna sing.

"*Fine, but stay within the lines.*"

I'm gonna dance.

"*Sure, but stay within the lines.*"

I'm gonna paint.

"*Yeah, but stay within the lines.*"

I'm gonna sing.

"*You'd better stay within the lines.*"

©Tim Seelig. Used with permission.

Chapter 7

Amahl to Bloody Mary

My life began with a combination of drama and music. But how in the world did I grow up to be a full-time opera singer? Had I grown up in one of the cities known as a bastion of the high art: New York City, Chicago, San Francisco? Nope, I grew up in Fort Worth, Texas. Cowtown. To be fair, both Fort Worth and Dallas have healthy regional opera companies for which I would perform in years to come.

Had I spent time listening to the Saturday broadcasts of the Met on the radio? That would also be a no. We were busy on Saturdays getting ready for church. "I take a bath every Saturday whether I need it or not."

Had I sung arias from the great operas? No. Thank goodness my voice teachers knew enough not to allow that. I cut my teeth on art songs. So what happened?

Well, I had seen some operas, but not many. I'd seen my mom sing in a few operas and musicals. I'll start with opera and move on to *The Sound of Music*, *Carousel*, and *South Pacific* (big tease).

I watched my mom win the regional Metropolitan Opera Auditions but decide not to move to the national finals because of her obligations to family and church. That brings up a big "What if?" and a "Should'a."

There is one opera I remember most vividly because my mom sang it every year. I can recite every line. It was Gian Carlo Menotti's *Amahl and the Night Visitors*. Mom played the lead role, the mother, every holiday. It was an annual staple in Fort Worth. The demand was so great that they gave multiple performances each year. I was at all of the rehearsals and performances.

Amahl was a young boy, usually played by a girl because of the vocal range. I so badly wanted to play that role opposite my mother. This was never spoken, but I'm pretty sure one of the reasons was my body shape. Amahl and his mother were starving. It wouldn't look right to have the well-fed, round boy with acne sprinkles in a faux Bible-era robe (more a Middle Eastern muumuu with a rope "cinched" at the nonexistent waist). And by the time I might have been ready, my voice began to change—dang it!

First, the role of the mother was not typecast in any way.

1. She was a single mother.

2. She was dirty.
3. She was penniless.
4. Her son was crippled.
5. She could fight!

None of those described my mom, but it was one of the really great mezzosoprano roles for a one-act opera based on a biblical theme. She was, in those respects, perfect. Downside: The production lasted over two weekends, meaning Mom could not keep her big Baptist hairdo teased within an inch of its life during that week. But here's the good news: Wigs were in, and many were sitting on wig forms all over the house, tempting me at every turn.

Here is the plot summary (bask in this for a moment): It was the year of our Savior's birth. Mother and her crippled son lived alone. They had nothing to their name but a bare room and a broom. No food. No hope. Lo and behold, what would happen next? The three kings passed through the village as they followed the star on their way to pay a visit to a baby whose name they did not know. They were bringing lots of bright, shiny things to Baby Anonymous. It is never explained what happened to her husband. We also don't know why the kings chose her tiny house. But they did.

My favorite part: While Mother was gathering villagers and munchies, she left Amahl with the kings, instructing him to leave the kings alone to rest. The minute she was out the door, Amahl became a total chatterbox. My favorite king was Caspar. He had the most fun aria: "This is my box. This is my box. I never travel without my box."

Upon her return, Mother asked, "Amahl, were you a nuisance?" Amahl innocently replied, "No, Mother. *They* kept asking me questions!" It was a visual and aural interpretation of a deep-seated trait of all Seeligs. We can literally talk until we think of something to say!

After snacks, being tired from their journey, they went to sleep. And what did Mother do but literally slink across that dirty floor like a Navy Seal, reaching for their gold to get her boy a new crutch, singing her *huge* aria, "All That Gold." Just as she almost grabbed a few shekels that the kings could certainly afford to lose, the kings' page catches her and literally throws her around the little abode.

She looked like Uhura flopping around the control room during a meteor storm in the original *Star Trek*. At first, it upset me—a lot. I actually saw the bruises on her arms during the run of the show. Even with preparation, I cried the first three or four times I watched rehearsal. But I soon got used to it and chalked it up to suffering for your art.

To wrap up, they forgave her for trying to steal Baby Anonymous's gifts, even though he was possibly already two years old. If they knew so little, maybe it was a girl and here they had brought blue myrrh. The Three Kings and Mom sang a gorgeous quartet about the baby they were looking for where the star was pointing.

"Have you seen a child the color of wheat, the color of corn?" *What?* There they go again making Baby Anonymous off-white (wheat) or yellow (corn). Well, the song was so beautiful that by the final chord, Amahl got himself healed and sang his aria, "Look, Mother, I can walk. I can dance."

As the kings prepared to leave and because he didn't need his crutch anymore, Amahl put it on the huge pile of gold, frankincense, and myrrh. He wanted Baby Anonymous to have his broken-down crutch should he need it. Everyone in the audience cried at the innocent generosity. They ignored the fact that if Baby Anonymous ever hurt a leg, he was the Son of God. But it's opera.

I mentioned that it was not just opera that I watched my mother sing—in addition to the recitals, concerts, oratorios, and Billy Graham crusades. She performed in musicals too (why didn't I catch that bug?). We had a first-rate professional musical theater company, Casa Mañana. It was in the round and hugely popular for decades, a true gem of the Fort Worth arts scene. Betty Buckley got her start there.

By this time, Mom was well-known—okay, famous—in the entire area. It was mostly the fact that she had performed at every Baptist church. She had also done concerts and recitals, sung with the symphony and the opera. Casting her would bring a huge new audience to the theater.

The first role Mom sang there was Mother Superior in *The Sound of Music.* Typecasting. And much better than the dirty single-mother thief. She brought the house down at every performance with her incredible vocal instrument as she sang "Climb Every Mountain." She brought both a stunning voice and her depth as a real mom and true minister. It was amazing. Chill bumps up and down, and not a few tears shed by every person in the audience—and rave reviews.

The next summer, they invited her back to play Nettie Fowler in *Carousel.* Again, the perfect role, replete with the show-stopping "You'll Never Walk Alone." It was incredible, even if it was my mother. The plot was obviously a little more worldly. Again, rave reviews.

The third summer, she was invited back (of course, smart people). So what showstopper would Virginia have this summer, inquiring minds wanted to know? Imagine her once again stopping the show every night singing "Bali Hai" from *South Pacific*.

Then the offer came. The offer was DOA. The song is sung by Bloody Mary! Okay, Mom obviously didn't drink. I'm not sure she even knew what a Bloody Mary was, but she knew there was some tomfoolery in that show. And Bloody Mary is not white, so there would be some serious pancake base being spread on with a trowel. The final straw: Bloody Mary doesn't brush her teeth and calls someone a "dirty bastard."

This was the end of Virginia's career in Broadway musicals. What a shame. But a girl's got principles!

Lessons:

- You must be willing to suffer for your art, even if you wind up with bruises.
- It's fun to dress in a costume and sing really loud.
- It's okay to steal if it's for a new crutch.
- It's okay to talk until you think of something to say. Thanks, Amahl.
- If you're Baptist, you can't play roles named after alcoholic beverages.
- Opera is good. Musicals can lead you down the wrong path.
- Music can heal. Save that one.

Chapter 8

My Father Figure...
Was a Woman

In 1958 the Seeligs had resettled from Dallas to Fort Worth. Mom and Dad were ensconced in the positions they would hold for the next thirty years. Mom was a voice professor, and Dad was vice president of Southwestern Baptist Theological Seminary, at that time the largest seminary in the world. They were fully engaged in full-time positions, and both had lots of outside engagements in their respective fields. There was little time for "normal" family things.

Steve and I didn't even notice. We had no idea what that looked like—never would. We were all busy doing our thing. We had lots of babysitters and a maid, Betty, whom we loved. She took care of "her" boys for years like a member of the family. Things were pretty good. Mom and Dad were quite high-profile in the Baptist world and beyond, making a huge mark on the Fort Worth community, and they were in demand.

In 1959 a new faculty member joined the music department at the seminary. Her name was Joe Ann Shelton (yes, Joe with an *e*). She hailed from Durant, Oklahoma, population 12,000, and had recently graduated from Oklahoma Baptist College in Shawnee, Oklahoma, population 15,000. She had done a lot of traveling across Oklahoma and Arkansas as the singer on tour with a young, trumpet-playing firebrand evangelist, Johnny Bisagno. He and Joe Ann had both graduated with music degrees. She hit Cowtown, population over 300,000, at the age of twenty-three. She was green under the collar in every way, but boy, could that girl sing.

In her first year of teaching, she ran into the refined, bigger-than-life Texas royalty named Virginia Garrett Seelig. They had little in common other than the music they were so very passionate about and the ministry that surrounded it. One day, they decided to try out a duet and never looked back. Their voices fit together smoothly and perfectly. Mom was a mezzosoprano, Joe Ann a dramatic soprano. They had huge voices that could cross over each other, and no one could tell who was singing which part. It was magic!

By the way, they were both funnier than hell—one-upping each other on the humor scale and barely flirting with the taste meter—that is, nothing risqué.

On a personal level, Joe Ann hit our house like an Oklahoma tornado—in all the good ways. The *Extreme Makeover 1959* episode was about to take place. This was a secret to no one. Cinderella was getting ready for the ball, moving from a farm in Durant to the world stage. Joe Ann was grateful for the help. She turned into a beautiful woman standing alongside another beautiful woman, singing their hearts out. I'm pretty sure it started with a manicure that was not available in rural Oklahoma. It moved to hair, makeup, and wardrobe. In no time, the swan emerged. They began singing together in 1959 and continued recording and performing around the world until 1975. It was quite a run.

Steve and I really didn't know it, but we were starved for attention from a strong, decisive figure. A male figure would have been ideal, but Dad had completely abdicated any direct role in our lives. I think he was uncomfortable showing any kind of soft side. He had had no male role model and was passing that on. From age seven, Dad had worked alongside his mother. He had no time for extracurricular things, other than marching band. His repertoire of manly things was woefully undiscovered. He soon began riding and raising Arabian horses.

Joe Ann's upbringing had been completely different from anything we had ever experienced. She found a family and two boys to bring into the more masculine side of living. We loved it (even though I was not exactly a Grizzly Adams in training).

She taught us to:

- Hunt (even how to clean a squirrel or two—there is that "Ewwwww" again from age five!).
- Fish (cleaning the fish was not nearly as gross as cleaning mammals).
- Gig frogs (which, yes, we would then eat).
- Ski and even jump the wake on a slalom.
- Drive a truck with a stick shift.
- Get dirty and have gross fingernails.
- Sleep under the stars (in a tent).
- Enjoy some Oklahoma food, although it was not much different from Texas food (red beans and cornbread, although her favorite was red beans on coconut cake).

She bought a lake house and a motorboat for our little family to enjoy when getting away was possible. Dad did not participate in a single activity I just listed. His defense was raising and owning the Arabian horses, which he did for forty years. I rode one of his horses once. I was not able to get the gist of how to communicate with the horse via knee and ankle pressure on that first time out. I never returned to the training ring.

Joe Ann stayed in our lives. She sang at my wedding and supported all my dreams and goals of professional singing. I am so grateful to have had Joe Ann in our lives for those sixteen years, from age eight to age twenty-four. I learned so very much that otherwise I would never have learned. Going back over the manly list, the only one I still do is eat Southern food.

Fast Forward. In 1975, everything changed. That year, Joe Ann received the second blessing. She was super-filled with the Holy Spirit. It included some of that speaking in tongues. She decided that anyone who didn't get the "fill 'er up" of the Spirit could no longer be part of her immediate life.

Joe Ann let my mother know that they could no longer perform together because Mom hadn't gotten the second blessing (like they were passing around seconds on gravy and Mom looked away for a nanosecond). Oops—sorry. No seconds on gravy? You're out. If that wasn't bad enough, she believed that the ministry she and Mom had had for all those years was for naught because they hadn't been filled with the Spirit.

It broke my mother's heart. She was never quite the same. The tie was severed. Mom died forty-plus years later, and to my knowledge there was never an apology or any reconciliation. I don't think they ever saw each other again.

As you will read later, my wife Vicki and I served as Southern Baptist missionaries for two years in Austria at this time. Getting selected was not hard; we were Seeligs. But when Joe Ann Shelton wrote a recommendation, we were so far in.

In 1975, when Joe Ann got the blessing, she wrote a letter to us in Austria. It was with a heavy heart that she needed to share with us that she had been noticing "leakage" in our Holy Spirit gas tank. She was concerned because our messages back home were filled with both stories of our mission work *and* the things each of us was experiencing in our respective studies. She said she felt it necessary to write to the Southern Baptist Mission Board and request that her recommendation be rescinded.

I never saw her again. Years later, the preacher who fired me and the man who lobbed the most evil, pious blows against me was none other than John Bisagno, Joe Ann's trumpet-playing evangelistic partner from 1958. Small world.

I will never forgive her for what she did to my mother. I would never try to define their bond, relationship, love for each other. They were as close as two good Christian women could be in that time. I also know that they were my role models for love between adults. I experienced firsthand what a person with a broken heart looks like. Worst of all, it was my mother's. And while she had many "friends" who adored her and surrounded her for the rest of her life, there was never another Joe Ann.

Chapter 9

Boys Choir and "Happy Talk"

Until I was eight, Dad worked in big churches. From the age of six through age eight, I often took the bus from school straight to the church. Mom was a full-time voice professor and wouldn't be home until later.

One day, as I entered the church, there was a poster that read, "Auditions for the world-famous Texas Boys Choir in room 214." Think of the Vienna Boys Choir, but instead of those adorable rosy cheeks and little-boy cassocks, our choir had cowboy hats and boots, the most adorable gingham shirts, plus a bandana. That was reason enough to join! They toured the world. They even had a choir school that was one of the best in Fort Worth. It was the real deal and a world-class musical organization.

I marched myself down there, walked in, and said, "I'd like to audition." They asked if I had an audition slot reserved. I did not. I told them my name, and the Seelig brand got me in. Of course, they knew my mother. I filled out the audition form.

I have no idea what I sang, but most definitely it was a soul-stirring medley of favorite hymns. I believe I had chosen a set centered on the cross. No "Caro Mio Ben" for me. After the audition, I went on my way, most likely heading to Fellowship Supper and the divine lemon icebox pie. I forgot to mention the audition.

A few days later, my parents received a letter inviting me to join the top chorus in the boys choir organization. The conductor, George Bragg, was a legend. Few brand-new boys were assigned to the top choir. There was a hierarchy of training choirs. I skipped it!

Before my parents could express joy or sorrow, the first question was, "Tim, how did this happen?" I relayed the story. They were surprised neither by my audacity nor the results. I was over the moon with excitement, jumping up and down and ready for my costume fitting!

They told me I would not be joining the chorus, offering lame excuses: time, energy, transportation. I was crestfallen. But there were no arguments to change their minds. This was strange since they really supported all my musical endeavors. I carried the disappointment around for quite some time.

Every time the Texas Boys Choir appeared on television or I heard they had taken some fabulous tour, the possibility that I might have been with them hurt. With that door closed and the strong "obey your parents" ethic, I just devoted myself even more to my church youth choir, bell choir, and music at school.

Decades later, I found out the reason. They knew Mr. Bragg in professional circles. They, along with some of their friends, had randomly decided he had gay tendencies. He was fifty and had never married. They did not want me around those influences. There was no proof—ever—just good-old Baptist innuendo, full of judgment, the kind that can ruin careers if spoken in the wrong place. There would be no further discussion.

They thought they had protected me. They felt quite pious for doing the right thing. I am still sorry I did not get to have that amazing experience working with Mr. Bragg. That pious thing would bite me in the ass many more times. Who gave it teeth?

Some of My Best Friends Are...Women

You have begun to get an inkling of my early relationships: a lot of estrogen and not much testosterone. In the early years, I had three matriarchs. My grandmother was my favorite. Her sister, Aunt Mary ("Aunt Mamie" to us), ran a close second. She was a live-in sorority house mother at Southern Methodist University. And my mom, of course, was the third. Meemaw, Mamie, and Mom.

Meemaw was soft and sweet and could envelop you in her arms and spirit with a single look or touch. Aunt Mamie was driven, a busy bee who did not leave her sorority "home" without gloves and a hat—ever. Mom, not soft or driven, lived her life with her head in the clouds thinking about music. I think I may be an amalgamation of all three of them!

Years later, the story would be told about how "special" little Tim was. Rather than play outdoors with the children, his very favorite activity was going with Mom and Aunt Mamie to Patsy's Fabric Barn, scrolling blissfully through dress patterns for hours. Who needed other children or bikes or balls? It just got you dirty. By the way, Aunt Mamie would sew. Mom would pay for the fabric.

Happy Talk

Elementary school was all about a pack of girlfriends on the playground (I may have had the biggest boy crush on Bobby Kellog.) My fourth-grade teacher was Mrs. Howington. She sang in our church and took voice lessons from my mom. When she decided to present a talent show, she paired me with a friend, Cathy, for a show-stopping duet of "Happy Talk" from the musical that was all the rage, *South Pacific*.

We were adorable doing the little hand motions. It wasn't a contest, but we won! And this began a long set of duets with girls, culminating in a husband/wife duo twenty-plus years later.

As a performer, Mom was always getting corsages for performances. She would put them in the refrigerator to keep a few days or longer, for no reason other than it seemed wasteful to throw away beautiful flowers. When the evening of the talent show arrived, she pulled one out and said, "Give this to Mrs. Howington as a thank you. She'll love it." It was fall, so it was lovely chrysanthemums in autumnal colors.

I presented it to her with great pomp and circumstance in front of the entire class as we gathered to put the final touches on our extravaganza. She immediately put it on to wear proudly through the show. She was truthfully overwhelmed at the thoughtfulness.

I'll never forget watching that corsage through the evening as, one by one, the petals dropped to the stage floor until pretty much all that remained was some florist tape and a few ribbons.

At the end of the evening, Mrs. Howington approached and said, "Oh, Tim, I am so very sorry about the beautiful corsage. Please ask your mother for the name of the florist so I can call them and ask for a replacement or a refund for her."

There was no way to tell her the corsage had been tucked between the Coca-Cola cherry Jell-O mold (dear non-Southerners, it's a thing: Coca-Cola, cherry Jell-O, and cherry pie filling) and the Rotel Velveeta dip for God only knows how long.

My mother called a florist and had a new one delivered to the school. I was crushed. But not as bad as those tragic chrysanthemums.

Did we learn a lesson from that saga? No, we did not.

Looking back now, "Happy Talk" was definitely an interesting choice of the songs in *South Pacific*. We had absolutely no idea there were racist overtones. We certainly had no idea there was another song in the musical with some of the most poignant lyrics of all time: "You've Got to Be Carefully Taught." We weren't ready for the message then, and, sadly, we're far from it now.

You've got to be taught before it's too late,
Before you are six or seven or eight,
To hate all the people your relatives hate.

Chapter 10

Cheerleading for "Jewsus"

Seventh grade is quite a shock in so many ways. My junior high encompassed grades seven through nine with more than 1,000 students. You changed classrooms every hour. How does one find a "place" to belong? It was clear I was going to have to find the nerd corner pretty quickly.

As the weeks passed, things began to sort out. It happened mostly in classrooms where the students had a chance to judge who might be a suitable gang to hang out with. It could have happened with affinity groups, but I was so busy at church that I didn't join anything at school. I was not in choir. I played in the orchestra, but those were *not* my people.

Have you ever thought about how precarious those weeks are in the life of a young person? I liked smart people, not snotty people or athletes. And I knew there was no need to try to fit in with the pretty people. I probably would have gravitated toward the colors of the rainbow, but our junior high was 100 percent white. Integration would not come until my senior year of high school.

Midway through fall, I had myself a buddy: Alan Hamill. So much to love.

- He was different from most. I loved that.
- He was Jewish. I came to love that.
- He was whipsmart and hilarious. We battled each other for the best grades.
- His parents owned the huge hardware/gift store near school.
- They had a gorgeous home on a hill.
- He had one sister.
- For me, his life was a total dream.
- He had Sunday mornings free and a religion with no hell.
- He had really hairy arms.
- It was perfect.

We began hanging out. I was invited to spend Friday nights at his house. His mother made the most delicious, exotic breakfasts ever: blintzes and latkes and schmear—oh my. That is not Baptist food! I don't remember a casserole unless noodle kugel qualifies. I was just in heaven. I felt like a Jew.

After breakfast, we would take a trip with Harriet, his gorgeous big sister, to Neiman Marcus. She was preparing for a lavish wedding. It was my first introduction to gorgeous things: Rosenthal, Christofle, Baccarat, and the like. It was a world I truly had not known existed.

While my family lived a comfortable life and Dad cooked amazing gourmet food as a hobby, we had—in the back of the kitchen cabinets—our share of Melmac plastic dishes and drinking glasses collected as incentives from the local gas station. That was not true of Alan. However, at the same time Mom and Dad were traveling the world—separately—our taste meter was rising with Lalique and Lladro tchotchkes brought home as souvenirs. No Precious Moments for us!

We discussed religion. Ours were so different from one another. He and his family looked at me with the Southern "bless your heart," but they were most kind. We discussed girls. Alan, with his social status and religion, was required to date more than I ever was. He went to dances. I didn't. He was expected to have girlfriends. I just had our church youth group as cover.

Alan and I did everything together. It was amazing having a best friend during those awkward junior high days. The Hamills invited me to Harriet's wedding, a fabulous Jewish affair. I shopped for this one! I was completely enamored with the canopy and the breaking of the glass. It was not a Baptist wedding. They had fun. They danced. They drank alcohol. I loved these people!

As Alan and I grew closer, we would make plans about things we wanted to do. Football was out—too rough. Wood and metal shop were eliminated—dirty fingernails. Home economics would have been amazing, but it was 1963. No marching band—too loud. The options were narrowing. Voilà! Harriet had been a college cheerleader. McLean Junior High had male cheerleaders in ninth grade. Why not go for it? We tried out, and—shock of shocks—we both made it.

My impetus, other than to do everything with Alan, was the fabulous outfits. Slimming, in fact. They even had the bright red leisure-suit-style jumpsuit in size "husky." By the way, that word was emblazoned in bold six-inch letters on the irremovable tag on JCPenney jeans. It was an entire line of clothing at Sears. So much for pretending I was petite by turning sideways all the time.

My junior high was the most prominent in Fort Worth. It advertised itself as a high school prep program for the 3,000-student R. L. Paschal High School, which would usher you right into Texas Christian University, mere blocks away, or the University of Texas in Austin if you wanted to party a lot, or had higher goals of going out of state! Not going to college was not an option for any child entering seventh grade at McLean.

Eight cheerleaders (four boys and four girls) were on the squad. I was best on the pom-poms, and I had rhythm. My voice already had a stentorian presence. I did not do tumbling. I was a spotter. That is the funniest thing ever. Had a girl ever started to fall off the shoulders of her partner, I would have screamed and run for the bleachers, no doubt.

It started with a weeklong cheerleading camp, which, of course, was held at Southern Methodist University. I hated it. It was a hot-as-hell summer. They made us do all kinds of contortions for which my short, stubby body was not built. My favorite part was the evening circle, when we would pass the spirit stick around and everyone would tell stories. They were not really that interesting, but we were seated on the floor in an air-conditioned building, all "snuggled up."

Then it was fall and football season started. We were ready to cheer the Cardinals to victory. I don't really remember watching any of the games. I was focused on my pom-poms—and Alan.

I guess the most important thing I can say is that I made it through the whole year of football and basketball games. The eight of us did become really good friends. Jeannie Pitman, one of the "other" girls on the squad, had a crush on me and tried to make a move. I'm pretty sure I relied on my pom-pom as a shield.

Alan and I became even closer. And I can't say there was not an exhilaration of standing on the field looking at thousands of people in the stands, turning occasionally to look at the field, my gaze not getting much farther than the jockstraps visible under the players' fabulous costumes/uniforms.

At the end of the year, we moved to the big-time high school, where my brother was a big deal. He would be selected as "Most Handsome" for his senior yearbook. That was not going to be his legacy for me. He didn't actually acknowledge my existence. That was fine.

But they had tenth-grade cheerleaders, and Alan and I were ready. We had the pom-poms! I was still a little clunky on the tumbling runs—which to me meant falling down. I am glad the audition didn't require knowledge of the rules of football.

We were not ready for so many to try out. The squad would be eight girls and eight boys. At prelims the judges narrowed it down to twelve girls and nine boys. The day of auditions came in the high school auditorium. I had fluffed my pom-poms with a frenzy, looking like Jimmy Hendrix on a humid day.

All students were invited to watch, and it seemed that at least 2,999 out of 3,000 were there.

First came the "group" auditions, where we did a choreographed routine. The Dallas Cowboys cheerleaders had been founded in 1960. The girls trying out for cheerleader were laser-focused on that as a career possibility. They were kickin' to heaven. We boys were just support for their fireworks of flying phalanges.

When the boys' turn came to lead a chant (more like yell leaders) we began: "Push 'em back, Panthers!" I began at a mezzoforte to get the crowd warmed up before putting the pedal to the metal with a fully supported diaphragmatic crescendo. My voice filled the auditorium to the rafters. It was *my* secret weapon. I had it in the bag.

Results were posted on the school office door at eight o'clock the next morning. Alan and I got to school early, filled with excitement for the next chapter to start. We read the eight names. Alan made it, but I did not. I was number nine. Some of the "mean girls" (boys included in that) took to calling me "Number Nine" in the halls as they passed.

It was a huge disappointment, but preparation for many of the difficult life lessons ahead for me. I didn't wallow in my loss. I joined PSOP, or Panther Spirit of Paschal. It was a group of forty students who sat in front of the cheerleaders at games. There were no tumbling runs—thank you, Jesus—but there were still great outfits, including white cowboy hats. I loved that.

Here's the funny thing: I have actually spent the rest of my life as a cheerleader. I traded in pom-poms for a baton, and while I don't shake it the same way, people do respond.

On an even more important level, I cheerlead someone every single day. Some days I get to cheerlead a fellow seeker with a word of encouragement. I cheerlead for music. I cheerlead for equal rights. I constantly cheerlead for anyone who feels like they are "other." I tell them to look their opponents in the eye across that field and chant with me, "Push 'em back; push 'em back! Go, Panthers!"

In high school, Alan and I drifted apart. We began focusing on other activities and making new friends. I just didn't see him much. We talked occasionally, and I knew he had settled on Boston College and premed. He knew I had chosen music and was off to—where else?—Abilene, Texas.

Toward the end of summer, I wrote a long letter to Alan. I'm sure in hindsight it felt like a love letter, although neither of us had ever hinted at any such thing. About halfway through the letter, the tone changed. The bottom line: The deepest regret in my life and certainly in our friendship was that I was unable to lead him to a saving knowledge of the Lord and Savior Jesus Christ. That failure, I said, would always be on my head and in my heart.

Oh, the regrets. I could have done it in the china aisle of Neiman's or on Saturday morning with his entire family. No, I had not wanted to change him one bit. But I had been taught to shove our religion down other people's throats. And I had not done that.

Showing the letter to my parents and others earned me praise and maybe bought me a few more years of peace. I had done what God wanted me to do. That very idea would haunt me in later years.

Chapter 11

Assassinations and the Shoe Salesman

The 1960s were colorful, yet one of the more troubled decades in American history. I missed out on almost all of it. Looking back, I had no idea how insular my life really was. Yet there were a couple events that cut right through the self-created fog.

A certain Friday in November 1963 was a day we had all looked forward to since September, when it was announced that President Kennedy was coming to Fort Worth. This was a big deal. Dallas was the "big city," but he had chosen to begin his morning in our very own town. Thousands greeted him at every turn. I was in seventh grade.

As soon as we got to school and settled into our classrooms, we listened on the intercom to the speech the president gave across from the Hotel Texas, where he was staying. Everyone was there: Congressman Jim Wright, Senator Yarborough, Governor Connally, and Vice President Johnson. Thousands had greeted his arrival late the night before. The whole city was electrified by his presence.

Even though the sound coming from the classroom intercom was not very good, we sat still, inspired by every word and that strange Bar Harbor accent. He was thrilling and called out Fort Worth's aviation enterprise. We were allowed to continue listening in as he and his entourage made their way to Fort Worth's Carswell Air Force Base for the ten-minute flight to Dallas's Love Field.

When they took off, the principal decided it was time to get back to our normal school day. Around 1:30 the principal came back on the intercom: "President Kennedy has been killed." It was anything but a normal day. School was being dismissed. The next three days, we did nothing. There was absolutely nothing on our three black-and-white network television channels but coverage of what would be one of the most devastating moments in our history. Or so we thought.

After three days, life returned to almost normal, filled with all the things that keep kids occupied and oblivious to the larger world around them.

In 1968, as a junior in high school, one of my part-time jobs was as a shoe salesman at Thom McAn. It was in one of the more diverse malls in Fort Worth.

It was wonderful getting out of my white church, white school, white neighborhood, white existence. I absolutely loved it. Other than Betty, the maid who had been with us for years, I had not had much contact with people of any other color except when my church youth group delivered Thanksgiving dinner to those "less fortunate." (Seriously, did we used to say that?)

I began to realize I was missing out on ninety percent of real life—the good stuff and the bad. I saw a little of that other life on television (now in color), and our fellow Texan Lyndon Baines Johnson was president. I spoke Texan just like he did. I vaguely knew there was a war going on and there were riots.

I did know there was a burgeoning movement of lost souls wandering around San Francisco. How did I know? Because in 1968 the youth choir from my church took a mission trip to San Francisco to witness to them. Oh boy— another ironic life-circle. The people I had prayed for in 1968 became my own people in 2011. I wish to God one of them had pulled me off the bus and saved me from the decades to come. I would have been a fabulous hippie (except for the personal hygiene part).

Back to 1968: It was Thursday, April 4, the day before Good Friday, and I was working at the shoe store. Catholics apparently had a name for it, which I would find out much, much later: Maundy Thursday. I had no idea who she was or what she had to do with Good Friday, but it was a pretty name, kind of like Mandy, but classier.

All employees were to work that evening because of the Easter rush. Easter required new shoes and a new hat at the very least. Most customers had procured their hats long ago. They knew what dress they were wearing. Now it was time to pull it all together in one symphony of pastels, like the colored Easter eggs that would hail the resurrection. The place was packed. We were frantically trying to keep the customers happy.

I had pretty much settled in with two specific customers. They were absolutely adorable. I wish I could remember their names all these years later. I will never forget how excited they were that Easter was here. We chatted each time I returned with new shoeboxes. They were so very excited that I was in church choir. They sang in their choir too.

It must have been around 7:30 that evening when a man came running in screaming, "Dr. King's been shot! Dr. King's been shot!" Everything in the store turned completely silent, as if earth was suspended and needed to catch its breath. Customers and employees streamed out into the mall, where it was no longer quiet.

Wails and sobs of disbelief bounced off the walls in one fathomless moment of horror. The woman I had been helping, her friend, and I walked out of the store. They turned to me and without a moment's hesitation took me in their arms. For a moment I was part of that family. I was not that white boy, part of a race that had subjugated them for centuries. I was not the spoiled and entitled teen who was planning his trip to Europe. No, I was Tim. They did not hold me responsible for being part of the almost-fatal blow to their spirit on that Maundy Thursday.

No, I was Tim, the nice boy who had been so friendly moments before, the one who sang in the church choir and who, without a single complaint, stacked boxes of shoes by their chairs. I was just a fellow traveler. I then got passed from small group to group. I had passed some sort of initiation by weeping with them. They could see the empathy in my eyes. They could feel it in my touch, my hug.

The mall stayed open for a while. It became almost completely silent, with people moving like zombies, with only an occasional outburst of grief. There was nothing to do. The news was not getting to the mall. We simply went home, not because we wanted to, but because we had run out of communal grief and desperately needed to move into a private space to even begin to comprehend what had just happened to our world.

For me, it suddenly became personal because I knew that this was the first time I had literally and figuratively put myself in the shoes of a community other than mine. That moment was one of the milestones on the way to my future life as an activist. It was that very fall of 1968, my senior year, when my high school integrated.

I wish I had had my Brownie camera to take a photo. But that would have somehow cheapened the moment, spoiled the authenticity of a very deep shift in this man. It would last throughout my life.

Chapter 12

Should Have Known

There is a moment when you actually realize you are spending more time looking at one particular character on a television show. It's just where your attention goes. You might be looking for role models, researching various ways to "be a man," or attempting to fill in the gap left by an "absent" father. Oops! That may have been just me.

In the 1950s and 1960s, television was a wonderland. We stepped from the black-and-white world of Auntie Em into the glorious Technicolor world of Dorothy, ruby red slippers and all. Women on TV were mostly portrayed as housewives or sisters. That fact was fine by me. June Cleaver was the perfect mom. I liked Sally Fields as Gidget. Marlo Thomas, with whom I would work forty-plus years later, was everyone's favorite *That Girl*.

The female bombshells on TV would come a bit later with the likes of *Charlie's Angels*. Many a young closeted teenage boy made his parents very happy with a poster of Farrah Fawcett in his room. They had no clue it was the feathered bangs to which he was attracted and aspired to emulate.

As an awkward teenager, hormones raging, voice breaking, I had a list of TV favorites. I was a huge fan of the four men of *Bonanza*: Daddy Ben, Adam, Hoss, Little Joe. Sadly, it predated VCRs and DVRs, so I could only watch them one time. It is perfect that "Hoss," a fellow Texan, started the Bonanza Steakhouse chain. Both television show and restaurant were a delicious smorgasbord.

While the women on TV in the 1960s were moms and sisters, the men were not exactly father figures or brothers. The list of gorgeous men is just too long: Paul Newman, Rock Hudson, Sean Connery, Omar Shariff, and Steve McQueen for something a little rougher.

As a teen, I cut out favorite pics of the stars and kept them in the very back of a dresser drawer. There was not a girl among them. These were lost in a house fire at age eighteen. Thank goodness! Those gentlemen were truly appreciated just for their acting skills. Should I have known? Nope. Surely I would start watching the women soon.

The next step in my "should have known" evolution was earth-shattering. It was no longer on the small screen. It was no longer a picture cut out of *Life* magazine. This was real life, people.

My parents were out of town at a Southern Baptist Convention meeting. I was sixteen and ridiculously responsible, so there was no babysitter. My brother was off at college, so I had the whole house to myself. Two of my friends from youth choir at church had occasionally talked about what it would be like to taste, or even drink, alcohol. It was the perfect time to use my empty house.

After a Wednesday night prayer meeting, we went home to give it a try. We knew *nothing* about what to drink, how much to drink, or what it would feel like to be tipsy. After all, the Baptist motto was, "I don't drink, and I don't chew, and I don't go with girls who do!"

One guy's older sister supplied the goods. I'm pretty sure she was intending to teach us a lesson. Speaking of smorgasbord, it was a variety of leftovers from someone's liquor cabinet. We had not eaten since the fellowship supper before the prayer meeting. In the brown paper bag she had clandestinely passed to her brother were whisky, vodka, and gin. Thank God there was no Everclear.

We thought whisky sounded masculine, so we chose that and mixed it with Dr Pepper (a Texas staple). Doing the bitter beer face with every sip, we proceeded with deadly focus on our goal. When we ran out of whisky, we switched to vodka and grape Crush. Somewhere along the way, we started a little teenage boy exploration—clothes remained on, just the pink parts barely exposed and a little Vaseline Intensive Care. The moment passed.

We were so drunk. I was the one who started throwing up first. My really good friends helped me to the bathtub and dumped me in, still throwing up. They were bona fide Florence Nightingales. They found the Pepto Bismol and, as a joke, mixed it with gin. Yes, that cocktail might be called a Pink Flamingo. The next morning, I felt like I had eaten one.

Chapter 13

And the House Came Burning Down

It was a hot summer in Texas. That's redundant and an understatement. I had just graduated from high school and spent the summer working, of course, but mostly getting ready to go off to college. I had new "college" clothes and everything to decorate my dorm room. I don't think there was ever a high school graduate more ready to shake some dust off his shoes at the Fort Worth city limits.

For the second year in a row, my parents had put together a group of family and friends to go to Europe. By leading the tour, Mom and Dad (and I) got to go for free. For the second year in a row, Steve didn't want to go. He stayed at school in Shawnee, Oklahoma.

Two weeks before we were to leave, we woke up on a Saturday morning to find that, sitting in our driveway, our three cars had been covered in oil-based paint. We were puzzled. We had to have all three cars towed to the auto repair shop. They were returned in a few days. Once again, they were parked in our driveway.

Saturday morning, neighbors came running over. All three cars had been set on fire—in our driveway. Firefighters came quickly. Whoever had done this had not done a very good job; only the inside was damaged. Luckily, there were no explosions.

It was no longer funny or just curious. The police got involved, but there was no way to trace anything. Three days later, we departed for a fourteen-day tour of Europe with our entourage of cousins, uncle, aunt, and a variety of church folks. We refueled in Nova Scotia and then landed in our first port of call, Amsterdam. This was a nonalcoholic trip of Baptists! Doobies would have been a mortal sin.

Our motor coach took us tired tourists to our hotel. Upon arrival, the office had a phone call waiting for Dad from the Fort Worth police. Our house had burned to the ground.

The question then was whether or not we could continue on our fourteen-day tour or whether we would need to go home. The police assured us that what was left of the house was "safe." My brother and some neighbors, with the help of the firefighters, would go through the scene to recover any valuables that could be found, such as jewelry.

Off we went to eight countries. While there, we kept in touch with the police, of course. They were in full-on investigation mode. When we finally arrived home, they met us at the airport and took us to an undisclosed hotel. They were taking no precautions with someone who would commit three crimes in a row—all obviously aimed at us. They sat with us for hours, grilling us about who we thought might have done this.

They focused in on me. Did I have any high school enemies? But my not making cheerleader because my tumbling runs ran out was no reason for revenge. It was horrible.

Other than everything I owned, I lost two irreplaceable items:

1. The stack of IOUs my brother had signed over the years. Those had become dust. No bill-collecting for me.
2. My tragic collection of photos of handsome men, torn from magazines. I was relieved to hear that everything in my desk was gone. Whew!

My frantic shopping spree to replace worldly goods was all covered by insurance. Then I would go college—driven by my father—the next week. I told him I didn't need his help setting up my room, so he turned around and drove back.

Mom and Dad rebuilt the house with the help of a fancy designer who talked them into turning the middle bedroom—the one my brother and I had shared all those years—into a TV room. No bed. It never felt the same to go back there.

About a month later, the police solved the crimes. My cousin Missy was one of the family members on tour with us. She was twenty-five at the time and had a boyfriend who did not want her to go. He thought the painted cars would stop us from going. When it did not, he thought the Roman candle cars would stop us. Nope.

When we left for the airport, he came along to say a tearful goodbye to Missy, then drove back to Fort Worth and went shopping for paraphernalia. He started the fire and waited, thinking surely we would come home. We did not. But before striking the match, he stole credit cards from my mother's top dresser drawer.

The next week, he used one of the stolen credit cards to buy gas. The attendant, thinking the boyfriend was acting strange, wrote down his license plate number. The billing statement showed gas charges while we were in Europe. We assumed the credit cards had burned up too.

The police tracked down the gas station, and voilà—cousin's boyfriend. He was charged with vandalism and theft. You can't prove arson if the arsonist does a good job! No fingerprints. He was put on a payment plan totaling something like $10,000. Missy did not marry the boyfriend.

It was only the first time I would lose everything.

Chapter 14

Phase or a Belt Notch?

Being an overachiever, I loved school except for the social aspect. I graduated near the top of my 900-student senior class in high school. My ACT and SAT scores were near the top. I could go to any university I wanted. And I had some in mind.

My parents were proud, of course. They added one word to "any university I wanted."

They simply said I could go to "any *Baptist* university I wanted." It was slim pickings in 1969. So I "chose" my parents' alma mater, Hardin-Simmons University in Abilene, Texas, for a few reasons:

1. full scholarship—either on talent or because "Seelig";
2. the temptation of an international USO tour;
3. an excellent voice teacher who had studied with my mom;
4. Mom and Dad had met there. Dad had gotten saved there. They had gotten married there. They had given my dad an honorary doctorate.

Off I went—with a brand-new wardrobe in tow. By the time I had arrived, my fate was set. My major would be music. It was one of the accepted majors on the list of future ministries that would guarantee the Seelig brand would live on. But in exactly which direction would I go?

All the new music majors gathered in a big room, bundles of nerves. This was our new "class" and our first gathering. All the music faculty were there as well. I looked fabulous—a real standout.

I observed as the professor in charge asked each student to stand, tell where he or she was from, and what each intended to study. I literally watched as a student stood, introduced himself, and rather apologetically said, "Music education." The next stood and shyly said, "Sacred music." The next stood, introduced himself, and boldly proclaimed, "Opera!"

There were murmurs of approval and envy all around. This continued. However, when it got to me, I wasn't going to slither into a major of which I was not proud. "I'll take opera for $1,000!" The die was cast. No other categories need be explored. *Die* was to become the operative word in that sentence. I pursued opera with a single-minded focus, until I won the pot of gold at the end of the rainbow—one of the few and coveted full-time opera jobs that existed. And I thought I would die.

Back to 1969 Abilene: Armed with my new focus on becoming an opera singer, I pulled out the "driven dad and talented mom" combo. Put them together and what do you get? Single-focused Tim, who would stop at nothing to advance toward that goal, taking no prisoners.

- From Hardin-Simmons University to Oklahoma Baptist University
- From OBU to North Texas State University
- From NTSU to the Mozarteum in Salzburg

Four schools and four degrees: a bachelor's, two masters, and a doctorate, all in vocal performance, with a minor in choral conducting. I was a natural. I had sung in choirs since I was in the cradle! The other choices back then were music theory and musicology. Conducting it would be. And this was a good thing, as it turned out. I was well educated if not well trained for the tasks ahead. Training would come on the job, whatever job, and I had a few. Four degrees in music had me singing all the time. The music—and my minor—would save my life.

I was off to college to expand my horizons and learn new things, as the school brochure said.

Things to bring: an open mind, a curious spirit, and a Bible. Meet young women and men of like mind, freshly scrubbed and ready for fellowship. Oh, and move from your small bedroom at home to live, for the first time, in same-sex dorms with communal showers. What could go wrong?

When I arrived at the music school of the small Baptist liberal arts school in Abilene, Texas, there were a couple older students who took me under their wing. It was interesting that I immediately thought they were a little creepy (too much, too soon). It's not surprising that I had *queer* written all over me.

Remember, our house had burned down two weeks before. I had been on the insurance-funded shopping spree of a lifetime. The latest fashions: big bell-bottom pants, shirts with collars that reached to my shoulders, matching shoes and belts, and even a few spiffy little scarves to add the final touch. I had lost my "baby weight." (Can you still call it that at eighteen?) It was hot (Abilene in August), and I was trying to be butch, although I only knew that word to mean a flat-top haircut.

It was all explained that I was there to become an opera singer and simply had a dramatic flair. Dear God, why didn't someone just sit me down and say, "Girl, if you are not gay, you need to take all those clothes back where you got them and start over"? No one dared. I was a Seelig at a Baptist school.

I won the freshman talent show, singing a duet with the cutest girl around, Betsy. We won with a breathtaking medley from *The Sound of Music*. Our "Edelweiss" brought down the house. Lord, is my life full of a bunch of self-fulfilling prophecies. It wouldn't be long before I was living on the beautiful "set" they built for the movie in Salzburg. Tourists actually believe that.

I didn't go home for any of the holidays, including Christmas. Anger at my father was at the seething point. I finally realized he had ignored me my entire life, showing more attention to his Arabian horses and the string of young Baptist preachers he mentored at the seminary than he ever showed me. Mom suffered because of my boycott of Dad and his lack of affection toward her. I stayed with my voice teacher and his wife over the holidays. Mom and Dad sent Christmas gifts. I sent them back.

When the end of the spring semester approached, I was still in no mind to grace my father with my presence for the summer, so I went to summer school. During my freshman year I had pledged a fraternity. I needed to belong to something so badly.

One of the older members of the fraternity, Grady, had graduated a few years before. He was twenty-five and trying to find himself. He had a big personality—funny, charming, handsome—and he was a big man on campus (although I should call him campus-adjacent because, by this point, he had no business hanging around, but I didn't even wonder). He approached me and said he was renting an apartment over the summer and needed a roommate to share it. That was perfect. He was responsible. I was nineteen and even more responsible. The bills would get paid.

Summers in Abilene are miserable. Wait, summers in Texas are miserable. He rented a tiny one-bedroom apartment with a single wheezing window unit, actually an evaporative cooler that just spewed water, in the living room, cooling the whole shotgun-style house: living room in the front, bedroom in the middle, and bathroom and sizzling kitchen farthest from the "air conditioner."

As the primary tenant, Grady would take the bedroom with an actual bed. I would sleep on a lumpy, sprung-spring sofa in the living room, closest to the blessed contraption that brought the daytime temperature of 110 down to a moist 80 or so for the night. These were absolutely miserable living conditions.

Even though I had been raised always to wear appropriate clothing and with enough body issues to fill a psychiatric tome on the topic, we just couldn't wear much clothing. One night was especially torrid. I was stretched out on my back with not even a sheet. Just as I was about to drift to sleep, Grady came in and said, "I just can't stay in the middle bedroom. There is no air at all. Is it okay if I sleep here on the floor next to the sofa?"

"Of course," I said.

Neither of us drifted anywhere. I lay there in the heat completely frozen—wide awake, wondering, and fearful. For those of you who have been suspended in this space between repulsion and curiosity, knowing that the next moments could change your life, you have my sympathy.

Then there was the possibility that I was making all of this up. Perhaps Grady had indeed fallen asleep and my worries were for naught. Everything I had been taught passed before my eyes, screaming, "Run! Your life is about to be ruined." On the other hand, there were *Bonanza* men, the pictures in the back of the dresser drawer, and the lotion.

I have absolutely no idea how long I hung suspended in slow motion. I heard a slight rustle. Then a hand reached up, resting on the side of the sofa/bed. He left it there for an eternity. I will assume that since I made no move to roll over or otherwise block the trajectory of his hand, he knew the struggle in my mind—and body. After maybe five more minutes, he moved his hand closer until it was barely touching my hip.

The battle within me was raging. I had three choices:

1. Take his hand and politely move it away.
2. Continue lying there as if I were a marble statue and maybe he would get the hint.
3. Roll away from him, pretending it was a natural sleep roll, which would telegraph my lack of interest.

I chose option three, which was not the right choice. Rather than seeing it as a refusal, Grady took it as an invitation. I was so ignorant. Within seconds he had moved up and was lying next to me, leading the moves from there. You don't need the details. It didn't last very long. There was nothing romantic or even sexy. It was certainly not tender, as I had always thought it would be. It hurt in every possible way. I do need to share with you how I felt. Dirty fills the bill. Used. Horrified. Violated. It was not consensual. Touching another man had been a fantasy for a very long time. It would be a long time before that fantasy returned.

He obviously knew that I had never done anything like that before. All the signs were there—before, during, and after. There had been no discussion before moving in. There had been no hint that this might be part of the apartment-sharing agreement. I feel confident that it was his goal. I was somewhat of a prize—a Seelig in a Baptist school. Was I just another young notch in his belt? I would find out soon enough.

When he was done, he moved back to the floor and fell soundly asleep, sated. I stayed in the bed, not sleeping. What would I do? What would I say? I had eight more weeks as his roommate. It turns out that I didn't have to say anything. Grady knew there would not be a repeat. It never was his goal. I stayed away from the apartment as much as possible. He never again asked to sleep on the floor of the living room.

This haunted me my entire sophomore year. I did not know where to put it. Was I gay? I didn't think so. Although I was completely torn apart inside, the Tim Show was in full bloom on the outside. Musically and academically, I was soaring. On the inside I was broken, desperately seeking some meaning. Why did this happen to me? Whatever signals I had sent to indicate it was something to which I was open needed to be searched out and eradicated. It was obviously my fault.

For years I struggled with this experience and my own shame. Even though it was not consensual, I wrestled with my own guilt. Why did I lie there and "take it"? Why couldn't I speak up for myself? Why was the psychological pain even greater than the physical pain, which healed itself? My entire next year was torturous. I still had to see Grady at fraternity events.

At the end of the year, I left Hardin-Simmons University. I left Grady, who had stopped all communication and was off to the new fraternity pledges. I saw it for what it was. He also knew that, in 1971, there was no one I could tell about a twenty-five-year-old man hunting his prey and finding it in a nineteen-year-old boy. There would be no repercussions for him.

I responded by running away. Next stop: Oklahoma Baptist University in Shawnee, Oklahoma. I thought I could escape the gay by moving. Surely it would not find me in a small town in Oklahoma, for heaven's sake. I would be safe and jump back on that narrow path.

My next physical homosexual encounter was thirteen years later. Grady went on to marry a prominent young woman in Abilene. It did not work out. He died of AIDS.

Epilogue: I am now nearing seventy. Sharing this story immediately brought back the emotional pain of that night. The shame is there as strong as it was after the event. One would hope that the repercussions of molestation would diminish over time. They have not. In fact, the more I learn to know myself, the more horror arises that this happened to me. If you have ever experienced anything like this, please tell someone you trust. If you have no one you trust, as I did for decades, look me up!

Chapter 15

Christian Counselor #1: Selecting a Wife

I had left Abilene and the gay in the dust as I struck out for greener—and straighter—pastures. My sudden departure from my parents' alma mater, Hardin-Simmons, was a bit of a surprise to all, but I did have cover in the form of a full music scholarship at Oklahoma Baptist University and a big USO trip. No one ever needed to know the real reason.

The physical move was pretty easy: my car, my string bass, and the now-two-year-old fashion wardrobe. I had added a few "normal" pieces along the way. That whole "look" was not going to work on the even more windswept plains of Oklahoma. I dodged that bullet.

The emotional move was not nearly as easy. I needed someone to talk to. I thought I knew the problem. I had done a whopper of a sin, or a whopper of a sin had been done on me, and I was devastated by it. I was also a little sad that it was not repeated. I felt that if I had had a second go at it, I could have, without doubt, known that it was not me and that I could forever walk away. But that did not happen.

I didn't know how to tell my parents I needed some counseling. That was not something good nineteen-year-old Baptist boys did. It was helpful that Mom, who suffered from depression her entire life, had broken the seal and begun her own forty-year journey through one therapist and medication after another. I would find out later that she never told any of them the root of her depression. Thanks to that, the stigma was not nearly as huge as it was for my fellow seekers.

I couldn't tell them the truth. (Can you say "reparative therapy"? You'll be saying it again in sixteen years.) So I told them I was having a difficult time with self-esteem. I was working really hard, and my singing was going really well, but I was having a hard time taking personal credit when I knew I was supposed to give God all the glory when complimented on my singing.

I needed to see someone to sort this out. After all, I was at the beginning of my career and was simply taking too much credit for being the one who went to the practice room every night, studied my foreign languages, memorized my music, and, most importantly, chose just the right outfit for every occasion.

The frightening part of the story was that they understood and supported my seeking help.

They said they would ask around for referrals to a good Christian psychiatrist in Oklahoma City, forty miles away. And they did. He was not a Baptist, but he was a Nazarene, and that passed their holy-smell test. The school, because "Seelig," allowed me to miss required chapel on every other Wednesday to drive to what we called "the city."

I dressed really nice. I walked into his office. We shook hands and sat down. He said, "So, Tim, why are you here?" I skipped the self-esteem/God part completely. I said, "I think I have homosexual tendencies," or something ridiculous like that. Jeez! I'm just surprised he didn't take one look at me and say, "Duh."

But no, he was kind and gentle and pulled out a few papers. He said it was a sexuality test. He wanted me to use the rest of our time taking the test and leave it with his receptionist when I was done. He would see me in two weeks. I have no idea if I told nothing but the truth, but considering the extent of my vast experience, there wasn't much to say.

I was so nervous for those two weeks. I went back over the questions and my answers one by one. Should I have said this or that? The effort was all for naught.

Two weeks went by. I made the drive to "the city." I may have dressed a little more "normally" this go-round. I sat down in front of him. He had my scores, right there in front of him. He had the very papers that would either send me careening out of control or allow me to stay the course.

Hands folded on my score sheet, he had a gentle smile as he said, "Tim, I have gone over your questionnaire. You are not a homosexual." I could have jumped right out of that chair and done one of my cheerleading tumbling runs.

I was relieved. He began going through scriptures with me, pointing out the ones that said homosexuality was really bad (not sure why he did that since we had both agreed I wasn't one). I think he thought it was kind of fun. Then he turned to scriptures about being a *man*, the ones about being the head of the household and procreating and so on (that sounded super-special).

It was a red-letter day. I was able to call my parents and tell them I was making wonderful progress on "Rise, shine, give God the glory, glory!" and all that. I continued for some time. Mom and Dad were happy to pay the psychiatrist's bill since it was going so well. And I still got to miss chapel every other week. All good.

The next visit to a Christian counselor, who was equally insightful, is coming up—in sixteen years.

Finding a Wife

I arrived at Oklahoma Baptist University as a transfer my junior year. I was a Tootsie Roll Pop: hard veneer of faux confidence, a soft mushy disaster on the inside.

OBU was a smorgasbord of eager college students looking to their future. As in all universities, there were plenty of "lady" students seeking their "Mrs. degree," I think more so than at a secular school, especially in that era. Women's lib was a fringe concept. Certainly, no nice young woman in Shawnee was about to burn her bra. Gloria Steinem had just begun her work, founding *Ms.* magazine in 1969. It was not among the periodicals at the library. Every young woman had been brainwashed into thinking her role was to support her husband. She was to be the ornament on his arm and basically shut up and do whatever he wanted for the rest of her life. Now, that's a degree worth seeking!

No one knew that I was running or what I could possibly have been trying to escape and replace. I had been recruited with a full-ride music scholarship with the specific plan to join "Tuneclippers," the show choir. It was exciting— a new place and new people. A fabulous USO concert trip was coming up to Korea, Japan, Guam, and the Philippines—for two months. I already had the international travel bug, and I couldn't wait.

The psychiatrist who had pronounced me "Free of the Gay," and for proof walked me through the scriptures, then turned from the Bible to the "Sears Catalogue of lady pickin'." He walked me through my acquaintances and friends at school as if he were trying to help me select the best model to suit my purposes, like a Kenmore vacuum cleaner. (I avoided looking at the male underwear pages as best I could. Been there, done that.)

He asked, "Are there any girls at the school who pique your interest?" That took some thought. I wanted to ask, "Pique in what way?" but changed my mind. There were. After a few weeks, we narrowed it down to two whom I liked, each presenting strong consumer guide reviews. They were Brenda and Vicki—both going on the two-month tour! They were both beautiful (some gay men tend to lean toward that). They actually competed against each other in the Miss Shawnee Beauty Pageant as a preliminary to Miss Oklahoma.

Brenda was down-to-earth, adorable (with freckles), brunette, funny, and approachable. A natural beauty emanated from her. She was from Sand Springs, Oklahoma, and grew up in an open, loving family. Not like mine. She had a beautiful voice. Not an ounce of pretense in her. What's not to love?

Vicki was more the sophisticated option. After all, she was from Midland, Texas, and beautiful, put-together, talented, a Barbie doll, and aloof. She grew up in a family that put her on a pedestal and polished her frequently. She never left home without full makeup. She drove a brand-new VW convertible. She was a princess who had a beautiful voice.

Decisions, Decisions

The Tuneclippers spent a lot of time together preparing for the long journey and making sure we were ready in every way. We bonded.

Every other week I would drive the thirty-five miles to Oklahoma City to discuss my future and what it might look like with each one of them. There was zero sexual chemistry with either of them. "Don't worry about that," the doctor said. "It is more important to find a companion, a friend who shares your goals and music. The other part will develop in time." (I waited thirteen years for that train to reach the station.)

Brenda scared me because she was real. She would require that from me in return. She had no pretense.

Vicki spent a lot of time on the outward picture of herself. She was the PR choice. And I think I realized deep down inside that if I chose her, I would not be required to be real or warm or intimate as long as the public picture was perfect. Boy, was I right!

Before the two-month trip, I began zeroing in. By the day the plane took off, I had pretty much made up my mind—almost. Two months later, by the end of the tour, Vicki was visiting my family. I have no idea if Brenda even cared. I can only imagine she now knows she dodged a bullet. My family was thrilled. "It's a girl!" We began plans for a big wedding—well, as big as it could be at the First Baptist Church of Shawnee, Oklahoma. And thus began the Tim and Vicki Show.

The wedding was a show replete with costumes, music, props, lighting, flowers, and a fabulous punch made of lime sherbet and ginger ale. All that the church allowed for the reception in the fellowship hall in the basement were the wedding cake, a bowl of mixed nuts, and peppermint meltaways.

It happened at two o'clock, the very day I graduated from OBU in the morning. The reasoning was that most of our friends would be heading home from college that day so they could attend the wedding and then head out. I jokingly say I rushed from graduation to wedding so as not to have time to stray. That was May 26, 1973.

The marriage had an expiration date like cottage cheese slowly gathering mold. The date was not posted anywhere. I had no idea it would be noon, Wednesday, November 5, 1986—13 years, 5 months, 9 days, and 20 hours. On that expiration date, the plastic tub blew its lid. I filed for divorce.

What filled those thirteen years of marriage? Lots and lots of activity, as we stayed as busy as possible so as not to have to sit down and face each other. Vicki attached herself fully to my dream of being on stage—the world stage, building my career brick by brick. She also benefited greatly from the once-in-a-lifetime opportunity to attend one of the most prestigious conservatories in the world: the International Orff Institute in Salzburg.

Chapter 16

Workaholism Is the Best "-ism"

This chapter begins with an uplifting, motivational scripture for you (you may want to print it out for your refrigerator, perhaps next to Tony Robbins, Brené Brown, or Marianne Williamson). Behold, the good news:

> *You lazy sluggard, look at an ant. Nobody has to tell it what to do. How long are you going to laze around doing nothing? How long before you get out of bed? A nap here, a nap there, a day off here, a day off there, sit back, take it easy—do you know what comes next? Just this: You can look forward to a dirt-poor life. Poverty will be your permanent houseguest!* Proverbs 6:6–11

Surely this makes you want to jump out of bed and show that little ant who's boss, perhaps even get a button to wear—"Lazy Sluggards United."

My brother, Steve, had a more difficult time embracing the German work ethic. He followed more in Mom's footsteps. She was a diva. She literally had "people." So did my brother. He was wildly charismatic and manipulative and could get anyone standing in the vicinity to do his work for him.

When I was fourteen, I got a learner's permit. My brother, sixteen, got his driver's license. He purchased a 1949 Ford for $700. It was financed by Mom and Dad for $50 a month. In no time, he defaulted on the loan. Rather than sell it, I took over the payments. However, I couldn't drive without Steve in the car. Unfortunately, I became his chauffeur. I would take various and sundry girls home from youth choir, both of them sitting in the back, Miss Daisy style. They were very quiet. I thought the fact that they were not talking was strange.

I needed money. Dad twisted the arms of a couple of his friends who owned a big cafeteria, Jetton's. It featured some of the best barbeque anywhere. They hired me as an underage dishwasher at eighty-one cents an hour. I spent many hours in the steamy bowels of the cafeteria with Juan. He didn't speak much English and had only one eye. I didn't ask if that happened in a dishwashing accident.

When the machine burned my arm, Juan would not let me go home or to the doctor. When my shift was over, Mom and Dad freaked. It was a pretty bad burn, and I had spent the rest of the shift handling filthy dishes caked with barbeque sauce, rib bones, and coleslaw. They made me quit. I'm sure Juan had a going-away party for me—the day after I left. I did not excel at dishwashing.

Lawn mowing in our section of Fort Worth was lucrative. Mom and Dad had been paying a pretty penny for a mow and an edge. In summer the yard had to be done every week. They said, "If you will do our yard for free, we will float you the money for a new lawnmower and edger. You can start your lawn-mowing service." Thus, I started my own business. I was off and running.

In no time I had the Ford paid off and soon upgraded to a 1957 Chevy. I haven't stopped working—or trading in cars—in the ensuing five decades plus. Some jobs were doozies: janitor, shoe salesman, singing waiter, apartment manager (in Switzerland), and Kelly Girl.

Nepotism

Dad got me a summer job as a full-time janitor at the student center at the seminary. In the beginning he would come down during my break and we'd get an RC Cola. Once, when we were walking along the grounds, Dad, up ahead, yelled (under his breath), "At least walk like you are working!" Ever since, I've been trying to pretend I was working even when taking a break.

From 1976–1979, during graduate school, I was a singing waiter at an Italian eatery in Dallas. I was the worst waiter ever (though a much better singer). I was horrible at my job because when it came my turn to perform (we were on rotation), I just didn't care one bit about my patrons' food getting cold or served at all. It was my time to sing, dang it.

It was a lovely place with a three-dollar bottomless wineglass. Many were the times when customers would literally fall out of their chairs. And they simply had to wait until I finished "Figaro" to be helped up—for a wine refill.

In 1980 my wife and I and our two children packed everything we had and moved to Switzerland. This tale fills an entire chapter later on.

In 1987 came Tim the Kelly Girl. For those unfamiliar, Kelly Girl was the top-of-the-line temporary office work agency. They used to have to wear gloves when they showed up for their assignment. My first assignment was inputting names and addresses for a pretty dirty car battery company. I have absolutely no idea what I was putting them into, but it was tedious. I learned nothing about batteries.

At one point I went to a psychiatrist to address my workaholism. He listened attentively to the list I wrote earlier. He asked if I loved all of it. I replied, "All of it."

He said he would normally encourage clients to slow down and find a hobby. But he wouldn't do that for me. The things I was doing all filled a different part of my soul. And they were all helping people. He suggested taking a nap every once in a while (which I have not done) and to keep going. I loved his advice and have faithfully followed it to this day.

Baptist Rocket

The years between arrival at Hardin-Simmons at eighteen and the life I left at thirty-five were crammed with wonderful opportunities. It was an amazing ride. I did what Mom and Dad had hoped. Even though my first goal was to become an opera singer—check—I was able to concertize all over the United States and many foreign countries. I was fulfilling their goal too: Rise as high in the Baptist diadem as possible; continue expanding the brand.

A dear friend said, "Tim, you never do things small." That was not my fault. I grew up in that environment. It was part of the brand.

Remember Betsy from the freshman talent show at Hardin-Simmons? After that duet, another freshman, Randall, asked if we might like to be a trio. He played guitar. I played string bass. We all sang. Thus, "Reality" was born. We learned music of the day (Peter, Paul, and Mary). We started getting very popular all over West Texas at after-football-game gatherings at big churches. There was no dancing, so they had entertainment at the Afterglow.

At the beginning of our sophomore year, a call went out for a small group of singers to perform at the United Nations Chapel on Christmas Eve. It would be broadcast nationally on NBC. We sent a tape and were selected. Up-and-coming composer Buryl Red composed a piece for us, "Instrument of Peace." We three nineteen-year-olds went to New York City; it was incredible. The narrator for the show was a Broadway playwright, Ragan Courtney.

In fall 1971 Buryl teamed up with Ragan again. They created what is known as the very first Christian musical *Celebrate Life*. They needed four disciples for the world premiere. I had transferred to OBU. They knew me and had heard the reputation of the school's music and theater departments, so they cast me and the other three disciples there. I was Matthew. Ragan played Jesus.

That summer we performed *Celebrate Life* in New Mexico and North Carolina every week—yes, back and forth between the two huge Baptist encampments. We also performed it in Nashville, where we welcomed a new Mary Magdalene to the cast, a gospel singer named Cynthia Clawson. It was life-changing.

In 1973, once again, Buryl was putting together a thirty-minute television variety show to be aired on NBC. He called and asked me to join the ensemble, which would appear in every episode. We would film in Nashville. We were called the "Spring Street Singers." He chose Betsy from Hardin-Simmons and Brenda from OBU, but not Vicki. It was a blast, and the guest artists were so much fun. More TV.

In 1974 Buryl composed another musical, *New Beginnings*. The world premiere was in Stockholm, Sweden. His favorite baritone had one of the leading roles. I am so grateful to him for all of those opportunities.

From there I began focusing more on opera. There were lots of opportunities at large conventions and churches and colleges. And I started performing small roles with opera companies in Dallas, Fort Worth, Beaumont, and Denton, among other locales.

I partnered with one of the most spectacular tenors I have ever heard, Karl Dent. We began singing together—recitals, operas, and the churches. We were on a roll—recording, headshots, the whole deal. Vicki and I were performing together and made our first gospel recording, an LP.

While in Salzburg, I won several prestigious competitions. One of them allowed me to do a recital at Schloss Mirabel (of *The Sound of Music* fame). Another was broadcast on Austrian State Radio.

All was going swimmingly as I was moved closer and closer to my goal, with the brass ring of opera right in front of me. I would keep my head down, stay on the narrow path, and keep working insanely hard at stepping up my game. It didn't matter what I had to do to get there. I don't think I was very nice.

Chapter 17

Salzburg: Missionary Position

There is story about me at age sixteen standing in front of the Mozarteum and pronouncing, "I will go to school here one day." It is now a huge part of the entire path my life took. Making that happen took a lot of magic, fairy dust, and money. In the end it all worked perfectly.

I was a little obsessed with Mozart. I sang every bit of his music I could. Having stood where he composed some of his best work, I was even more inspired. Moving there to study was not then so much an *if* as a *when*. Vicki was fully on board. She had not been there, but my stories—and *The Sound of Music*—convinced her to join in the effort.

After we got married in 1973, I immediately began my master's degree study at the University of North Texas. We were poor graduate students and happy with the ramen. That fall, with my real goal still burning, I wrote to the Southern Baptist missionaries stationed in Salzburg. Basically, they ran a German-speaking Baptist church and an English-speaking Baptist church. Austrians have as many Catholic churches as we do Baptist ones.

There was not much for the missionaries to do. As Southern Baptists they tried to save Austrians from their main sin: drinking beer (how'd that go?). The Austrian youth, who became our very close friends, also had a very loose freedom of sexual expression. This irked the missionaries to no end. The fact that the Austrians were happy and unencumbered by guilt was just too much.

In my letter I told them about myself and Vicki—letting them know it was my dream to live there and go to school one day. Immediately, I got a letter back. The mission group in Salzburg had put in a request to the Southern Baptist Missionary Board for a young couple who would be willing to move to Salzburg to help them for two years. They were called "missionary journeymen." They were looking for this couple to work with, and increase in numbers, the youth in the German-speaking church and to help with music in the English-speaking church.

When we told them I hoped to attend the Mozarteum and Vicki hoped to attend the Carl Orff Institute, they flipped. They had never had inroads to either of these two main conservatories. It was exactly what they were looking for. We were set—almost. We applied to the Mission Board. They wrote to the Mozarteum. It was a match made in heaven.

There was one hurdle. We had to spend the entire summer isolated on a small college campus in North Carolina training with the other young missionary journeymen. It was a spiritual boot camp intended to prepare us. But more than that, it was supposed to weed out those who were not strong enough to move to a foreign country. They made it rough. It was all-day-long therapy with the Bible as the textbook. Vicki and I both bristled at the artificial "world" they set up to try to trick us into running screaming into the night. We banded together, determined to get the prize: Salzburg.

There was one tiny hurdle left. At the end of the twelve weeks, they wanted a group photo to post in all the Baptist newspapers with "their" new mini-missionaries. I had worn a beard throughout college. A few others had beards or mustaches. We were told the day before that the men could not have any facial hair for the photo. They wanted scrubbed and squeaky-clean young people. I went to the leader and showed him the pictures of my two missionary leaders in Salzburg. Both had full beards. That didn't matter. Either I shaved or Vicki and I would have to stay home and be released. I will say my reaction probably did not fit the actual requirement. They told me the only reason I didn't want to shave was because I had issues with authority figures. I told them it was scars from teenage acne.

Anyway, we really, really wanted to go to Austria, so the night before the photo, all of us with facial hair had a shaving party and appeared the next morning shaved and shorn, presenting "our bodies a living sacrifice, holy and acceptable unto God, which is your reasonable service" (Rom 12:1). If shaving got us the golden ticket, I was prepared to shave whatever needed to be shaved.

There was a good life lesson in there: "If you can't beat 'em, join 'em." At least let them think you did.

Our two years were absolutely incredible. We fulfilled the hopes and dreams of the missionaries and then some. We started a singing group made up of Austrian teens. We toured Austria, Switzerland, and Germany. They had never dreamed of such. We helped open a youth center for kids to hang out mere blocks from the Mozarteum. We led music in church and sang a lot. Our superiors were thrilled.

In return we went to school and both received the equivalent to master's degrees. Vicki's was as a music education expert, having studied Carl Orff methods. We were privileged enough to meet him and hear him speak. He was eighty at the time.

I did not get to meet the man my school was named after, but I graduated with a degree in lieder and oratorio, and I spent two years with the most amazing voice teacher anywhere on earth.

We both served the Baptists well. And they allowed us to further our education. It was a huge win for all.

Audition

When we first arrived in Salzburg, the missionaries had an apartment ready for us. It was adorable, if cold. We actually sat on the furnace to have morning coffee, but it was a dream come true.

First thing up was to learn German. Our jobs and our schools depended on that. The classes at both of our conservatories were all taught in German, of course. We started intensive study as soon as we got there. We had both taken German before, so it was not from square one. We did that in earnest from August until December. Somewhere along the way, we actually began to understand the television. That was a milestone. We were majoring in German language and Austrian pastries.

During fall I had the chance to go to the Mozarteum for concerts and recitals and to fully research the voice teachers. The most famous one of all was Frau Kammersängerin Hanna Ludwig. She was a mezzosoprano who'd had a successful career as a singer and eventually teacher. Kammersängerin was like having tenure on steroids. To fulfill her position, she only had to have four or five voice students.

What to do? Her schedule was posted on her studio door, so after several days of nerve-building, I knocked as a lesson was ending. I told her who I was and that I would love to be considered as one of her voice students. She said, "That's nice. I will have you sing at my home next Wednesday evening." She gave me the address. I left and did everything possible for my knees not to buckle in the hallowed marble halls of the conservatory named for none other than Wolfie.

When Wednesday came, I tried on three—okay, maybe five—outfits and got a cab. When the driver pulled up at our destination, I said, "You need to check the address." He confirmed we were there. I was looking at the most stunning palatial home, sitting on a brook with a view of the Alps out the windows. It was the von Trapp family home without the gazebo. My knees buckled again.

I rang the doorbell, and Frau Kammersängerin Ludwig answered the door and invited me in. She led me down a long hall with floor-to-ceiling posters from her international career. As we turned the corner, there was a stunning sunken living room with huge floor-to-ceiling windows, totally filled with people. She introduced me as a possible new student in her studio. She did not say who the "people" were. I thought I would just assume the worst: They were all ultra-famous opera singers. A grand piano was nestled among the oriental carpets. She introduced the accompanist. I gave him my music. Here I was, a boy from Fort Worth, Texas—doing what?

She asked what I would be singing. "'Der Vogelfanger' from *The Magic Flute*," said I. Now, how stupid was that? Mozart composed *The Magic Flute* in Salzburg, at the site that is now the Mozarteum. The people in the room didn't cut their teeth on "Itsy Bitsy Spider." They grew up singing highlights of *The Magic Flute*. They can sing it in their sleep! I could have chosen some obscure American piece they would not have known, but no.

I took my place in the crook of the piano, basically holding on for dear life. I sang it. At the completion, I thought it wasn't bad and that I would soon be sent out to await the verdict. There was polite "golf tournament" applause.

But Frau Kammersängerin Hanna Ludwig had different thoughts. She asked if I knew what the aria was about. Of course I did. It is about a bird catcher (the actual title of the aria!) who is full of life, knows few boundaries, and loves to sing and dance and whistle.

"Then why, pray tell, did you stand in the crook of the piano singing as if you were the saddest, scaredest person on earth?" She asked me to repeat the aria, but this time to dance and sing and strut and do whatever my heart desired—but to be true to Papageno.

My life passed before my eyes! I was suddenly sitting outside the set of *Romper Room*.

I was standing on the high dive. What would the people in the room think if I made a fool of myself?

I had two choices:

1. Start crying—and be sent home like at *Romper Room*, or
2. Give it my best shot, knowing I couldn't die from it and might never see these people again.

I sang my heart out. I acted. I danced a little. I sat on the floor. I did everything but give Frau Kammersängerin Hanna Ludwig a lap dance.

At the end of the aria, there was resounding applause. She walked over, took my hand, and said, "I'll see you in January." Thus began one of the most amazing opportunities of my life.

The next years were nothing short of incredible as I finished a second master's degree at the Mozarteum. At the end of my studies, I did a few auditions. I was offered a job at a small opera company in Vienna. Hanna said, "No, you are not ready. Your voice needs to settle. Another opportunity will come."

I trusted her. We returned home, and I began work on my doctorate. I took the job as a singing waiter. Someone had to pay the bills as the babies started popping out.

Lessons from two years in Austria were too many to enumerate. In addition to the invaluable musical experiences, the lesson of separation from our family would be important. Surviving in a distant land was empowering. The challenge of making your way with a completely new circle of friends would come in handy. Those two years prepared me in so many ways for my life ahead.

Chapter 18

Linz: Big Austrian Fail

Hanna Ludwig had told me to trust the process, go home, continue developing my voice and allowing it to mature. Lo and behold, three years later Hanna called. "There is the perfect position for you in Linz, Austria. They are looking for a Figaro, and you're perfect. You must get here!"

We had no money. During our schooling, we had created two children. I had financed most of my own education up to that point, so I did the unthinkable and asked my parents for a loan. Off I went, leaving Vicki and the two kids at home in Denton, Texas—all of this on a financial shoestring.

Full-time jobs as opera singers are as difficult to get as a job playing in the NBA. It was a big leap of faith. But I trusted Hanna that Linz, Austria, was waiting just for me and I would finally fulfill my dream of singing opera in Europe.

I flew to Salzburg to brush up my audition pieces with Hanna. Then I got on the train to Linz, a stunningly beautiful city. I walked to the opera house and warmed up in the bathroom on the fourth floor. It was my turn.

I entered the stage, gave my music to the accompanist, and looked out at a darkened theater. A voice from the dark welcomed me in German and asked for my first piece. I sang a killer aria from *The Marriage of Figaro*, knowing that was what they were looking for. After that he asked for another aria and then another. When I finished, he said, "Your voice is beautiful. Your acting is extraordinary. You would be perfect for the opening we have. Unfortunately, we filled that position last week. *Danke.*"

I barely remember walking off the stage. I do remember returning to the fourth-floor bathroom, locking the door, and weeping, falling into the fetal position. I wept because of my folly, my selfishness, and my family back home, who had sacrificed everything so I could chase this dream.

On the train back to Salzburg, I threw myself a fabulous pity party for one. Hanna was having none of it. When I got back to her home, she said, "Stop feeling sorry for yourself. Worse things will happen in your life. Get up and finish the audition tour we set up for you. Off you go!"

Throughout the remainder of the audition trip through Austria, Germany, and then Switzerland, I thought, "Whatever. I can't change my flight home. I might as well sing for my schnitzel."

St. Gallen was my last stop. Even though defeated and ready to go home, I sang my heart out, knowing it was probably the last time I would ever sing in Europe. They said, "*Danke*. Don't call us. We'll call you." And I headed home, tail tucked firmly between my legs.

That fall of 1979 I started my first full-time teaching job at Houston Baptist University. I had no more begun teaching than a telegram arrived: "Lieber Herr Seelig. (stop) It is our pleasure to offer you the position of lead baritone in the Swiss National Opera in St. Gallen, Switzerland. (stop) Please respond. (stop)." All of that in German, and no, dang it, I did not save it!

I told the school I was leaving after one year, and we spent the next nine months preparing for a move to Europe. My next train ride to St. Gallen was a year later, 1980, armed with a contract with the Swiss National Opera; a wife and two kids, ages one and three; diapers; formula; and heavy winter clothes (hard to find in Houston). I was ready to conquer the operatic world!

St. Gallen represents both the pinnacle and the end of my dream of singing opera. On so many levels it was not for me. My personality profile is the complete opposite of what it takes to be an opera singer. I was destined to be a teacher, and (who knew?) a conductor. We came home in 1981. Once again, my tail tucked. But I learned valuable life lessons:

1. Never say never. Upon leaving St. Gallen, I had said I would never return there.
2. Time heals. The pain of the experience has been replaced with amazing, joyful memories.
3. You *can* go home.
4. Don't dwell on the failures. It is not the successes in life that build character; it's the failures and how you respond to them.

Looking back, it was Hanna who helped me respond to this failure with the courage I didn't have at that time. She said, "Get up. Dust yourself off. Get on the next train." I learned that sometimes, when you don't have the strength to pick yourself up, there are countless people and angels to help with that.

Melinda

Living in a foreign country, while exciting, can also be exhausting. Spending all day conversing in a second language wears on your brain. One of the things people do is gather with friends or strangers who speak English. We did this in Salzburg as part of our outreach from the English-speaking Baptist church.

We gathered at a local beer garden. We never knew who would show up because one person would tell another. We had an absolutely delightful group on this occasion. As the conversation developed, each person told where he or she was from and what he or she was doing in St. Gallen.

A friend, George, brought one of his friends, Melinda, who was spending a semester studying. It was a "semester abroad" from her university. Her major was accounting. When it came my time to reveal what I did, she went crazy. She told us how she and her family loved music and how she couldn't sing a lick. Then she asked me to please, please, please sing something—just a simple song of some kind.

I told her how happy I was that she loved music, but I declined the request to sing a song, embarrassed to do that in a beer garden. She begged. I asked her, as an accounting major, if anyone had ever asked her to count in public. That was, admittedly, a little snotty. She begged again. I said, "No. But I can get you tickets to a concert I'm singing next week." She was disappointed not to get the live performance on the spot but was clearly excited to see me in a whole opera. She couldn't wait to tell her family. Having made plans to meet the next week at my performance, we all went our separate ways.

The next morning, George called. I assumed it was to redeem my offer of tickets. However, that was not his message. He let us know that Melinda had been tragically killed the night before while riding her bicycle back to the hostel. She never heard me sing. Why? Because I was worried about what people in the restaurant would think, people I would never see again. It was Melinda I would never see again.

I had been unfaithful to my gift and to my calling. There would be no going back, no fixing this. It was over—for her. Too late. Done.

"What will people think?" That question is the curse of our existence.

Chapter 19

Beautiful, Bouncing Babies

In 1976 Vicki and I headed home from our two-year Austrian adventure. We stopped in the Bahamas for a short R&R. I'm pretty sure we made a baby on that trip. We discovered rum punch on the gorgeous beach; we had probably been watching too many commercials for a Sandals romantic beach getaway.

Vicki was pregnant. We weren't sure how we were going to manage the finances, but to make ends meet I was a teaching assistant at the University of North Texas and a singing waiter. Vicki worked for a while at the university but then had to quit due to a tricky pregnancy. Her parents were most generous and helped us buy a small, brand-new house in a new development in Denton. It was an investment for them and a way to provide a home for the new one that was more suitable than college apartments.

We were excited, expectant parents—making plans, buying cute things. I'm not sure how we found out it was a girl, but we knew. We couldn't decide on a name. We actually liked the old-fashioned *Sadie* and the newly popular *Brooke*. My father said if we named her that, he would never visit. He actually didn't visit anyway. Corianna could have been Sadie Brooke.

Six weeks before her due date, we arose to go to church. Vicki, who was in the bathroom, said, "I think my water broke." I responded, "You're crazy! Come back and sit on the bed." She did. Her water finished breaking like the Hoover Dam (at least to my eyes).

She grabbed a towel, put it between her legs, and applied makeup while I was freaking out. I took her to the hospital and got her settled as much as possible. Since fathers were not allowed in the delivery room, I went home to get some coffee, a newspaper, and schoolbooks for the long wait. When I got back—after maybe an hour—they called me up to the window and said, "Here's your baby." I looked, saw the umbilical cord, and thought, "It's a boy." I should have looked a little lower.

Well, it was a girl. Labor had been less than two hours. She was a preemie—right at five pounds—but she was perfect. She stayed a few extra days at the hospital to gain some weight and then came home, our princess.

Life was great as she grew. She was sweet and funny. We did all the things people knew to do in 1977. She loved her Johnny Jump Up attached to the door frame. I believe they banned those in later years because it scrambled babies' brains. If true, a good scramble it was.

We were fully of the mind that "a baby will save a marriage," for a while. We jumped into it. Vicki's parents were amazing. They loved their first grandchild so much and visited from Lamesa, a six-hour drive, often. My parents sent thoughts and prayers (not the diaper-changing kind).

But what was not to love about this gorgeous child? She was very smart. Her personality shone long before it should have. Her mom, who stayed home with her, got her walking, talking, and even singing, something she would later deny because her mother and father were singers. When she figured that out, there was no more singing until the singing group her uncle put together later. She loved *The Sound of Music*, which was her mother's favorite movie since we had just returned from living inside the movie. She also loved the *Music Machine* song "Have Patience," sung by Herbert the Snail:

> *Have patience. Have patience.*
> *Don't be in such a hurry.*
> *When you get impatient,*
> *You only start to worry.*
> *Remember, remember that God is patient too.*
> *And think of all the times when others have to wait for you.*

Those words, sung countless times every day, did not apply to Corianna or her dad. She could literally walk into any room of people and be perfectly at home. Vicki also dressed her to the nines. She would walk into daycare, church, and eventually school with no hesitation.

On her first day of school, we walked her to the door expecting and hoping she would turn with lingering looks in her eye, maybe tears. Nope. She turned only slightly, a small wave indicating, "Y'all can go now." And off she went into kindergarten.

She was independent and confident. Kindergarten simply represented groups of people she could entertain or take care of. She loved being with her daddy and would be Daddy's little girl the rest of her life. She sat through countless hours of rehearsals and performances, just as her dad had done with his mom.

Having a little girl brought us together. It gave us something to unite around. She was absolutely the light of our lives. We were no longer a struggling couple. We were a family unit. This gave me even more dedication to walk the narrow path and be the best dad I possibly could.

Bouncing Baby Boy Judson

Soon, Corianna's little brother arrived (I don't remember the vacation or beverage that resulted in his birth). He was also small, but not as small as his big sis. He was two years and three months younger than Corianna.

We named him Judson, even though everyone was starting to use Justin. We wanted his name to be a little different than everyone in his class. We searched and found Adoniram Judson, one the first Baptist foreign missionaries. He and his third wife, Ann, were sent to Burma in 1812 to save the heathens there. It was perfect. Not only were we naming him after a Baptist, but a *big* Baptist, one who is on the list of "Ten Baptists Everyone Should Know." There is also a book titled *The Lives of the Three Mrs. Judsons*.

If Corianna came in like a storm, Judson snuck in the backdoor. Corianna was seemingly confident and strong from the moment she popped out. Judson was quite different. Some of that may have been because his sister smothered him and directed his every move. She would say, "I want to hold him and squeeze him and love him!" It's a wonder he survived. But she was a great sister, and he let her hold, squeeze, and *boss* him. He allowed that until things changed.

Proud papa just has to say that Judson was the most adorable child on the planet. He was just pretty. He had huge eyes and would duck his chin with a little quiver. The world was at his command. He was also the much more sensitive of the two. From the time he was speaking, one of his favorite remarks was, "You hurt my feelers." Most of the time we had no idea what we had done to hurt his feelers. But we tried to make amends.

He also loved to be held. Okay, demanded. He would be tired of walking—or maybe just breathing—and look up with those eyes of his, reach up his hands, and say, "Hold you?" It came out more as, "Ho jew?," but we said nothing because it was so damn cute. Seriously, I'm sure he did not know the fine turn of phrase he was using, but it melted hearts. If a small child says "Hold me," it is easy to reply, "Not now." But when he offers to "Hold you"—I was done every time.

Learning bedtime protocol is tough. Judson, like most children, did not want to go to bed alone or on time or at all. He was five years old when this just got exhausting. He would holler from his room, "Hold my hand!" One of us would go in, sit on the floor, and hold his hand until he fell asleep.

One night, we were just tired. We put him to bed, and not five minutes later came the tell-tale "Please hold my hand." I had had enough. I marched myself to his bedroom door, and in my absolutely most paternal voice said, "Judson Seelig, if I hear from you again, I am going to spank your bottom." After a pause of maybe two minutes of pondering came, "Daddy, would you come spank me and hold my hand?" Having weighed the fact that actions have consequences, he made a calculated decision that it was worth it (I think he knew my bark was way more than my spank). I melted and held his hand for the next two years.

So we had two perfect children, a girl and a boy, Corianna Seelig and Judson Standefer Seelig. Both would change their names.

Corianna was the protector who bossed him with love and took over his early training. There was not a shred of jealousy. She was a very grownup and precocious toddler. She held his hands through the adventures to come—even moving to Switzerland, where they were the most adorable children in lederhosen and dirndl anyone had ever seen.

Probably the cutest thing ever was his role in the Singing Seeligs. My brother, who also had a girl and a boy, envisioned the Baptist version of the Osmonds (who were Mormons). So he got them going.

Stephanie, Steve's oldest, took control. They went to the other room to practice a surprise song. When they came back to the den, Stephanie was Marie, John Mark was Donnie, and Corianna and Judson were embarrassed to death. They sang "Goin' to the Chapel."

It was really adorable. Judson looked as if in death's grip. I don't think he sang a note. They were not ready for their close-up, and the dreams of television royalty switched back to the Osmonds.

Corianna and the cousins tormented Judson by dressing him up, putting him in girls' bathing suits, and smearing him with shaving cream. We have all these pictures as reminders. Some of this was on his own. One year, for months after Halloween, he insisted on wearing his Underoos, Superman cape and mask, and cowboy boots. He also insisted on wearing them everywhere we went, except church. That took negotiation. And (aside) for two years, Corianna refused to wear anything but jelly shoes—even to church.

Hindsight is so good. Looking back, I ask: Why shouldn't they have worn what they wanted to? It wasn't their problem; it was ours. They hadn't learned "What will people think?" Somehow in our "present a perfect picture" world, we were embarrassed by our children's originality and uniqueness. They were just being themselves. That frightened us. What if Judson never wanted to trade in his Underoos for real clothes? What if, like us, people thought that jelly shoes were redneck and caused mold to grow between the toes? We thought it somehow shined a negative light on us. It threatened our own insistence that conformity was a bona fide "law of nature."

One friend, rather than force her children to dress as she wanted them to, simply made a big button for them to wear when they went out in their "creative attire" that said:

"I CHOSE MY OWN CLOTHES." Win/win.

It took Judson a long time to come into his own. When he did, he became the most amazing man I know. He is still choosing his own clothes.

Chapter 20

Two Roads, One Dead End

My big break came in 1980, when I was hired as the lead baritone for the Swiss National Opera in St. Gallen, Switzerland. All the years of hard work and determination paid off. Vicki and I had spent the better part of a year raising funds to be able to make this move for the four of us.

Unlike in Austria, this was not a two-year commitment. It was going to be our life. This had always been my dream, and we were all in. With a three-year-old and a one-year-old, we were setting sail (okay, we flew) to a new life. Everything was put in boxes and shipped. The furniture was sold. We were not coming back. It was 1980. It was Europe. We had two toddlers. We knew nothing about what Swiss diapers looked like.

What was our first contact in this quaint little city in the Alps? The Baptist church, of course. There is one in every town in the world. We told the pastor our situation and that we would be attending his church and would be looking for housing.

There was an older Swiss man in the congregation who had an enormous house, and he was the only resident. He agreed to allow us to stay there while we looked for an apartment. The church would hold our boxes for us. We could live out of our suitcases. Perfect—except for one thing: He didn't like children. As a lifelong bachelor, he was not accustomed to noise of any kind. And he was grumpy and didn't like any clutter. Oh dear! We tiptoed around trying to be as quiet as possible. All of that put our apartment search on a fast track.

We looked at quaint apartments downtown. I thought they were charming with their big windows and cranky furnaces. I was voted down three to one. We kept looking. We found a brand-new, modern apartment house on a hill outside of town a bit. It was sleek, and everything was sparkling—except the price. I was the only breadwinner. Not only did we have two small children, but also the laws are very strict in Switzerland about foreigners working, so that was not an option for Vicki.

Just as we were about to decline the apartment, the agent said, "There is one other possibility." At that point I was willing to work the corner down by the opera house if necessary. "We need an onsite maintenance man. It would reduce your rent to where you need it to be." Done! I had always been a hard worker.

How hard could this be? I needed to mop the stairs regularly and, in autumn, rake the leaves around the apartment. Then the snow would come. I had to shovel the sidewalks and mop the stairs as a result of wet, snowy boots coming in from outside. No problem.

I had lived two winters in Austria, in the city center, with lots of people and cars. I was not prepared for an apartment complex in the hills above St. Gallen. We lived on the side of an Alp, for heaven's sake. Then the snow came. I would keep up with it as best I could before heading to opera rehearsal during the day. I sang almost every night, so I would do a little mopping when I got home. I thought I was doing great.

Apparently, I was not doing so great. The apartment owner was getting complaints that the sidewalks were not clean enough and the inside stairs needed a lot more tender loving care than I was giving them. The Austrians are chill compared to the Swiss. They wanted their stairs to be as clean as their Swiss watches and mopped as often as their Swiss trains ran. I upped my game: a snow shovel in one hand, a mop in the other, practicing Mozart as I went.

One great thing: There was a young couple that owned a bakery next door. They lived above it. They had a little girl who befriended Corianna. We encouraged her to play with her friend as often as possible because they sent her home with fresh baked goods every time. I needed the extra nourishment to shovel some more!

That was home life. Then there was the work life. As a full-time member of the resident cast, I would be singing in three to four different operas at the same time. They alternated nights. We rehearsed during the day and sang at night. Our rotation included operas in German, Italian, and French. I shoveled in between. One of the big regrets was that the kids would often beg me to play in the snow (which I hated). I had to say "no" every time because my primary goal was not to get sick.

The resident cast members were all young. Everyone was getting their start. I was the only one married with kids. While they bonded over trips to the beer garden after performances, I would go home. They bonded over sleeping together in random groupings. I did not. So I did not get to know them outside the opera house. I was a little jealous on the inside and ridiculously judgmental on the outside. I was not a pleasant colleague.

Then there was the singing. I was good at my job. I had far more training than any of my colleagues. But something was missing from most of the singing

I had done before—in churches, in concert halls, in English! And there was the teaching, making a difference.

Every night, I put on the costume and makeup of a different character. I went out and sang, took a bow at the end, and went home and mopped. Rinse and repeat. If I stayed with this career path, it would be years before I broke into anything that might resemble the "big time." I was doing the same thing over and over—just in different languages.

I became disillusioned quickly. The life of an opera singer requires massive introvert time studying languages and learning the music for the next opera. In school, there were people to help. When I got out, there were no people. The company told me they would begin rehearsals for *The Marriage of Figaro* on January 3, and I had to show up with it memorized. This required hours and hours of quiet study, all alone. No one had ever told me that part of the story.

We were all miserable. There was no end in sight. And the money was incredibly tight. In fact, we were not making ends meet. If we were to stay, we would have to ask our parents to help. They probably would have, but we were a family of four. I had a full-time career. We should not be depending on our parents for support.

I truly did not know what to do. We had raised a lot of money from friends and family and by giving house concerts all over Houston. Everyone was so proud of us—and me.

I wrote a friend and spilled it all. He was a writer and poet. He wrote back with a paraphrase of Robert Frost's "The Road Not Taken" that has done me well ever since: *Two roads diverged in a yellow wood. I looked down one as far as I could, then took the other. I found out the one I had chosen was a dead end.* How long should I beat my head against the wall before going back and taking the other?

The "other" was the life I had waiting at home: teaching, singing, inspiring others where I could.

I resigned my dream job and broke my two-year contract midway through the season. I tucked my tail between my legs and prepared to eat copious amounts of crow and humble pie. And I started all over again.

This would not be the last time I had that meal.

Chapter 21

Cesspool Behind the Baptistry

My struggles were real. But others had struggles as well. It was quite the standard topic of discussion among church employees. Who had fallen from grace this week? Who had merely backslidden? Who was divorced, disgraced, or just dissed (not a word we used back then). Sometimes it was in the spirit of "bless their hearts," but most often it was pretty vicious gossip. It was not benign water cooler conversation. It was far from Christlike.

Have you wondered why one fundamentalist leader after another falls from grace, succumbing to the exact thing they all rail against every Sunday morning and on television 24/7 and around the world? In setting the stage for my own indiscretions, I must mention the pandemic of holier-than-thou hypocrites gracing the halls and annals of organized religion. When young, I remember bullying kids we thought were effeminate. Surely my intention was to identify and make fun of them to distract from my fears about myself. The bullied become the bully. The church is a different place from the schoolyard. Or is it? Obviously, there are similarities. The preacher raises his voice to decry/bully those sinners while sometimes secretly committing the same sins or wishing he could.

Ted Haggard, once a leading evangelical pastor, was removed from his own megachurch in 2006 after admitting to a gay sex scandal. Now he has set up a new ministry with his wife, Gayle, who has stood by him throughout his troubles, as the church's co-pastor. "We realized that I am a sinner and she is a saint, but that way we do have a very broad appeal," he joked in an interview from his home in Colorado Springs, a city that has been described as the Vatican of America's evangelical movement. "I feel we have moved past the scandal. We have forgiveness. It is a second chance," he said.

Did those whose lives he harmed forgive him? Or was it just the "sheeple" stupid enough to be hypnotized by his idiocy? Sorry, I feel strongly about this. And it drives me crazy that others don't.

The real crime is how churches are set up as bastions of secrecy and protection, where sexual predators can hide and be shielded. Catholics are a special case here. The horrific abuse of young boys for centuries deserves only the worst punishment possible. But as we are finding, it was the church hierarchy that created a "safe space" for priests to do whatever they wished with the young boys who came thinking they were serving God, not the physical needs of the priest they trusted.

But it's not just the Catholics. In 2019 *The Houston Chronicle* published a six-part exposé of the pattern of abuse and cover-up within the Southern Baptist Convention. At the core of Southern Baptist doctrine, as the report noted, is local church autonomy, the idea that each church is independent and self-governing. It's a perfect profession for a con artist—or a predator—because "all a man has to do is talk a good talk and convince people that he's been called by God, and, bingo, he's a Southern Baptist minister. He can move from church to church, from state to state. It's a porous sieve of a denomination" (Robert Downen, Lise Olsen, and John Tedesco, Multimedia by Jon Shapley, "Abuse of Faith," *Houston Chronicle*, February 10, 2019, hhttps://www.houstonchronicle.com/news/investigations/article/Southern-Baptist-sexual-abuse-spreads-as-leaders-13588038.php).

Which brings us closer—really close—to home for me. Let's call it, "Who's on First [Baptist] and Who's on Second [Baptist]?" More on that to come.

"Several Southern Baptist leaders and their churches have been criticized for ignoring the abused or covering for alleged predators, including at Houston's Second Baptist, where former SBC president Ed Young has been pastor since 1978," the newspaper reported. "Young built the church into one of the largest and most important in the SBC; today, it counts more than 60,000 members who attend at multiple campuses." (This was the church my brother "served" until his death from brain cancer.)

According to court documents, a fourteen-year-old named Heather Schneider was raped inside Second Baptist by one of the staff members, John Forse, who directed pageants and plays at the church. He lured the teen with the promise of acting lessons. She immediately told her mother.

Young called the next morning to offer whatever he could do to help. According to Heather's mother, he hung up when she told him she had already called the police. She immediately faced the church's formidable legal team. She was David facing Second Baptist's Goliath. She had no stone for her slingshot. Heather died by suicide (drug overdose). John Forse got probation.

The Southern Baptist Convention distanced itself from any responsibility. And Young expressed concern that his "deposition testimony could unfavorably affect [his] television ministry, which now is seen on a daily basis in the greater Houston area."

Ed's TV ministry was safe. He can now be seen on television around the world.

It seemed churches were exploding with hypocrisy—especially in 1986, the year my ministry and life crashed. In that very year, the U.S. Supreme Court passed *Bowers v. Hardwick*, which criminalized oral and anal sex in private between consenting adults. I was confused by all of it, and I had no place to turn.

Chapter 22

Walk of Shame

When I escaped the curse of homosexuality by moving from Abilene, Texas, to Shawnee, Oklahoma, my brother was there. He would help by introducing me to the right people, ultra-straight. He did. I pledged his fraternity. All was well.

Unfortunately, when I entered the school of music, it became clear that my escape had not worked. Oklahoma Baptist University had a large theater department. What did that mean? Gays. What was more, they seemed almost comfortable in their unfortunate state.

There is no question in my mind that they thought, "How great is this! Our tribe has increased by one." I felt it. What would I do? Counter it by being even more aloof, distant, and sometimes downright rude by ignoring even their efforts at friendship. Guilt by association was not going to happen to me.

So I made it through my last two years of college with no dangerous liaisons, not even close. And, as you know, I married on the day of my graduation. I was good, except, of course, for the psychiatrist in Oklahoma City. I arrived at the marriage bed unscathed—almost. There was Abilene.

I dove into my work, dedicating every waking moment to my career and then the kids. We moved a lot, but we did our best to keep the kids feeling safe and secure in their family unit, in spite of the lack of human warmth or authentic affection between their parents. We had married at twenty-two and had had no indiscretions for ten years and also no physical passion. It is definitely one of the regrets I have for Vicki, who never experienced that from me, ever, from our wedding night, when the marriage was not consummated, and forward.

I am a very passionate man. I had this love of life and love of music and love for humans building up but with no valve to allow for occasional release of all those emotions. There were furtive glances shared with men walking along the street. I have no doubt that for them it was merely a little flirtation, whereas I was thinking, "Oh, my goodness, you looked at me twice. You must love me. Can you take me away?" By the time I finished that tragic thought, they were gone.

Alert: These are the things I shared with my third Christian counselor at my first one-on-one session. These are the things he then shared with Vicki the next day at her one-on-one.

I had experienced the devastation of all my work hopes and dreams falling apart when I gave up on St. Gallen. Not only had it been my big chance to be an opera singer, but it had also saved me from the Baptist hamster wheel, round and round, going nowhere. And what happened? Houston Baptist University took me back as a professor. Second Baptist Church, "fellowship of excitement," hired me as interim minister of music. Ed Young was pastor.

While I had jobs, I was really broken down. I had been saying "I want to be an opera singer" since at least 1969. I had gotten the degrees to prepare me. It wasn't just what I did; it was who I was. I started looking hard inside myself to find out who I was.

Vicki and the kids were out of town visiting her parents. I was scared to death, but I decided to drive around Montrose, the gay section of Houston. I knew there was what I called a "dirty bookstore" down there. I parked in the corner of the lot. I had no idea what was going on with the men who were coming and going, so I left.

The next night I returned and walked through the halls and booths, completely freaked out. I still couldn't figure out exactly what the protocol was. Were there invitations? Negotiations? Chitchat, perhaps?

I went back to the parking lot and waited until a nice-looking man got out of his car. I approached and said, "Excuse me, I'm new to this. Could you tell me a little about what happens in there?" He literally ran back to his car and sped off. Maybe he was a Baptist minister too!

I'm a determined type, so I went back in and lurked around until I figured it out. There was an electric feeling of danger. Because I was a public figure in a huge Baptist church, there was a pretty good chance someone would know me. That didn't matter. I needed the touch of another human being. It was a tragic substitute for the dreams I had been having about what it would be like. That kind of brief, anonymous tête-à-tête would never fill in for real human connection. But it was something—*liaisons dangéreuses*.

I didn't go often, but any visit was too many. Of course, I grabbed the local gay magazine while there and devoured it in the car before throwing it away. If I was never going to "meet" any gays, I could at least read about them and live vicariously. They looked so happy. They were so fit. There was no Internet, so everything had a phone number or an address. And there were personals. But I really didn't get that and didn't want anyone to have my phone number.

I discovered there were such things as gay saunas. I went to one. It was way too bright! I tried the park—literally around the corner from First Baptist.

Oh, boy, that was bright and dangerous, filled with desperate men like me—plus a few exhibitionists, voyeurs, and undercover policemen. I was walking on a very dangerous edge.

All of the foregoing was completely unsatisfying. A twenty-minute tryst was only making me feel more alone and more guilty about what I was potentially doing to my family. It also made me more desperate for a real connection. I was desperate for human contact, as meaningless as that might have been. The danger was intoxicating, and very real.

My entire tenure in the church had been filled with lingering glances here and there and looking away as fast as I could. There were plenty of closeted, married gay men who were on church staffs everywhere. From what I understand after I came out, I had really been missing out on quite a network of "ministers having sex" from coast to coast. I just never took the step past the glances or signed up for the "Baptist Minister Gay Closet Club" with members from around the world.

Then one of those glances lasted a little longer. It was from someone I had known for a long time in Baptist circles. He was an artist as well. He was married with kids. Perfect! We had been social friends as families for a long time.

Our encounter happened when our wives and kids were out of town. We decided to go to a movie and to meet at his house to head out. We did not get to the movie. It was a brand-new experience for me, but not for him, to "be with someone" whose name I knew. We got together off and on for months, always brief encounters in various locations, including a locked church office. I think I fell in love. He did not.

We managed to be on a trip together, just the two of us. We had separate rooms, of course. We had a brief moment together, and then he requested that I leave. "I don't like sleeping with others." I was heartbroken. I had wanted to actually sleep with him throughout our "romance." Eventually, it became too difficult to arrange a rendezvous, so we stopped. Our families remained friends until I came out.

In summer 1986 I lived with my parents in Fort Worth while I finished my doctorate in Denton. I was studying really hard. I took a break from studying every once in a while. On one of those breaks, I met a very nice, handsome man named Paul who lived in Dallas. He was an active member at Prestonwood Baptist Church. Whew!

He kept inviting me to spend the night with him. I had never done that. I was scared to death to take that leap. One night, I finally decided I would avoid it no longer. I made some excuse to my parents about studying late and drove to Dallas to spend my very first night in the arms of a man.

In the morning, I knew there would be no going back. It felt completely natural. I felt taken care of in the most fulfilling way. The cares of the world went away for eight whole hours. It wasn't any of the many roles I played in my real life. I was just Tim. Paul stayed in the background, living in Dallas and helping me to negotiate the hard stuff from a distance. He was also named in divorce filing number two as my "partner in sodomy."

But now what? My plan was to take my time helping the family adjust, even if that might be a full school year. I wanted to protect the kids, Vicki, and our income while we made the transition.

Ah, the best-laid plans of mice and men often go awry. I was about to become a pariah. I do not remember a hand grenade anywhere in those meticulous plans I had created.

Chapter 23

Christian Counselor #2: Altar Call

I am a man of second chances—and have needed many more than two. The first Christian counselor had not gone that well at the age of nineteen, but I thought I'd give Christian counselors another chance.

Things at Houston's First Baptist Church, where I was now serving, were a mess. With a huge staff—approximately 180 full- and part-timers—there were obviously going to be wanderers, hypocrites, and ladies of the night. Early summer 1986 was particularly steamy. The minister of education was caught in a prostitution sting and filmed exiting a lovely motel room.

Put yourself in Texas in 1986, or any time for that matter. The church folks all over Houston had to judge the wayward minister. I think they would have forgiven him had he not chosen an African-American prostitute.

Pastor John Bisagno's staff was falling apart, all on the nightly news, so he hired a psychiatrist for the staff to use on an as-needed and free-of-charge basis. The psychiatrist was from out of town (we were never told what town). He knew no one at the church, so information was completely safe in his hands. He was set up in an office with a separate entrance so that clients would not have to wear a trench coat and fake nose/eyeglasses to enter. Client appointments were set with thirty-minute breaks so that we wouldn't pass each other in the waiting room and pontificate about each individual's particular problem or proclivity.

I may have signed up too quickly, like the kid in class who raises his hand too often, desperate for attention, or like a second tenor who suffers the same malady in choir rehearsal. When my time came, I entered the private entrance. I spoke the private code word through the small opening in the inner door. It was like a speakeasy. Looking back, I suppose the code phrase should have been, "You're nuts." (The code phrase for Christian counselor number three should have been, "I'm screwed." But I get ahead of myself.)

This was supposed to be anonymous. I said, "I am a musician." The "therapist" (we were never actually told his credentials because we weren't supposed to know who he was from that "other" town) said, "I know who you are and the amazing music ministry you have." Holy crap! That made the next statement even harder. I said, "I think I'm gay."

He did not give me a test or walk me through Scripture like contestant number one. Nope, he got right to it: "What makes you think so? How have you acted on that?"

I told him the Cliffs Notes version: about the recent indiscretions at the "dirty" bookstore and even at the park within spitting distance of the church. After an indeterminate period of time, with his nodding occasionally and uttering "I see" here and there, he was ready for his prognosis to my self-diagnosis: "Tim, I have followed you and your wife for some time," he said. "Your music and your leadership are amazing. You are doing wonderful work at this church and all over the country. My advice to you is not to upset that applecart you've built so carefully."

Then, leaning forward in his chair as if telling me an intimate secret (because we had bonded in those fifty minutes), he gave the final encouraging words of wisdom: "Continue what you are doing with your wife and your music. Take care of those urges when they arise, as you have been. But don't let it ruin your ministry."

This was just the slap in the face I needed. It made me sick. It made me look at myself. His words actually held up a mirror so that I could see my life and the wreck I was making of it. He did me a huge favor that day. My own hypocrisy could not have been unveiled in a brighter light.

I was done. I was done with the church. I was done lying and cheating and fornicating and sneaking around and hurting everyone—and they didn't even know it.

Christian counselor number two was another one whose license I could have had removed. But who was I going to tell? Who would believe me? It didn't matter. My ugly truth was in front of me in neon lights.

Altar Call: Redecorate

For those not familiar with the innards of Southern Baptist church life, here's a quick primer: The church has put the "fun" in dysfunction. Southern Baptists have an altar call at the end of every church service, with the congregation singing a song encouraging compliance and reminding you of what a wretch you are ("Amazing grace, how sweet the sound that saved a wretch like me"). During the altar call, people can come forward for three reasons:

1. to get saved (normally only once);
2. to join the church and share in the fun;
3. to "rededicate" their life to the Lord.

Behind the scenes, we often jokingly changed "rededicate your life" to "redecorate your life." All of this is based on guilt and how much of it can be spread around. It's a lot like sunscreen; you have to reapply often or you'll get burned.

But the altar call became something different for me. When I did not physically go to the altar, I was there in my mind, actually praying. I asked God all about being gay. God didn't actually answer. I asked God to please take my desires away. Nope. I claimed that my "sexual preference" was heterosexual—really. I would weep. I'm pretty sure everyone just thought I was praying for the starving people in Africa, for them to see the light and listen to the missionaries better so that they could go to heaven, even if they had to starve to get there. *Nada*.

I reverted to Jesus's words: "Father, take this cup from me." That has confused scholars to no end. Jesus was saying, "Look, this is going to be extremely unpleasant. I don't want to go through with this. If there's any other way to save humanity from their sins, let's do that instead. Yet I want to do what *you* want to do, not what *I* want to do."

That was the same request as mine: "Coming out is going to be extremely unpleasant. I don't want to go through with this." I mean, my next day had no comparison to Jesus's. Still, I wasn't keen on my future either.

My tears were not about the lost souls; they were about me. I was the lost soul for whom I was weeping. I asked God to take this from me. Maybe one more verse of that invitational hymn would do the trick. But God did not remove it.

The top guilt-inducing hit was "Just As I Am." Every Baptist can sing this on demand. Verses 1 and 2 are pretty good. Verse 3 was mine:

> *Just as I am, and waiting not*
> *to rid my soul of one dark blot*
> *to thee whose blood can cleanse each spot*
> *O Lamb of God, I come, I come.*

Yup, I was that guy. I couldn't believe everyone couldn't see it. It was massive. It pervaded my every thought. I thought it would soon ruin my life. Little did I know that admitting what the church folks called my big old blot would make it go away. The truth will set you free after all.

It was years before I finally accepted the fact that God did not change me because I was already whole—and a homosexual.

Even with the sky falling around me, I was still grateful for so many things.

Grateful

I've got a roof over my head
I've got a warm place to sleep
Some nights I lie awake counting gifts
Instead of counting sheep
I've got a heart that can hold love
I've got a mind that can think
There may be times when I lose the light
And let my spirits sink
But I can't stay depressed
When I remember how I'm blessed

In a city of strangers, I've got a family of friends.
No matter what rocks and brambles fill the way,
I know that they will stay until the end.

I have a hand holding my hand,
It's not a hand you can see
But on the road of Life,
This hand will shepherd me
Through delight and despair
Holding tight and always there.

Grateful, grateful
Truly grateful I am
Grateful, grateful
Truly blessed
And duly grateful

Words and music by John Buccino from *Urban Myths*. Used by permission.

The Song of Myself

One day, I awoke, all grown up,
No idea where the time had gone,
Set adrift by fear, nowhere to turn.
No light to lead me home.

This is the song of myself,
The musical memoir of my life.
These are the words that I wrote of myself.
My song. My hymn. My serenade.

Sitting in a chair in a darkened room,
Scrolling through the pain in my life,
Looking for something to hang on to,
Some rock of ages or amazing grace.

There was no rock, no grace.
There was no home but me.
So many melodies that others chose for me.
I had to find my own.

A new song replaced those past,
As unique as my own hand or eye,
Springing deep from within:
The song of myself

Clear, vibrant, soaring,
It is a hymn of hope, it is my ode to joy,
A serenade of love and thanks.

It is the song that led me home to me.
My song, My hymn. My life.
Perfect just as it is.
My serenade. Now my gift to you.

©Tim Seelig, from *Serenade of Life*. Music by James Eakin.

Chapter 24

Christian Counselor #3: Rip the Band-Aid Off

It had been sixteen years since Christian counselor one—the nice Nazarene psychiatrist—stamped me "Not Gay." And only months since Christian counselor two—the smart fellow who told me just to scratch the itch when needed. Surely the third time would be the charm.

In fall 1986 my marriage was really falling apart. I had finally experienced a true connection with a male-gendered person. I had no idea what to do with that. Vicki and I were still singing the special music and then fighting the rest of the time. I finally told Vicki we needed help. We had never had any counseling in our thirteen years.

I told her I would go to anyone she selected. Her only resources were First Baptist Church, which was a little embarrassing, but she confided in one of the counselors on staff. He recommended a Christian counselor who was not on the staff.

Monday Morning

Vicki made the appointment. We went, having no idea what to say or what possible path we might find to stop the fighting. He talked to us and got the background of our lives. He knew who we were and of our ministry together. We talked and shared some "precious moments." At the end of the session, he rather jovially said, "I'd like to see each of you individually, and then we'll come back together and see where we are. Tim, why don't we start with you? How about tomorrow morning? Vicki, I can see you on Wednesday."

I thought, "How strange that this man has so many open appointments to make room for us." I was soon to find out why.

Tuesday Morning

I showed up for the session, sat down, and quite literally said, "I'm gay." He said, "I knew that. So why are you here?" I said that what I needed from him, and hoped he would provide, was an exit strategy. I didn't have to explain, but did, that I was the Baptist breadwinner and we needed time to deal with all the jobs and entanglements. It was late October. With some great care, we might be able to make it until the end of the school year. We could transition our entire lives piece by piece to cause the least collateral damage.

He said, "That's a good plan. Tell me about your experiences that brought you to this point." And I did. I pretty much regurgitated it, needing someone to hear it. And he was a professional. Surely he would be impartial. No. He immediately went to Vicki's defense.

"Vicki is a beautiful woman. She deserves a full life and someone who can love her fully—emotionally and physically." It got a little creepy, but, hey, it was already creepy.

At the end of the session, he said, "I have my one-on-one with Vicki tomorrow. This evening, I would like for you to tell her what's going on with you. Tell her about your struggle with the gay thing. That way, she'll know when she arrives for her appointment and we can take it from there."

Yes, I was being blackmailed. There was no veiled implication that if I did not tell Vicki, he would. I had a stinking (and sinking) feeling that this may be why he had so much free time. Friends would later say I could have had his license taken away. But to what end?

Tuesday Night

We put the kids to bed. I held Judson's hand until he went to sleep. The plan was to share a little from my appointment to give Vicki a bit of a heads-up for the next morning. We sat on the green velour settee in the living room of our brand-new house. I couldn't dilly-dally. I cut right to the chase: "I have been struggling with homosexual feelings."

Vicki's face froze. I could have knocked her over with a feather. When she regained her composure a bit, she was very empathetic. "How long have you had these feelings?" she queried. She asked for no specifics, no names, dates, or places. She was completely surprised by this news.

Later, some of my friends were shocked that she was shocked. They all said the closet you were hiding in must have been huge, big enough for some enormous gestures and pretty awesome wardrobe. A closet is a closet, people.

We ended with a little "bless your heart!" hug, not unlike all our hugs for thirteen years.

Wednesday Morning

I went to teach all day at Houston Baptist University. Then I headed directly to church to get ready for adult choir rehearsal and to meet Vicki and the kids for fellowship supper around 5:30 at the church's in-house restaurant, The Garden of Eatin' (I'm not making this up). We all went our ways to various activities.

We had a babysitter who often took the kids home so that we could party after rehearsal at Waffle House with two of our friends. That is when I learned what had happened Wednesday morning and throughout the afternoon, right up to fellowship supper time.

First, the Christian counselor had asked Vicki what I had said. That was apparently not good enough for him, so he unloaded the entire catalogue of Tim's dalliances over the last three years. He must have extended the hour session to fit it in—or he just talked really fast. Vicki got it all, including some bookstores and saunas and parks, oh my! There would obviously be no plan to dissolve the marriage and salvage our finances. We went from the six-month layaway plan to the "Pay the Piper Now" plan.

She was in shock and was very angry. Who wouldn't be? Her natural reaction was to call our pastor, Dr. John Bisagno—yup, the trumpet-playing, Bible-banging little Johnny Bisagno from 1958. She went right over to his office, having no idea what kind of snowball that set into motion that would continue for the better part of a year. He told her he would handle the church's response and actions from there. She went home to call family and friends until it was time for the fellowship supper.

She was stoic. I was curious. But we decided to wait until the Waffle House to share how her session went. At nine o'clock, when choir rehearsal finished, I had no idea what the day had held, none whatsoever. We splurged on a pecan waffle, and the saga began to unfold. Vicki had obviously not only shared the news with our friends, but they were prepared. The plan was that I would pack my things and leave the house. They would tell the kids I was leaving on a concert tour. It would give us time to sort things out. I simply acquiesced. I had no way to protest or disagree.

We never communicated with Christian counselor three again. His work was done. I have no doubt he felt he had struck one for God's army.

There was a better way—seriously. Perhaps we could have taken a month (November) or even made it through the holidays and addressed it between semesters, after the First Baptist Church pageant was over and the camels and donkeys went back into their stalls.

That was not to be.

ACT II

Chapter 25

Trip to the Pastor's Office

There were a lot of difficult hurdles and roadblocks ahead—with visible and invisible items of torture attached to them. Some caused a minor sting while others were meant to do more damage—like the second divorce filing with the big "S" word in all caps and bold: SODOMY! That letter is permanently affixed to my choir robe, should I ever attempt to put it on again, which I have not done.

In the "go forward" plan that was shared with me, the first stop was the pastor's office. I did not pass "go." Instead of collecting $200, I actually had all my money taken away and put in a "community chest to help ruin Tim." Yay!

Let me be clear: The church had every right in the world to fire me. I was not leading a life that was compatible with serving on a church staff of a Baptist church. What they did not have the right to do was crucify me in every way possible and tear my children apart.

There is a First Baptist, often a Second, and sometimes Third and Fourth Baptist churches in towns across America. These often result from unresolved arguments. Usually First Baptist is the biggest. Second is not an indication of size, however, in Houston.

When my brother ended his tenure at Second Baptist, they had five campuses and 60,000 members. When I went to the pastor's office that day, First Baptist had 22,000 members. To get this, you'll have to concentrate.

I had been interim minister of music at Second Baptist Church, fellowship of excitement (Ed Young, pastor). When they hired a new minister of music, the minister of music at First Baptist (John Bisagno, pastor) called and said, "You don't want to work for him; come over to First Baptist." I did. I became associate minister of music there.

When I was fired, my brother was hired by First Baptist (John Bisagno). After a few years, he was recruited by Ed Young, pastor, to come work for him at Second Baptist.

Let's review: I had done Second, then First; Steve had done First, then Second. Now you know "Who's on First!"

My trip to the pastor's office was at First Baptist Church—going as a lamb heading for the slaughter. I obviously had *nothing* to hide after the avalanche of information from my lips to Christian counselor number three to Vicki to John Bisagno and then to friends and family around the country.

Resignation Written

Given the short preparation time, Johnnie Bisagno, the trumpeting evangelist turned pastor, was quite prepared. There was some preliminary chitchat about how sorry he was that circumstances had brought us here, how sad it all was, Vicki deserved better, etc. For a minute, from his somber tone, I thought we were discussing a funeral. Any minute, I expected him to pull out the catalogue of caskets in which to bury the old Tim.

It turns out he didn't need a casket. The church's money was going to be used for other things: ruining Tim's life and helping the victim squeeze as much blood as possible out of Tim the turnip.

A gargantuan man, Bisagno, sat across from me at his gargantuan desk. He said there had been much discussion—no doubt that was true—and there were some things that, if I agreed to them, would enable me to take a leave of absence and return when my report card was all A's. I heard, "We are going to take away the urges so you don't ruin your ministry."

Pastor John handed me the printed list and read it aloud in his best evangelist voice, for extra punch.

1. Reparative therapy (so predicable). They had found a place in Arizona that could take me right away. I researched it later. They used all means, including shock therapy. This was like an intervention. I expected my family to walk in any minute.

2. Sharing in Jesus's name. I was to make a list of all church staff members—and highly visible volunteers who either were gay or whom I suspected were gay. Dale Garrett would have been one of those on the list.

3. I would stand in front of the church (not on the street in front of the church in front of the thousands) and allow two members of the ministerial staff to accuse me of the sin of homosexuality. I would acknowledge my sin and ask forgiveness—from the whole congregation. I was way too much in shock to have even pondered the music for that service. Later, I would!

4. I was to cease my friendship with Barbara Bamberg, one of the assistant accompanists, because she was considered to have aided and abetted

my behavior. That one hurt, and maybe was the one I was least willing to do.

John continued: "If you refuse any of these, you will need to resign your position at the church. In fact, the resignation letter has already been penned and will be in the church paper."

They knew they had made the conditions so ridiculous that the letter was a nonstarter for anyone but a crazy person. They were going to fire me anyway. They just thought they could emasculate me and get me to accuse innocent people on my way out the door.

Even though I was floating somewhere between disbelief and shock, I had not lost my center. I somehow found the courage to thank him for his time. I said something to the effect of: "I will not be completing the requirements on your list. Actually, none of the above." I walked out of his office, and I walked out of life as I knew it. It was October 1986.

Oh, I could have stayed and done the things I was asked to do. I could have lived a lie to keep the house of cards from falling—and the sky with them. I'd done that and learned the names of so many others who were doing the same. But that was not who I was. Dad always said one of my Achilles' heels was my penchant for telling the truth even when it's not popular. This was one enormous truth.

I was thrown under the church bus. It then rolled over me, backed up, and rolled over me again. It was a disaster. No FEMA. No Red Cross. No safety net. No community. No resources. I was displaced, completely. I knew one single out gay person in Houston, Texas: my hair stylist, Dale Garrett. Even though he shared my middle name, we had little else in common.

The plan was for me to move out the following Friday. I packed my things, said goodbye to the kids as they went to school, and found refuge in a place I could afford: Motel 6. As I sat in that room on a dreary November night, I had a peace of mind no one could ever understand. Yet it was there.

I had told the whole truth for the first time in my life and created a foundation on which to build. I also had enough quarters to allow me to watch TV and take a turn on the "massage" bed, available only to exclusive Motel 6 patrons—those with quarters. Turned on the TV to catch the latest episode of *Dallas*. Premonition?

The displacement was not just the removal/destruction of physical things or even my occupation. It was a displacement of my center, my being. Thirty-five years of living one truth had turned out to be a lie. The building block at the very bottom of the structure was pulled out. The emotional house of cards came tumbling down.

I was alone, without resources or the knowledge of how to get any, adrift—physically and emotionally.

Yet I had left the pastor's office with a with a few things he, nor anyone else, could take away:

Truth.

Music.

Humor.

And a newly discovered sense of empathy.

When I was fired from the First Baptist Church of Houston, the pastor who fired me tipped the scales at well over 300 pounds. In our discussions as I was being let go, I simply asked him about the list of "sins" the church regarded with such unequal importance. I asked whether gluttony and homosexuality were perhaps on the list together.

I happened to mention they were, but my belief that gluttony was a choice and homosexuality was not. So, I asked, what gave him the authority to fire me in Jesus's name? He gave me a great answer: "Well, you know the fact that gluttony is a sin may be biblical, but it is just not very practical."

As I have discovered over the ensuing years, religious folks have used this very argument against the LGBTQ community: "Homosexuality may not be a sin according to the Scripture, but it sure is practical to use as one."

Chapter 26

Wife's Dreams Dashed

In many ways, Vicki was simply a tool of the church and her upbringing. She was not evil, just malleable. She had spent her life doing what people wanted her or told her to do. She, too, grew up in the bosom of the church. As a young woman, she was taught: Don't think, don't feel, don't explore, don't dream; just love the Lord and do what your husband says—unless he comes out, and then you don't have to anymore. We had both been indoctrinated thoroughly. I cannot fault her for that.

Our marriage, while busy, too busy, was never fulfilling. I don't know if Vicki will ever realize what a blessing it was to divorce. There are really only three things I fault her for:

1. Doing unthinkable damage in one fell swoop, in one day, really just a few hours. But I know she was in shock and had no place to turn other than everyone we knew. She could have been a little more selective.

2. Choosing John Bisagno and other leaders at the church, who, while under the pretext of protecting her, were actually out to punish me and make sure everyone saw what their wrath looked like when someone strayed that far. Their portrayal of me as the most evil person on earth did not match the man to whom she had been married for thirteen years.

3. Going against our agreement to wait until the dust settled to tell the children the real reason I left. Corianna confided in me that it was only days until that information came out. She remembered it with astounding clarity. For some reason Vicki took the kids into the palatial master bath, sat them on the side of the huge Jacuzzi tub, and told them their daddy left them for a man. They had no way to comprehend that at ages seven and nine.

Other than that, we were stumbling around. The odds were stacked, with the entire church sitting on the bride's side. This scene would be repeated at the courthouse two months later during divorce proceedings.

Several weeks passed at home between the big announcement and when I moved out, maybe a week or two at the most. Those were tense times, full of arguments, not unlike leading up to the divorce. But, boy, did we now have a huge elephant in the room to chew into bits and pieces.

I regret every word and everything I said and the way I delivered it. Vicki knew a lot. She knew way too much from the nice counselor who had shared the most intimate and horrifying details of the "latter days." One big blessing: In baring my soul about my indiscretions, I had not named names. I am so grateful I did not. The counselor would have had no problem sharing those with Vicki, none whatsoever. She wanted names. She wanted the number of indiscretions.

Because we were both in shock and it had been so dramatic and *so* many people had been brought into the discussion, we were raw. Rather than go to our corners, we fought many rounds, with no sexy woman to ring a bell so we could swish out our mouths and wipe off the blood. We brought out the worst in each other in every way.

It was horrible, and I am so sorry for being a participant in that. You know that old kind of tragic warning: Be careful what you say. "Words are like nails hammered into wood. You can remove the nails, but the holes will be there forever." I have no doubt that the damage caused by some of my words is still there.

My fate with the church was sealed very quickly. I was especially popular at meetings of the Woman's Missionary Union, made up of the matriarchs of each Baptist church. They basically ran the church, although women were not allowed in any positions of leadership. It was apparently okay for them to lead themselves.

It probably went something like this, in hushed tones: "I have a burden to share. Dear John and Virginia Seelig have suffered such a blow. Their son, Tim, has turned into a homosexual. We need to pray for them, God's dear servants."

Once I left the house on that dreadful Friday morning, I didn't see much of Vicki except when I was allowed to be with the kids—mostly picking them up for court-mandated therapy. We exchanged frozen looks and as little conversation as possible (mostly, "What time will they be home?"). I don't blame her.

Then Vicki's prized possessions began to slip away: the Mercedes (yes, new), the beautiful home in southwest Houston (yes, new). Other possessions had to go because they would be in a relatively small apartment rather than a gorgeous big house. Probably the worst thing that slipped away was the appearance of perfection she treasured beyond anything.

It takes a sixty-one-day waiting period in Texas to get a divorce, from the original filing date, even if the parameters change in the document along the way. And, boy, did they. I filed on November 6, 1987. Vicki's church posse got busy.

The custodial parent, Vicki, had the right to choose the kids' court-mandated therapist and reject three therapists before the court would step in. Vicki found a woman through a referral. It was my responsibility to take them. Of course, I loved getting to see them more.

We went to the woman's office in the Montrose (gay) area of town. The first time we walked in, I knew we were sunk. The office smelled of patchouli and had bright "foreign" wall hangings, rugs, and statues. The kids felt immediately at home when this warm woman who radiated kindness put her arm around the two of them and took them into her office. They loved her and looked forward to every session.

She told them that their dad was okay. That he was not the evil man some said he was. This resonated deeply with them. Finally, someone was saying what they felt. After eight sessions, Vicki took her turn bringing them to the therapist. After that session, Vicki let the court know she would be looking for another. When I asked the kids about it, they simply said, "Mom doesn't want us going back to her. She is obviously not a Christian."

Before she chose another therapist, Vicki moved in with her parents in West Texas. She moved the kids 496.2 miles away, a drive of seven hours and fifty-one minutes, without a stop at Dairy Queen for a chilidog and a Blizzard. There would be no more visits to a therapist that far drive away. There probably wasn't a therapist in Lamesa.

All other information was filtered through Corianna and Judson, mostly Corianna. Judson was the quiet one. He would join in with his sister, but never started the conversation. He felt alone. He was angry. He was moody. He only had a part-time dad.

They visited me once a month for quite some time. It was difficult. The first summer after the divorce, I came to pick up the kids for what was going to be our first two-week stretch together. My partner at the time had a beautiful lake house. He had invited us to join him there to relax, swim, ski. When I picked them up, instead of excited kids with bathing suits and sunscreen, I was met by a constable serving me with an injunction.

The kids were upstairs with Vicki and a couple from the church in case Dad got angry or even violent. I was neither. No, I was gut-punched and, even more, heartbroken. The injunction stated that, until they were eighteen, the kids were not to sleep under the roof with anyone who was not a blood relative. That was that. Plans changed dramatically for years to come.

Judson did "all the things." He didn't have male role models. His Uncle Steve had moved to a megachurch in Arizona. He tried playing trumpet in the school band. They thanked him when he turned in the borrowed trumpet! He played football for a while. He never found his footing and was angry much of the time. He stopped the monthly visits with Dad for the most part. He was becoming uncomfortable around Dad's friends, who were all gay, of course.

Once a month, Vicki took the kids to Houston Hobby Airport, filled out all the forms, and loaded them on a Southwest Airlines flight from Houston to Dallas. There was no TSA, so we were always able to take them right to the gate. I would put them on their flight on Sunday. My biggest challenge was doing an O. J. Simpson through Dallas Love Field to try to make it to the car before completely falling apart—tearing my insides out that I would not be there for them for another month.

I learned about Vicki's boyfriends. I'm certain she learned about mine. Some of that had been revealed in the amended second divorce filing and the court injunction. I learned about her job. I'm certain she heard about mine. Corianna loved it!

I found out Vicki had made two new friends—gay friends. She found out I had made, oh, hundreds of gay friends.

Vicki and I discussed child support—and the "extras" child support would not cover. We discussed education beyond high school. The kids had no one to tell them it was going to be okay. They certainly had no one to tell them that Dad is okay as a human.

I do not believe Vicki intentionally badmouthed me to the kids. She didn't have to. Everyone she surrounded herself with by staying an active member of First Baptist Church of Houston did a good enough job. There was no way to be friends.

Twenty years later, I received a beautiful letter from one of Corianna's church friends during my time of coming out. It was heartbreaking for this little girl. She said one day I was everywhere at the church, singing, conducting, parenting. Then one day I was not there anymore. And she never heard my name spoken again. In her mind, "there was something you could do that was so bad, it would make you disappear."

She went on to share how that one event had shaken her deeply. She changed her belief system completely. If God, in his wrath and judgment, would just make someone disappear, then that was not a god she would worship. She had become an agnostic. She had looked me up to see where I had disappeared. She was thrilled and thanked me for what I do.

Lives were changed that fateful day I was outed and ousted from First Baptist. With the wisdom brought only by age, the ultimate impact of that day has been amazing. It is impossible to see when you are in the middle of pain like this. Trust is tested mightily. Would I throw the proverbial baby out with the dirty bathwater?

Chapter 27

Corianna's Single Focus

As will become increasingly evident throughout Act II, Corianna stayed as close to my side, supporting me as she could. Actually, she reveled in every part of it. It was not easy. She got to spend one weekend a month with what she came to call her "logical" family. The rest of the time she spent with people who hated both the sin and the sinner in this case. And, as Corianna would tell it, they spared not a moment in reviewing how their lives had been ruined.

She was nine years old and mature beyond her years. You could look in her eyes and know she "got it," whatever "it" was. Beautiful from birth, she swore not to let anyone see her sweat or even a crack in her armor where her dad was concerned.

The day I said goodbye to them at our house, she absolutely knew it was not for a two-week concert tour. The couple of weeks before that had been difficult—okay, years. She absorbed all of it. By nine she had established a comprehensive inventory of her dad, her mom, and the two of them together. She knew it was coming to an end.

I don't think Judson knew. He was seven and had been treated as the little brother, not expecting him to grasp deep, unspoken things. Looking back, I see we were much more protective of his "feelers" than Corianna's. She seemed self-sufficient. She didn't "need" to be held or coddled in any way, or so we thought. Judson did need the attention. He found it in his sister and mother. I was soon to lose intimate daily contact, as I guess all divorced dads do.

Corianna took things in stride, moving around a lot, including Europe, and changing schools. She adjusted to all of it, at least externally. She wanted everything and everyone to be okay. This would be one of her life themes: Take care of everyone else first.

She swam on the neighborhood swim team, winning a number of trophies and ribbons. But being a great team member was her first goal. If a swimmer was having a bad day or feeling pain or had an injury, Corianna was right there, encouraging him or her, even at the cost of her next race. She had mastered empathy by this point, including the menagerie she kept around the house.

When I got my first tragic little apartment, she saw it as an adventure. I had nothing on the walls. She suggested we paint something. We bought a stretched canvas and some acrylic paints in her choice of colors and took it all home. She chose black, gray, and red (oh, dear!). We decided that something avant-garde and contemporary was our best choice.

We painted the canvas in the building's parking lot. We let it dry—patience not being any of our spiritual gifts—and hung it over the sprung-spring pullout sofa. You would have thought it was a Jackson Pollock; it made about as much sense as one. Judson helped, but, as usual, he stood back a bit, letting big sister take the lead. He was also not as adaptive and couldn't grasp that this little abode would be my home.

She wanted me to feel okay about our new lives together. She went to great lengths to assure me that what mattered was us. Months turned into years, and that never changed. Through some very turbulent times ahead, she had one thing at the forefront of her mind and actions and made sure I heard her saying loud and clear, "Daddy, everything is okay, 'cause I love you!"

Unwavering for the Next 32 Years

Corianna had taken care of, protected, even mothered her little brother, and her pets, and her team, and her classmates. Much of that caring she focused on me. What a lucky dad I was, and I knew it! And, boy, did that carry us both through some murky water ahead.

The year after coming out, the following song was released—on audiocassette—composed by Fred Small and performed by The Flirtations. The first time the kids came to visit after the recording came out, I played it for them, over and over. It was my little antidote to the brainwashing they were getting at home.

Everything Possible

We have cleared off the table, the leftovers saved,
Washed the dishes and put them away
I have told you a story and tucked you in tight
At the end of your knockabout day
As the moon sets its sails to carry you to sleep
Over the midnight sea
I will sing you a song no one sang to me
May it keep you good company.

You can be anybody you want to be,
You can love whomever you will
You can travel any country where your heart leads
And know I will love you still
You can live by yourself, you can gather friends around,
You can choose one special one
And the only measure of your words and your deeds
Will be the love you leave behind when you're done.

Some girls grow up strong and bold
Some boys are quiet and kind
Some race on ahead, some follow behind
Some grow in their own way and time
Some women love women, some men love men
Some raise children, some never do
You can dream all the day never reaching the end
Of everything possible for you.

Don't be rattled by names, by taunts, by games
But seek out spirits true
If you give your friends the best part of yourself
They will give the same back to you.

You can be anybody you want to be,
You can love whomever you will
You can travel any country where your heart leads
And know I will love you still
You can live by yourself, you can gather friends around,
You can choose one special one
And the only measure of your words and your deeds
Will be the love you leave behind when you're done.

Chapter 28

Judson's Long Journey

My son, Judson, was a different story. From day one, he remained close to his mom. This split was an absolutely tragic result of the divorce and the gay. Not only did it erode the relationship between Judson and me, but it also did the same to Judson and Corianna—the most unfortunate of all results. I really "lost" Judson at different levels from age seven until twenty-four.

The first two years of the divorce were brutal. No redeeming moment to be found. From the kids' vantage point, I can only imagine what it did to them. During that time I had limited contact with them. It was better in the beginning because I had gotten an apartment in Houston, but soon they moved to West Texas to live with Vicki's grandmother in the small, remote, dusty town of Lamesa. Yes, it was as isolated and desolate as it sounds. They moved from a church of 22,000 members, where they were literally adored, to a town of 9,000, where they knew no one. There were no cellphones or Internet, only a landline in the kitchen.

Visitation stopped for months due to distance, cost, unwilling grandparents. I know Vicki made that decision because our beautiful house in Houston was gone. Our car had been repossessed. She had no job. It was a terrible, terrible time for her to have to mother her two children. Retreating, licking wounds, and protecting the kids were her goals, of course. It did none of that, at least through Corianna's eyes. They were being sent to living hell because of what Dad did.

It was not long until they moved back to Houston. It made sense, because my brother and The Singing Seeligs were there. I had abdicated all decision-making. Had I had any input, I would never have moved the kids back into the judgmental arms of the First Baptist Church. The church had no choice but to fall all over the poor little Seelig children bearing the burden of their dad's decision every time they entered. By that time I had resettled in Dallas, so we remained physically apart.

As the kids traversed middle school and high school, they maintained a modicum of normalcy. That is probably a stretch, and only from my perspective, because they didn't want to hurt me by airing or sharing their deepest struggle. They had moved into an apartment in one of the most exclusive parts of town and went to one of the wealthiest Republican high schools anywhere. They cut through the property of outrageous mansions to get to school.

In his early teens, Judson became very angry. Vicki took him to a therapist. Judson was angry at his dad. He was angry that he had to take care of his mom. But most of all, he was angry that at the age of seven, the implication was strong that he was now the man of the house. That was what worried him and angered him. The therapist allowed him to voice those things and work through them. And he got better with the knowledge and the support that it was okay just to be a teenager.

By his final years in high school, his mother was dating a man from out of town. As an out-of-towner, he spent a great deal of time at Judson's house. He became that missing onsite male role model. There was a hitch in the plan: He was a pretty devout fundamentalist and subtly reinforced the negative judgment regarding his gay dad.

I do not know what went on to bring Judson to his next decision, but it absolutely could not have happened in a vacuum. Surely my absence in his life had been a contributing factor in his decision-making.

Along the way, Vicki had gotten a really great job as a recruiter for a major law firm in Houston. Our incomes were more equal. We agreed that each of us would pay half of Corianna's and Judson's education beyond high school. It would be difficult, but fair.

That brings us to the years beyond high school. The story continues in the chapter titled "Worst Cup of Coffee Ever."

Chapter 29

Brother's Difficulty

The day the Band-Aid was ripped off, my brother was obviously on the top of the list for Vicki to inform. During the immediate aftermath, I remember only one phone call from Steve. It was the Baptist version of "WTF? What have you done to our family?"

Our "brand," built over fifty years, was strong. I was threatening it. WWTSD? (What Would The Seeligs Do?)

To give context, after high school graduation Steve had gone off to a Baptist college, leaving me with two years of bliss. Having sent him on the road to Oklahoma, I had just one worried thought: "Please don't screw up and be sent home."

Steve did what Mom and Dad had so hoped both of us would do. He married a lovely Baptist girl from Kansas. Her name was Bonita. He started to travel up the stairway to heaven, meaning a bigger and bigger church each step of the way. He was awesome at it, having larger and larger churches in Houston; Little Rock, Arkansas; Tempe, Arizona; ultimately settling back in Houston.

Steve and Bonita had two beautiful children: Stephanie and John Mark. Once again, I followed in big brother's footsteps with two children, a girl and a boy. Steve and I were not really close. We didn't call each other to chat. It was always some kind of four-way competition with Dad and Mom.

Most of the conversations centered on how many people were at Steve's summer camp, or at Dad's Sunday school class or at a convention he was in charge of, or at Mom's last concert. I fell into the trap. Rather than discuss the differences each of us was making in people's lives, we counted such efforts as though they were in a poll. Who's winning this week? It is one of the patterns I regret so deeply because I do know that each of us, in his or her own way, was about the business of changing people's lives for the better. But that became an assumption that went unspoken.

There was nothing inherently wrong about always talking about how size matters. In some strange way, it could work if we had taken the time to talk about individual stories or, God forbid, our own problems in life. We were in competition with each other every step of the way. Steve would often win, thanks to the huge budgets of megachurches versus nonprofits. Moving on.

I can say with certainty that Steve never approached me as my only brother with a "Can you share your story with me? It must have been terrible." He never even approached as a loving, caring minister with a "What can I do to help?"

That being said, by 1986, few in the church were prepared for the gays coming out. There was little attempt at empathy or understanding. By that point there was certainly no preparation for organized religion to face the AIDS pandemic, just peeking its ugly head out of its closet.

Our fate as brothers was somewhat sealed by the board game moves of the church. As the associate minister of music, my major function was starting and conducting Single Singers, a choir for single adults, who often find no place in the fabric of a family church. It was a very large choir, and we were having a blast, just having returned with 200 singers from a mission trip to Costa Rica. We had a fifth anniversary concert. I came out.

Steve was the minister for single adults at a megachurch in the Phoenix area. He was an amazing pied piper for them. John Bisagno thought, for some reason, it would be good to replace a Seelig with a Seelig. So three months after I was fired, Steve was hired. Part of his duties was to step into the directorship of the single-adult choir. Part of the deal was that Steve would publicly denounce the actions of his brother and his homosexual lifestyle. Steve accepted the terms of employment.

The move to Houston allowed Steve and his wife, Bonita, to be close to my kids. Their cousins now lived in the same city. Steve jumped into high gear, the only gear he had, creating a family unit as best as he could. That came with some control and large doses of "your daddy's bad" inferences.

A few months after the coming-out hurricane had settled into about Category 2, and was just hovering, I procured a small apartment with a pullout bed. The kids came over for our first weekend together—alone. They were visibly upset. We retrieved a blanket and got up on the sofa bed. I asked what was going on. They said that their cousins had pulled them aside and told them their daddy had told them Uncle Tim was a sinner and "the Bible told me so" kind of message.

They knew about sin. It's why they had to get dunked, because they were committing their own mortal sins. I was also already very familiar with scriptures being used as a weapon (still today). The kids had been through enough. At that time Steve was morbidly obese, with mounting health issues that would plague him the rest of his life.

I tried to calm the kids with a broad discussion of sin. But they were seven and nine, for heaven's sake. I told them that, according to the church, there was indeed a list of sins—explaining them as best I could while trying not to emphasize any one: (1) wrath, (2) greed, (3) sloth, (4) pride, (5) lust, (6) envy, and (7) gluttony.

Two days later, I got an irate phone call from Steve warning me not to discuss theology with my children. He was livid that I had dared to share with them a list of sins that "undermined his position as head of the household." He was furious to have his hand caught in the cookie jar, pointing the cookie at his brother (or was I really his brother then?). "For all have sinned." I guess not.

Thanksgiving seems to bring out the worst in us. We put such pressure on the whole thing, trying our best to be that Norman Rockwell picture. Thanksgiving would never be the same. It probably never is when a divorce is involved.

When Thanksgiving came around, Mom and Dad invited my partner, Louis, to join Corianna, Judson, and me. That was not going to happen. Steve told my parents he did not want his children exposed to homosexuality and did not want to pretend it was okay by attending Thanksgiving lunch. My parents, wanting to see all the grandchildren for the holiday, worked around it. They served the first full Thanksgiving dinner at noon for my family. Then they completely reset for a second dinner for Steve's family. This tradition lasted for several years.

A year later, when I was living in Dallas, we were awakened in the middle of the night by a phone call from my brother. The things he spewed were vile, ending with, "I never want to see you again." Later, when Steve finally came to me with an apology for the way he had treated me repeatedly, I told him what it would take to gain my forgiveness.

As a high-profile minister (of a church that would soon boast of 60,000 members), he would need to write a book or manual titled *What Not to Do When a Family Member Comes Out* and get Broadman Press, the publishing arm of the Southern Baptist Convention, to publish it. That had a snowball's chance in hell, on so many levels, not the least of which was that I already had one foot in the fires of hell.

To this day, I fully believe that a manual such as that, perhaps penned by Steve and Tim together, could have changed family dynamics for countless Baptist young people who were struggling and, most probably, saved lives.

The years rolled on. The cousins, who went to different schools, continued to share their experiences. By this time Steve had moved to the staff of

Second Baptist Church, so they no longer went to the same church. Opportunities to see each other diminished, and finally all went off to college and their separate ways.

I know there are many things for which my kids are grateful to Steve, and especially Bonita. There was no roadmap for any of this. I do regret that some of the routes we all took were without lights as we struggled mightily to find common ground. Steve and I never found it, but pretended to have done just that. We would be friendly and even say "Love you" when hanging up the phone. The four-way competition that motivated family conversations lost a contestant. Only three were all up in the church still. I was just waving my conductor's arms at the gays.

Easter weekend 2011 the most delicious thing happened. It was enough to make you believe there is a God and she has a sense of humor. This was the all-time pinnacle of ironies and the ultimate competition for the boys.

On Saturday night, I was on Jon Stewart's *The Daily Show*, defending San Francisco as the gayest city in America. An audience of 2.3 million people watched that show. The only other event of this magnitude was the documentary *After Goodbye: An AIDS Story*, seen by 20 million people the first night it aired on PBS.

The next morning, Easter, Steve was on CNN talking about Second Baptist's YouTube sensation "Dance Your Shoes Off." He had produced the video, which at that point had over a million hits. It wasn't really "dancing" (Baptists), but more a choreographed exercise routine. We called it Jeezercise. I doubt there was much overlap in our TV audiences.

Steve was a fighter; Bonita was Florence Nightingale. She stood by his side during the worst of days. Brain cancer is the worst, or one of the worst. He lived almost four more years.

His funeral was held at the main campus of Second Baptist Church. There were 2,000 attendees, and it was livestreamed. Gospel stars performed. And there were lots of preachers.

Corianna and I attended the funeral. It was hard for us both. We marched in with the family, sitting on the second row. Neither had seen the people from First or Second Baptist in decades. It was hard, but we wanted to honor our brother and uncle and be there for family.

One preacher told of meeting Steve for the first time at a church camp. He walked in on Steve talking to a young man who he later found out "had made some bad decisions and ended up with AIDS. This is the kind of heart

Steve had." We knew the message was for me. There was no other reason he could have possibly inserted AIDS. It's not as if Steve got the Baptist church to open a clinic or information center. Corianna was so angry that this preacher felt it was appropriate to take a jab like that, she leaned over and said, "We are walking out!"

I told her "no." We were on the second row. Again, the motivation was: "What will people think?" Expunging that from life is a lesson I am still trying to learn.

Although we never really bonded as brothers, Steve touched tens of thousands of people with his humor and big heart.

Chapter 30

Parents: Bless Their Hearts

When I came out, Mom and Dad—the super Baptists—asked what they had done to make me a homosexual. I told them, "Absolutely nothing." What they had done was instill a deep sense of telling the truth that would not allow me to live a lie anymore. I am not sure they were happy with that either. But let me tell you how they have reacted over these years.

The first year was really rough. Mostly, they had to negotiate the animus between their two sons. No parent wants that. I will have to say it was ninety percent on Dad's side. There was an episode of going through the list of sins in the Bible. They wanted nothing to do with me or my "sexual preference," as they called it. (Of course I woke up one day and, like ordering brunch, thought, "Being a heterosexual is not my preference today. I think I'll have the homosexual. What fun it would be to lose everything!")

I don't believe my brother or most of his family ever acknowledged the fact that I was born this way. It just didn't fit into their rigid, narrow belief system. Dear God, if they believed that one thing, wouldn't all of it unravel? (Yes, it would, in a good way.)

The second year, they decided to purchase eight season tickets to the TCC, the gay chorus I had started directing. They got a group together and attended for years. That was a wow! It was also a shocker, since they never came to any performances when I was growing up. They were truly too busy.

They started making up for lost time by attending this chorus's concerts, but seldom critiqued them. One concert was all psalms. They were in heaven. It was with a full brass symphonic band and the mind-blowing (and ear-blowing) organ at the Meyerson Symphony Center. Their critique was only about one piece.

The phenomenal Bobby McFerrin had composed a piece based on Psalm 23. It was like a chant—a cappella and breathtaking. The singers killed it. My parents pointed out a fatal flaw in it: McFerrin had changed a lyric and thereby almost ruined the whole concert for them.

Bobby had changed God's gender (even though God has no gender): "The Lord is my Shepherd, I have all I need. She makes me lie down in green meadows." *Blasphemy!* God was a white man, for heaven's sake!

I tried to explain that my singers and the audience were moved by this. The mean, judgmental God who would exterminate almost every living being in a flood was tough to swallow for the gays. The hope that God also embodied what are assumed to be feminine qualities of a mother brought much comfort and a greater possibility that they would feel more inclined to believe in that God. Still, blasphemy. Move on and enjoy the "wins" of their attending at all.

They did what Christians should do: They prayed for me. They knew it is not their job to convict me of sin. They believed in a God big enough to do that should the need arise! They simply loved me and encouraged me to be the best person I could be.

At one point they asked why I kept talking about my coming out. I reminded them of what they had always told me: that the day they accepted Jesus as their Lord and Savior was the most important day of their lives. From that moment forward, every single day for them had been different from those before. And they gave witness to that at every opportunity. And so it was with my coming out. From that day forward, everything changed. I'm just bearing witness!

Mom and Dad are gone now. He lived to be ninety-four, and we became best friends when we were all we had left. I know my parents wished things had been different, but they were not.

At the funeral home when Mom died, we reviewed the obituary Dad had written to be printed in the Fort Worth paper. It said Virginia was survived by two sons: Stephen, associate pastor of Second Baptist Church of Houston; and Timothy, artistic director of the San Francisco Men's Chorus. I did everything I could to avoid my head exploding all over the caskets displayed so beautifully around the room.

I pulled Dad aside and simply said, "It's okay to leave what I do out of the obituary. I'd rather be left out completely than not be truthful about the chorus I conduct and of which I am so proud." He looked like a kid caught with his hand in the cookie jar and asked the funeral coordinator to come over.

He said, "The obituary needs editing before it goes to the paper. Please add the word *Gay* to the San Francisco Gay Men's Chorus." She didn't blink. She walked away, and nothing was ever said about it again. It appeared in the newspaper and the funeral program for all the Baptists to read.

Many may not understand the enormity of this, but many will. This is a newspaper that every one of their friends and colleagues in their hometown read. My parents had come a long, long way. I am so proud of them and the journey we were on together.

Chapter 31

Turtles for the Save

Music had been my rock at every twist and turn. It was one of the things about which I said *"You can't take that away from me."* Those are music, humor, empathy, and truth-telling.

I started at the age three singing "You Are My Sunshine" while standing on the piano bench. This evolved into *The Marriage of Figaro* in Switzerland and a solo recital singing Rachmaninov at Carnegie Hall. It was at my very core. It became my life, both "what I do" and "who I am."

I had come out in late October 1986. I knew nothing. I would visit Paul in Dallas from time to time, one of those being for Memorial Day. Paul was a part of the sober community, and every Memorial Day they held the Texas Roundup. It was a gay old time with hundreds in attendance. People not in AA were not allowed to attend the sessions, except for the big banquet. Paul and his next-door neighbor, Charles Hodnet, had something up their sleeve.

I arrived for the mocktail hour—perfect for a little Baptist boy who knew only the piña colada. As we strolled around, Paul and Charles introduced me to the chairman of some group called the TCC. He said they were looking for a conductor. They were paying $35,000. It was a little late to turn in an application, but if I dropped it by his office the next day, he would add it to the pile.

We went into the banquet where members of the TCC would be singing. This was perfect since I had never heard a gay men's chorus sing. I didn't even know there was such a thing.

After more mocktails, the emcee introduced the chorale. About twenty-five guys filed onto risers. As I recall, they sang "Big D," one of their standards. For their big closer, they sang F. Melius Christiansen's arrangement of "Beautiful Savior" ("Fairest Lord Jesus"). No! That had been a standard in my previous life. I had hoped never to hear it again. Were this a church choir made up of gays (aren't they all?), I needed to think about that.

The dean at Houston Baptist University called me in as the school year ended to let me know I had two years left on my three-year contract. Because I was a member of an organization of professors, they could not fire me without hard evidence. They would allow me to teach my last two years, as uncomfortable as that might be.

The chorale's $35,000 was the same salary I was making as a full-time professor. If I got the job, I could quit teaching and shake the dust off my Houston boots. My application was submitted; it even had a video of my conducting my 200-voice singles choir. The days dragged on, and I met with only one person, the president of the chorus, Michael Sullivan. He was wonderful and very helpful. I was selected as one of two finalists and asked to audition. The day before the audition, Michael invited me to lunch at The Black-Eyed Pea, famous for grits and cornbread. I ordered the vegetable plate, passing on the chicken-fried steak.

Michael launched into the details about the time and place: 7:30 at Thanksgiving Square. I would be the second of the two finalists to audition. As we finished up a shared banana pudding, he said, "Oh, there is one more detail. The chorus has fallen into some financial difficulty. We have, unfortunately, had to change the salary from $35,000 to $12,000."

What? I had to decide if I even wanted to audition. I couldn't quit my job in Houston for that. I sure couldn't pay child support. I went ahead and auditioned.

Oh, my goodness gracious! For the first time in my life I was conducting men like myself! It was absolutely exhilarating. For the last thirty-plus years I have had the privilege of welcoming hundreds of gay men and lesbians into my choruses. Many, if not most, enter the room and, with the first note, cry! Many have loved music their whole lives and have sung in school choruses or church choirs where they had to be in the closet. The music may have been touching their soul, but against a backdrop of living a lie. Finally, bringing the love of music and being oneself is a dream come true. It is very emotional. That's how I felt that night.

They offered me the job, but I had a mixed response. What would I do? Well, I decided to do both. I taught at HBU from Monday through Thursday afternoon. I then ran to Hobby Airport and flew to Dallas on low-cost Southwest Airlines for chorus's Thursday evening rehearsal.

If I had events back in Houston or could see the kids, I would fly home. If not, I stayed at Paul's house. That was July 1987. It was my very first conducting audition ever. The next one would be in November 2010. I'm pretty sure I won't be doing another.

I walked the tightrope of teaching at a Baptist university and moonlighting with a gay chorus. The chorus was bankrupt, codependent, and dysfunctional, so it was a match made in heaven. I had nothing to lose, most definitely the money that was just enough for my flights.

I jumped in with both feet. Meeting the board members for the first time, they asked about my vision for the chorus. It was everything I could do not to say, "Try to help get you all out of debt so you can pay me the salary you teased me with two months ago." Instead, I poured my heart out.

I told them I had come out just nine months earlier, an event witnessed by thousands of people. I simply did not have the luxury to fail since so many were expecting just that. They would love to see me in the gutter for my betrayal and the hurt I had caused them. I would not stop until the chorale was recognized as the finest men's chorus anywhere. I could tell they were not listening.

They said, "That's nice," and asked me to leave. I was completely gobsmacked. I was their new artistic director. I think I may have said, "Are you serious?" They were. I got up, red-faced, and walked out. I found out only later that it was because they needed to discuss the dire (really dire) financial straits the chorus was in. And they didn't want me to know. The former manager had not paid payroll taxes—for some time. The IRS seized their bank account. It would be cash for a while. Oh, Lord, is this how the gays operated their business?

My first concert—named "Hello, Dallas!"—was in October. When I arrived at the venue for dress rehearsal, there was no piano. The board chair explained, "You know, we are running on a cash basis. We passed the hat at the last board meeting but raised only enough for one night of piano rental. We had our choice: performance or dress rehearsal."

I planned to stay just one year, and this helped solidify that decision. I applied for two other jobs the next summer. At that time the chorale raised my salary to $20,000. I stayed for twenty years! It would be several years before my salary climbed to the original offer.

One of the jobs I should have gotten was as head of choral studies at a really great university. I sang a recital; the professor loved it. I conducted the chorus; the kids loved it. I had meetings with my future colleagues; we got along great. I shared with them my vision for the choral program: beautiful singing, creative programming, and performances at Carnegie Hall.

I went home and started packing; it was that good. A week later, the dean called. I was ready with my "I'm thrilled. I accept. When do I start?" Instead, I got, "Tim, we all loved you and everything about you in the application process. You are quite a force. In the end we realized that you are a racehorse. What we need at this time is a milk cow, someone to show up every day and feed the students (cows). Best of luck to you."

This is the best reason ever for losing a job. I've thought of it often. I never tried to be a milk cow. The second reason was an invitation to come to San Francisco for a final audition for the professional men's ensemble Chanticleer. The invitation came from Louis Botto. The salary was terrible, not enough for child support. The travel schedule was brutal. I would never see my kids. Most of the singers rented apartments together, with maybe four or more roommates. Oh, dear! Louis and I talked a lot (he had tapes of my singing), but in the end I just couldn't do it.

I didn't really care about those other jobs. I was in love with this thing called the Turtle Creek Chorale. First concert? Check. Holiday concert? Check. Some people left because I was demanding. Others left because I was comfortable being gay (although perhaps a little overexuberant, having been out of the closet for only ten months).

Spring came, and I decided to have some fun and shake things up. We did a concert titled "Bach to Bach." The first half was classical, starting with J. S. Bach. They sang really well. The audience loved it. For the second half, we featured P. D. Q. Bach (aka Peter Schickele). It is a hilarious oratorio titled *Oedipus Tex*. It presents the story of Ed (Oedipus) set before a country-western backdrop. I had been fortunate to sing the lead role in the world premiere, conducted by Peter himself. It is quite a romp. Cast members included Billie Jo Casta and Madame Peep, backed by The Okay Chorale. It was perfect for us. Mr. Schickele was gracious enough to allow us to arrange it for a men's chorus.

They all thought that sounded nice, until I told them that everyone would be changing outfits at intermission into cowboy hats (check), cowboy boots (check), and togas! "This man's lost his mind; this is not who we are. Blah, blah, blah." Half the chorus was all in, with another quarter willing to go along. As to the last quarter, "Bye, Felicia!"

The fifty singers we started with began to dwindle. We added a few after the holiday concert. "Bach to Bach" was a huge hit. The audience screamed. When the singers saw how much the audience loved it, their whole demeanor changed. It was as if this had been their idea!

A huge number of people auditioned after that with more in the summer. We hit 100 and never looked back. It was as if the chorus had been listening to my vision, stated at the first board meeting.

We were all looking for something to lift us from the horrors of the AIDS pandemic exploding around us. We needed each other. We were no longer just gay brothers in song. We were caregivers. We were mourners. We were ministers.

Chapter 32

From Gutter to Glitter

The TCC continued to find its footing while experiencing meteoric growth that no one knew how to handle. An original member, Ed Young (not the preacher), invited me for coffee and told me all about GALA Choruses, the Gay and Lesbian Association of Choruses. They were having their triennial festival (every three years, now four) in Seattle in 1989.

We wondered aloud, "Don't you think we should be members of GALA?" I said, "Of course. Why aren't we?" Ed hemmed and hawed and said, "Well, the board doesn't think we should be so blatant with our orientation. We'd have to put it in the program."

Excuse me! I did not go through my incredibly painful coming out, losing everything, to go back in the closet for anyone, board or not. Ed said he would pay the initial fee to join. I said, "Do it." He did.

At the next board meeting, I excitedly announced the generous gift by Ed and that we were starting fundraising to go to Seattle in eighteen months. The members with whom I had spoken were fully on board and excited. Nothing was said. But they knew the ship had at least pulled away from the dock. The same thing happened with the Alan Ross Freedom Parade, Dallas' gay pride parade. The board didn't want the chorus to march in it. A singer paid the entry fee, and we marched.

The world didn't fall in. This is, after all, a member-driven organization. This is the same board that had the audacity, when the local ABC affiliate broadcast our holiday shows, to ponder whether or not we should take off our AIDS ribbons. I threatened to walk out. Years later, Bitter Beverlys would blame me for dragging the chorus out of the closet. You're welcome.

The next twenty years were filled with the anguish of AIDS, the growing pains of any group with the triple whammy of dysfunction: nonprofit, arts, and gay. But with all of that, the chorus soared in those twenty years:

- Thirty-seven recordings, including:
  Billboard Top 10 Classical Chart for John Rutter's *Requiem*
  Chorus! Magazine's "Best Choral Recording" of 1990
  The only recording of Richard Strauss's *Die Tageszeiten*
  with the Fort Worth Symphony Orchestra

The only recording of Gyorgy Orban's *Missa III* with the
Meadows Symphony Orchestra, SMU
- Two documentaries:
  After Goodbye: An AIDS Story, PBS, Emmy Award for Best
  Documentary
  The Power of Harmony, Best Documentary, USA Film
  Festival
- Eight prestigious invitations to perform for the American Choral Directors Association (three national, three regional, two state)
- Four performances at Carnegie Hall
- Performances in Barcelona, Berlin, Prague, and London
- Budget growth from $69,000 in 1987 to $1.7 million in 2007
- Season subscribership growth from 125 to over 2,000
- Growth in the number of singers from 50 to 250
- The chorus becoming a shining jewel in the tiara of the Dallas arts scene
- Conducting the chorus in a performance for Her Majesty Queen Elizabeth II. The headline accompanying the pic of me shaking her hand was "Lucky Queen"!

We were living our dream—and fulfilling a mission. And we were doing all of that gay stuff in Dallas, which some consider the buckle of the Bible Belt. We did some crazy things in our quest to put TCC on the map.

Along the way, when I turned fifty, I had turned to Juanelle Teague for help. I also went to a hypnotist/therapist to try to unblock some of my past that continued to haunt me. I did what I was asked. Put on the special flashing "blindfolds," put on the headphones so I could only hear the hypnotist. We began. I fell right in.

He began taking me back little by little to my fifth birthday party. Blocked. He continued. "What kind of cake did you have?" "What friends were there?" Nothing. Finally, he said, "Let's go in another direction. Let's begin work on your life's mission."

I literally said (because he recorded it all on cassettes), "I already know what that is: 'I will use whatever medium I am given to make sure every person with whom I have contact knows they are worthy and full just as they are.'"

It's hard to keep a large nonprofit gay chorus in the black. It is expensive to run such an organization. We do all sorts of things, from bake sales to auctions, car washes to online, individual fundraising pages for big trips. One day I was driving along Turtle Creek (yes, there is an actual Turtle Creek) and saw a banner for a marathon raising money for a worthy cause. I thought, "We should do a marathon. They apparently make pretty good money, or people wouldn't keep doing them. You just need to know a lot of athletic people who like to run long distances." I couldn't think of any, but I thought some of our members might know some.

By the time I got to the office, it had dawned on me that we were not "called" to run. We were called to sing. And thus was born the idea of trying to set the Guinness World Record for "longest choral concert" in history. It was a marathon of sorts. No one had to run. No blisters. No sweating even!

In hindsight I realize that it may have been easier to run a marathon. Because no one had ever tried what we were planning, the Guinness folks had no previous history to guide them in setting up the rules. They were making it up as they went along, as were we. Their team of rule-makers was tough. They wanted to make it difficult, as they should.

We could have set the record with five hours, since none had gone before. But it was our twentieth anniversary. Why not try for twenty hours? We rented a movie theater to hold the event. We decided we would sing, nonstop, from midnight on Friday night until eight o'clock on Saturday night. We set these hours because we wanted to have a huge celebration with the chorus members and friends and patrons.

The singers each got pledges based on how many hours they would sing. We got corporate sponsors for the event. And we sold tickets to hear the chorus. You could purchase a two-hour ticket, a four-hour ticket, or a pass that allowed you to come and go the entire time.

The rules that caught us a little off guard were that the chorus had to sing, nonstop; could not repeat songs within a two-hour break; could not stop for longer than thirty seconds; and could not sing "filler" songs (such as "Happy Birthday"). Each singer could take a fifteen-minute break each hour and had to "clock in" and out to prove he was there and singing. We put 100 chairs on the stage. We had six notebooks under each chair. Each had approximately ninety minutes of music.

It was amazing. The entire time we had volunteers with food for when the singers took a break. If that was not enough, we had wardrobe changes every four hours, from pajamas at midnight to holiday garb in the morning. We ended the evening in formal attire, champagne all around. We had two accompanists who swapped off. I conducted most of the time, spelled by my assistant when I had to take a bio break.

Guinness sent proctors to make sure we followed the rules. Off they went to "talk among themselves" and decide if we qualified. It took about six weeks, but we did it: twenty hours and twenty-two minutes. And we're in the big shiny book!

We had more fun than humans are allowed to have—in the very middle of the tragic impact of AIDS on our chorus, in the struggle for equality, in the fight to keep up with memorizing our music, and while trying to fulfill my dream to become the best in the world. We paused to laugh. We introduced hilarity to our audience, and some bawdiness too, and irreverence. It was no longer your mother's church choir concert. We were out, way out. Thank goodness!

Most importantly, I grew. What I didn't know in those first few weeks, I would learn over time. I learned with John Thomas's mentorship. I learned from every single member. I already knew how to push and be demanding and not to settle. But I also learned about volunteers. I learned about how to get along with boards (mostly after I left). I can look back and see my self-growth soaring with the chorus. I am so grateful to the hundreds of men who were patient enough to stay the course as I learned.

From the first rehearsal, I majored in learning empathy—with every singer who died; with every singer whose pain was palpable as he was rejected by family and church; with those who lived with HIV and struggled with survivor's guilt and becoming invisible; with those who struggled financially. Empathy. This course was not offered in my first thirty-five years in the church. Faux empathy is still their game as we watch many line up behind policies and people who have no empathy and hold them up as role models, because they still hate the gays, abortion, and immigrants. I was saved from that by the most loving, empathetic people on the planet.

Was it all rainbows and unicorns? No, it was not. I was hired to be a vision-ary artistic director, at least after the first year, when we finally got in the black. But I was a racehorse, after all. Many were hoping for a milk cow. Throughout my twenty years at the artistic helm of the TCC, people disagreed with my vision. Often, it was not the vision they disliked but how to get there. My Myers-Briggs profile type is ENFJ: big picture, soft heart, top down, list maker. This personality profile often clashes with board members, school administra-tors, deacons, and the like.

There were a few people during my tenure who were hellbent on control-ling or thwarting me and my vision. They were unhappy, although setting that vision was what I was hired to do. During the twenty years, there was one attempted coup by four board members. They did not succeed, and resigned from the board, then asking the newspaper to investigate their charges against me. Indeed, several media outlets did the deep dive of research. None of it stood up to the spotlight. But the struggle truly wore me down and led to my retirement announcement a year later.

Regardless, there is no question my life had been saved by the TCC. I could never tell them fully how much I owe and love them.

Chapter 33

Then Came the Women

Two years into my tenure with the chorale, in June 1989, I was asked to judge the Mr./Ms. Razzle Dazzle Contest. I was seated by Lory Masters and Barbara O'Brien. I was unfamiliar with both of them. I didn't know Lory "owned" Dallas as *the* realtor to the gays (but I would soon learn). I didn't know Barbara owned a piece of Dallas, a fabulous lesbian bar, The Desert Moon. I was pretty ignorant.

Lory turned to me between contestants and said, in her best gravelly baritone voice, "You're doing pretty good with the turtles. Why isn't there a women's chorus in Dallas?" She kind of scared me. Barbara said if anything like that were to happen, and we should ever decide to start one, she would offer the bar as a meeting place and margaritas. I seriously gave it little thought.

In July 1989, when TCC attended its first GALA Festival in Seattle, I was overwhelmed. What blew me away was watching the San Diego Men's Chorus on stage. Halfway through their set, they invited the newly formed San Diego Women's Chorus to join them. The audience was blown away. I cried and cried. I saw a vision of something that could happen in Dallas.

When I got home, I first talked to the leadership of TCC about starting a sister chorus. For the most part, everyone was thrilled about the possibility and willing to lend their support. The only concerns were about how it would be set up. Would The Women's Chorus of Dallas (TWCD) be a part of TCC? It turned out that it was best to keep the siblings separate financially. Without that enthusiasm and support, the women's chorus might not have happened. It certainly would not have had the spectacular growth and success without being arm in arm with its brother chorus.

With that green light, I talked about it with my best girlfriend, who also had moved up from Houston. We decided to just do it. We met at the Desert Moon and had margaritas, of course. This was interesting because TCC was started with margaritas in a gay bar. In that case, it was three church musicians after choir rehearsal on Wednesday night.

We kept telling people about the new chorus, and they told people. By the time we had our first official meeting, there were probably thirty passionate, opinionated, strong-willed women present. I would learn that was not unusual. We didn't have a conductor or an accompanist or a penny.

I was asked to bring a sample starter budget to the next meeting. I was happy to do that, but the chorus didn't exist yet. It had zero dollars. Everyone there was willing to pass the hat. The next meeting, I brought a very simple budget that a startup might have. I listed something like $400 for the conductor, $300 for the accompanist, purchase of music, and rent at Sammons. It was the bare minimum.

After I presented it, Colleen, whom I did not know, stood and asked, "Would you conduct the TCC for that much money?" I replied, "No." She said, "Well, we are not going to pay a woman less than a man is making!" I just love that so much. Indeed, the group did raise the first salary for an artistic director. Thus began a long history of Tim being put in his place—and the tremendous patience everyone had, as I learned. I continued to learn important lessons.

I was in my second year of conducting the men and had gotten very comfortable with the camp element of our intercourse. I consistently called them "girls" in jest—and to get their attention. They thought it was fun.

I believe it was the first or second rehearsal conducting the women when I said, "Girls, pay attention." There was no laughter, not even a chuckle. Heads either spun or exploded. I moved on with rehearsal. I was schooled on the fact that using that term is offensive and patriarchal. I had no clue. At the next rehearsal, I apologized profusely and told them nothing was meant by it and that I had lots to learn from them. Over the months, they began to trust me. The barriers began to break down. Soon, they were calling me "girl."

One performance issue I ran into early was getting the chorus members to open their hearts. I needed them to be vulnerable in order for the gorgeous music they were making to touch the audience's hearts. I worked at it from every direction. Finally, at my wit's end, one of the singers stepped forward with an incredible "testimony." She shared how difficult it was to grow up and know you were a lesbian. Most men were not role models (an understatement). The response was to close off the areas of vulnerability to protect their hearts. I learned something important that night. Others spoke as well. We had a major breakthrough. From that time on, the women changed. And so did I.

There were so many incredible musical moments and so much stupid fun. At one of our parties when raspberry f***ers were served (much like Long Island tea, with five clear liquors mixed with raspberry lemonade), a rumor started that one singer peed in her pants in the front yard. At the next rehearsal, to set the record straight, she stood and said, "I did not pee my pants. I took my pants off before I peed." Oh, so much fun!

The goal of any LGBTQ chorus is to provide a safe space and to create an environment like none other, a place where every single person is allowed to be exactly who she or he is, no judgment, no bullying. This created some absolutely wild moments in each of the two choruses.

I was able to conduct 100 women on Mondays and over 200 men on Tuesdays. I could write a book. Wait, I am.

There is so much heart that went into bringing TWCD to where it is. The members carried their brothers through the AIDS pandemic. They loved, cared for, fed, healed, and sang for them—changing the heart of the chorus. It brought the chorus to a new level of care and empathy such that when Jeri Lynne was the first woman in the chorus to be diagnosed with breast cancer, TWCD was ready to gather around her in every way. Thanks to her, we commissioned a huge work in her honor, arguably the chorus's finest work of all time. It compelled the chorus's brothers to change their red AIDS ribbons to share half with pink, in solidarity with our sisters.

It was the best of times. I had a spectacular men's chorus and a fabulous women's chorus. And when we joined, "Heaven came down, and glory filled my soul."

Chapter 34

AIDS and LGBTQ Activism

It was an absolutely scorching August evening when, bright-eyed and bushy-tailed, I walked into my first rehearsal as the new conductor of Dallas's gay men's chorus. Nine months before, I was married and working for the Baptists. Three months before, I had no idea that there was such a thing as a gay chorus. But there I was, called upon to get up to speed really quickly.

After a short introduction, I took the podium. Around forty singers were assembled that night. As I raised my arms to conduct, I looked down to see a beautiful young man in the front row covered in sores. I could not imagine what was wrong with him and why he would come to rehearsal like that. That wouldn't have happened in the Baptist choir. If a soprano's hair had fallen due to the humidity in Houston, she would stay home!

At break I asked John, one of the singers, about it. He gave me a pitying southern "Bless your heart" look, trying not to be too judgmental, and he explained that Jeff had full-blown AIDS. Singing with his brothers each week was keeping him alive. It was the music and the family and, most importantly, the unconditional love they showered on him—no shame, no guilt, no fear of touching him because they might catch it. It was his home once a week.

My life changed that night. I witnessed the power of this "singing together" thing we do. Oh, I had preached it before, but now it was right there in front of me. Jeff was the proof. It turns out that John was the executive director of the AIDS Resource Center. He said, "You really need help!" I agreed. He gets his own chapter in this book because of what he did for me over the next twelve years before his death.

I will never forget the glow in Jeff's face as he sang that night. I would see it for only a few weeks because he became too ill to attend rehearsals. Over the next years, I watched as this chorus family took care of countless brothers, helped them get to doctors' appointments, eat, go to the bathroom, and just hold their hands. It was the life lesson I needed. I saw what Christians talk about but seldom do. This was the real thing.

I vowed to do what I could to ease the pain, slow the disease, provide a place for all to come who needed the music—and much more. An AIDS activist was born.

Our days back then were filled with little other than dealing with this dreadful disease. The SFGMC was hit especially hard. Choruses across the country were called on to sing memorial service after memorial service—for members, their partners, and their friends. Every rehearsal included announcements about who had died, who had entered hospice, or who needed care at home or a visit in the hospital. And then we sang some more. We were in every stage of grief— all at once.

When I began conducting in Dallas, we had lost eleven singers. When I left, the number was around 175. In San Francisco, members of the Fifth Section— those lost to HIV/AIDS—now number 300. The chorus sang, raised money and awareness, and fought the fight every day. And I led them.

An Emmy for AIDS

As the TCC began to grow, many singers came for the healing power of music and community. Many had AIDS/HIV. It was 1989. The local ABC-TV affiliate asked to do a short segment on the chorus and the healing power of music. The board balked. They feared the chorus might become known as "that AIDS Choir." They were voted down overwhelmingly because of the chorus's desire to allow it.

The proposed three-minute segment turned into more than seven minutes. It was beautiful. Yes, music is healing and was making a difference. No one ever called us "that AIDS Choir." Our own fears were abated; they were a waste of time and energy.

In spring 1991 TCC invited the Seattle Men's Chorus to sing with us in Dallas. We wanted something for double chorus to perform together. We had an assistant conductor, Kris Anthony, who was also an arranger. He said he had something in mind. Not long after, he walked in with a manuscript titled "I Shall Miss Loving You." It had one chorus singing a stunning English text and a different chorus singing *Agnus Dei* from the Latin mass. It was amazing!

Kris then told me it was really just one movement of a longer work he had been thinking about for a long time. I said, "Great, we'll do the whole thing this coming fall." He was hesitant. I went ahead and put it in the season brochure for the next season (extortion), and Kris got to work.

One of Kris's favorite books was a best-seller by Peter McWilliams titled *How to Survive the Loss of a Love*. The book was based on Dr. Elisabeth Kübler-Ross's stages of grief. Kris had already contacted Peter and asked if he could set some of his book to music, juxtaposed with Latin mass text. Peter was thrilled, and Kris completed the forty-minute work between March and August.

When we gathered for the first rehearsal in August, we knew something very special was being birthed. We sang. We wept. The piece began to take hold, and by the time we performed the world premiere at the symphony hall in October, it was sold out—and there happened to be an entire row of people from our local PBS station in attendance.

Immediately after the performance, the PBS folks called to tell us they wanted to do a documentary on the music and the chorus and this amazing piece that was helping us grieve the loss of singers at a staggering rate. Kris was again reticent. We didn't know why. He was a minister of music at a local church but was out to them. What could be the problem? Then we found out. In order for him to allow this story to be told, he had to "come out" again. He had full-blown AIDS. No one knew. He then confessed that he had composed *When We No Longer Touch* as his own requiem.

The filming began. In June 1992 PBS shot the actual performance for the documentary—it was the final step in its completion. It was, once again, back at the symphony hall. It was, in fact, just before we left for the GALA Festival in Denver. Our guest chorus was the Gay Men's Chorus of Los Angeles (GMCLA), and Jake Heggie was one of their synthesizer players.

Peter McWilliams flew in two days before. He had never met Kris. They created this massive work over the phone. Kris died just before Peter arrived. With Kris's death still so fresh, the performance was numbing. Once it was heard in Denver, it was performed by choruses for many years, including SFGMC in 1995. Just a few years later, Peter McWilliams died of complications from AIDS.

The documentary is titled *After Goodbye: An AIDS Story*. It worked its way through the PBS hierarchy and ultimately was selected for a national broadcast. An audience of twenty million people watched the first airing. It went on to win twelve national awards and, ultimately, the national Emmy for Best Documentary in 1994.

I didn't attend the Emmys because we didn't think there was a chance—and it was rehearsal night. A big mistake on my part.

Olympic Torch, 1996 Olympics

It was 1995, a year before Atlanta would host the Summer Olympics. A huge amount of planning goes into the transport of the actual flame from Greece to the site of the Olympics. The flame flew from Greece to Los Angeles before beginning its trek through forty-two states—16,000 miles—to Atlanta.

I didn't know how Olympic torchbearers were selected until I received an invitation to be one. And I don't run. I had been selected as a community hero for my work in the fight against AIDS and HIV and my activism in the fight for equality for the LGBTQ community.

I was completely overwhelmed when I found out my best friend and mentor, John Thomas, had spearheaded the people who had signed on to the nomination. It was incredibly humbling, but now I had to run.

Each torchbearer carries the torch one-sixth of a mile. You scoff. But it was June in Dallas, and I would be running in downtown Dallas with crowds of people lining the street and police escorts in front and back.

Did I say I don't run? My friend Robert Steele didn't run either, but he said he would help. We went to Bachman Lake in Dallas and looked at the running path, 3.1 miles long, and thought that would be a good start. We got a little way but turned back. We were good. We went for margaritas.

The day came. All torchbearers met at a location outside downtown. It was early. We got on buses with lots of water. We were then dropped off one by one at the location where we would accept our torch. Peeing was the biggest challenge. But once it got closer to time, I was so nervous that I was all dried up anyway!

Tons of fans from the TCC and the TWCD were there to encourage me along my route. We waited. It was hot as hell. Nothing was happening. Just me in some adorable running shorts I would never wear again, the official t-shirt, and my very own torch.

Soon we heard a commotion, then police motorcycles. We could see the entourage surrounding the person who would light my torch! It all happened so quickly. The torch lit, I turned and, smiling, "ran" my one-sixth mile. I was on stage—running. It was my marathon!

It was over before we knew it. We celebrated, in part, over the fact that I had somehow pulled it off. It was a great day. I have not run since.

Chapter 35

One Man Changed My Life

John Thomas was my best friend. He made everyone feel like a best friend. But it was I who was the recipient of the greatest gift anyone can give: time. John and I had lunch together almost every Wednesday for ten years. I was honored to be holding his hand when he took his final breath on this earth.

John was one of the first people I met when I moved to Dallas in 1987, even before the first rehearsal of the TCC. He was one of the movers and shakers they wanted me to meet. I liked him instantly.

It was John whom I would ask what was wrong with that man in the front row and why he was at rehearsal with all those sores. John was gentle in his instruction. He could have called me an idiot (and it would have been deserved). But he did not. He was very patient in his "You need help."

At a subsequent rehearsal I used the term *sexual preference*. Rather than correct me in public—and seeing before him a true gay neophyte just out of the closet and thrust into the limelight for which I was nowhere near prepared—he invited me to lunch. He explained that by using the term *sexual preference*, I was implying that our orientation was a choice. A preference? What a blunder. At that point my whole life had been upended because my orientation was *not* a choice. I've been schooling folks on that one ever since.

The final straw was a note I wrote to my new chorus telling them how moved I was by their struggle with and their response to Aids. John's head must have exploded. I may have written "Ayds," the 1960s diet candy! I needed him much more than I knew. But he knew.

John began modeling life for me. I soaked it up. For months we tried to have lunch here or there, calendars becoming a nightmare. Finally, John said, "Let's go to lunch every Wednesday." I was over the moon. I had no idea what he saw in me that he was willing to give that much of his sought-after time. And we did have lunch, at the same restaurant—Lucky's—almost every Wednesday for a decade until he was too sick. What's more, he is still fixing me. Every decision I make in my life will always be weighed against the incredibly wise influence of my friend John.

The son of a Baptist pastor, John sang in church and in school and then in the TCC. John was also instrumental in the formation of the TWCD. He loved women. The chorus made him an honorary lesbian.

John was an activist's activist. He did it with a kind, thoughtful demeanor and often with a disarming, impish smile. He was arrested a lot—at AIDS protests in Dallas, New York, Washington, and San Francisco. He became part of the lawsuits that first challenged Texas's sodomy law and Parkland Memorial Hospital's treatment of AIDS patients.

He was ridiculously handsome, with steel blue eyes and prematurely gray hair. He was a gentle giant: selfless, tireless, a crusader, a feminist, and a big old huggy bear. His signature props included random coffee cups, cigarettes, a dirty truck, rainbows, and wrinkled, soiled ties. He kept an assortment of ties on the floor of his truck for when he needed to "dress up." As the executive director of the AIDS Resource Center, he was followed everywhere by news media and cameras for comments. They often stationed themselves outside Lucky's on Wednesdays.

John could listen better than anyone I have ever met. And when he wrapped his long arms around me, the cares of the world vanished.

I learned a very important lesson from John. One night, my partner and I went to dinner with John (at his invitation) at Mi Cocina in Highland Park Village. It was packed and noisy. We ordered margaritas and were chowing down on the chips and salsa when John put his drink down.

The look on his face told us to do the same. He had a very simple announcement: After all these years on the front lines of educating people about AIDS and its prevention, he, the godfather of the movement in Dallas, had just found out he had seroconverted. He had HIV. It was 1992. We sat in stunned silence. We held his hands.

As the immediate shock wore off, we began to cry into our chips. It was as close to a death sentence as you could get. How would he tell the thousands for whom he had been a light, a role model? Luckily, John had spoken to our mutual friend William Waybourn, an amazing LGBTQ activist and PR guru. William had convinced John that no announcement was needed.

John wrote a weekly newspaper column about AIDS. William instructed him to simply change the way he wrote—change "those with AIDS/HIV" to "those of us with AIDS/HIV." As William said, "You never announced you were negative, so no one knows." And John did as William had advised. Of course, those close to John, who knew, were devastated. It meant there was a shorter time with John and we had better cram it all in. And we did.

In 1994 John and I attended a friend's memorial service. It was pretty dreary and did not reflect the person we had known. We left quite disturbed. On the way home he said, "Don't even think of doing that to me when I am gone. I'm going home and will spell it out for you." And he did.

On May 31, 1994, John wrote his own service. He did not want the TCC or TWCD (both of which he loved dearly) to sing because he said it was too hard on us to have to sing at our brothers' services. He and I argued about this until the very end. He knew he couldn't win that one. Hundreds sang in the choir that day!

He gave his own service a title: "Rally for the integrity, dignity, and rights of gay people and those living with AIDS and HIV." These were the words he wrote to be shared after his passing:

> Don't celebrate my life. Live whatever part of my life you can and pass it on to others. Hurry on through the stages of loss and grief and mourning. There is really not time.
>
> Know the depth of sorrow that I felt leaving you far surpasses whatever you may feel.
>
> My greatest sadness, and therefore tears, always came with a thought of letting you down or hurting you or disappointing you.
>
> Please support organizations advancing the self-esteem and value of the gay and lesbian community and people with AIDS/HIV.
>
> I would rather you do this from your own commitment to making a difference to improve the lives of others than as a memorial to me.

John died Wednesday, January 21, 1999, held by friends: Rev. Michael Piazza, Lory Masters, William Waybourn, and me. He had changed my life. He had decided, with his limited time, that he would spend a lot of it on me. I thought we were just best friends. As it turns out, he was passing the baton.

Epilogue: John disliked fussy people and things. He refused to have us pay for an urn. Fine. We divided his ashes into six Tupperware containers. They were spread around the country by his besties. I got two, one for me to keep (I cannot tell you how many house cleaners have almost thrown my part of

John away). The other was to spread in Kauai, a place John, Louis, and Corianna had visited often.

Corianna and I found a beautiful, peaceful rocky spot in Poipu. We took a baggie down to the calm water. We were hugging each other, sharing stories, and crying. John was having none of this. From nowhere came a giant wave that knocked both of us on our butts, and the baggie got drenched. Laughing so hard, we didn't notice the bag had emptied itself. He got his way.

One of the traditions in Hawaii is to throw a lei into the ocean for the person who has passed and keep one for yourself. I was not one to have dried flowers sitting around, so I decided to have a lei tattooed around my ankle so John would always be with me. I love it so much that I don't want to wear socks. It would not be my last tattoo.

Chapter 36

Eating Jewish Crow

Back to 1969, when my close friend Alan Hamill went off to college in Boston: I went to the fabulously exotic paradise of Abilene, Texas, from which I had sent Alan, a Jew, my "You're going to hellfire and brimstone" letter as a parting gift.

Between 1969 and 1987 I would occasionally visit his parents' hardware store/gift shop to ask about Alan. They were wonderfully warm, but there always seemed to be a slightly awkward moment when I assumed they were thinking: "You little pompous, pious, self-righteous ass. After all the things we did together, you had to go and break your best friend's heart." But they didn't do that, although I felt pretty sure Alan would have shared the letter with his family, including Harriett, my girl crush.

In 1988, after arriving in Dallas the year before, I was in need of a doctor, mostly to get me through my allergies. I had asked John Thomas for a referral. Even though John and I were HIV-negative, John said his doctor was on the cutting edge of HIV treatment. He serves on the board at the AIDS Resource Center and spent countless hours taking care of AIDS patients who couldn't afford the care.

The doc sounded like a saint, and John said, "I'll give him a call and ask if he has any openings in his practice. By the way, if you hadn't figured it out, he's gay." As an afterthought, John remarked over his shoulder, "By the way, his name is Dr. Alan Hamill."

After I caught my breath, I began to cry. I *was* that pompous little pious, self-righteous ass. Alan, on the other hand, had studied years and years to give back. "Who's the big Christian now?" I thought.

How could I make amends? What would I say? Would he take me as a patient? If the tables had been turned and he had done that to me, would I forgive him? From the gay press, Alan surely knew I was in Dallas. And he loved music. When I contacted his office, he wondered if I might reach out, knowing our paths would cross one another's sooner or later. I made an appointment.

I was so nervous. His nurse led me to an examination room. I was sweating. The two to three minutes I waited felt like a lifetime. Then he knocked lightly and came in, looking all handsome and official in his white lab coat.

He flashed that beautiful smile, unchanged in the missing eighteen years. He placed my charts on the counter, looked at me, and opened his arms to hold me in "Forgiveness's Embrace" (the title of a song by Stephen Schwartz).

I said I was sorry. He countered, "Let's keep you healthy. The work you are doing is important." In that moment I realized *that* is what Jesus would have done—no judgment.

Alan died of AIDS. I was invited as a special guest, seated with the family at the synagogue, as I had been for Harriet's wedding. I think I became on honorary Jew that very day.

Chapter 37

Lovers, Boyfriends, and a Husband

It is a disappointment to me that I couldn't make one relationship last. I had watched my parents survive sixty-five years of marriage. I wanted something better. But as the poet Maya Angelou said, "To grow up is to stop putting blame on parents." However, I wasn't helped by watching them stumble through life with zero passion for each other.

Without success I tried to talk my mother into leaving my dad. She said she would rather stay and suffer through it than risk what people would think. She also knew that when and if she got sick, Dad would wait on her hand and foot to try to make up for the lack of affection or passion. The fact that she never had that kind of love is what sent her to therapists for fifty years. Yet she never told them the truth about what was lacking or what was going on.

So what did I do? I married my mother in Vicki. Corianna and Judson spent the first part of their lives watching the same thing: a marriage without passion between husband and wife and no public displays of affection, no warmth.

And, according to conventional wisdom, I suck at boyfriends. Unconventional wisdom says I have had just the right partner for just the right time frame for us to share each other's lives and to teach and learn from each other. Some lessons just take less time than others. I echo Stephen Schwartz: "People come into your life for a reason." And with every one of them, I have been changed for good.

I never liked being single and wanted that to be as brief as possible. I am my best self and find my greatest fulfillment in relation to another. I love that connection. I am a good partner. I am the biggest mama bear, homemaker, and cook, and I keep a ridiculously ordered and straight, if not spotless, house (hello, OCD).

This was not something Dan was particularly adept at. At one point, the cabinet with pots and pans was a total mess. I put it all in *proper* order, took a picture, and, with it, wrote a poem:

Pots on the left
Pans on the right
Lids in the back
No need to fight!

This came with the implication that if it did not happen, there would be consequences. That said, there is a Big Tim to contend with. That's clear throughout this book. All of that said, these are the people with whom I have cohabitated and a brief description of the gifts they gave:

Vicki: Thirteen years. Two perfect children. Traveling duet partner.

Paul: Two years. A safety net and mentor through the worst of times. Paul was a CPA, and those gifts helped guide me "out" of the mess I was in.

Single: One year. Shopping, eating, and burying my singleness in work.

Louis: Nine years. Helped raise two teens in distress. Supported my growing into myself. Best friends with my best friend, John Thomas. Weathered AIDS together. Louis was a lawyer. He taught me—and the kids—order and honesty.

Single: One year. Shopping, eating, and burying my singleness in work.

Shawn: Twelve years. Brilliance and creativity. Light and dark. Mountaintops and deep valleys. Shawn was a brilliant photographer, videographer, and graphic designer. His gift was to help me stretch, to see the stars and go for them.

Single: One year. My physician asked, "Are you eating your way through San Francisco?" I said "yes" and found a new doctor.

Dan: Six years. Best friend imaginable. We did everything together. He was involved in every aspect of my life from chorus to kids. Dan is a tech guy. He tried to teach me things such as Excel, Alexa, and remotes. I never learned.

Bobby: One year (so far). Deepest soul and heart a man could have. Singer, songwriter, guitarist extraordinaire.

My Second Marriage

When Dan and I got together after thirteen years of friendship, we thought it would be forever. We met in 2000 at an LGBTQ choral festival. His parents actually introduced us. They had heard TCC and TWCD in a concert. They ran to Dan and said, "You have to come with us to the next concert. Their conductor is so funny!" They found him and introduced us.

We were with various partners for the ensuing years, eyeing each other over the fence. In 2013 we found ourselves single at the same time. We were such great friends that we decided to try being more than that. We literally sat at lunch one day and checked off the boxes for a great friendship/relationship. Dan loved music and the chorus. Dan was also an AIDS activist. He has done the AIDS ride in California twelve times.

There was one box we didn't check because we had no experience with each other in this area: the passion-and-romance box. We were doing things completely opposite of most gay relationships, starting with friendship while hoping the sexual attraction and romance would come. Most gay relationships start with the sexual attraction and perhaps physical intimacy, then, pretending to be in a relationship, trying to squeeze the square pegs into round holes. We had all the friend/compatibility/life activities aced on the test.

We married in 2014. He was amazing. We had a blast. In 2019 there was something missing. All the friendship boxes were checked, but the passion box had half a check. Always a dreamer, I still wanted to score 100, and 95 was never good enough for me. I did not see that box suddenly being filled in.

In October 2018 we met a wonderful man at one of our concerts. It was a difficult time for us, and he brought a new warmth and openness to the table. We were both attracted to him. Dan and I looked at each other and asked, "What do we do with this?" The answer was to let it unfold as it will.

We began to spend time with him, and our affection grew equally among the three of us. We had many discussions about polyamory and felt we were good candidates. We dove in. This part of our journey as a thruple was fairly brief in the big scheme but filled with love and amazing growth for all of us. We learned a lot from the book *More than Two*. I share this because I think it is a hugely important part of my story. It was new and exhilarating and challenging. Three people in love with each other. Three very dynamic people.

Being in a polyamorous relationship provided a catalyst on the pieces that were missing. Along the way I had realized, before Dan did, that we were better friends than husbands. If we stayed married, there was a possibility the friendship we had shared for nineteen years would be damaged. I filed for divorce.

Dan did not want it, but he was a perfect gentleman. We weathered it with the most amazing generosity of spirit. We were gentle with each other, showing love every step of the way. The way we handled our divorce has become a model for many across the nation, thanks to Facebook. Now we get to be best friends for the rest of our lives.

I have not yet been able to break the pattern of serial relationships. I'm not dead yet, and hope springs eternal. And I'm still learning and growing and loving.

Chapter 38

Dolphins to Kids with Cancer

Corianna, like every seventeen-year-old girl, wanted to train dolphins for the rest of her life. When we did a college tour, we had no choice but to only look at schools on or near the ocean with some kind of marine biology program. We took her to the University of Miami, Stanford, USC, UCSD (San Diego and Scripps). She applied to most and was accepted. But she couldn't make up her mind.

She didn't accept any early admittance letters. Spring wore on, and then one day she said she would go to the University of Hawaii. They certainly had dolphin studies, and we all loved Hawaii, and this would be a great reason to visit. So Vicki and I said yes.

Because she had waited so long in deciding, there were no dorm rooms left. To be fair, they have a priority list of who gets rooms. It starts with native Hawaiians and goes to various island and Pacific cultures, ending with nice Caucasian girls, *Haoles*, who say they want to study dolphins.

We searched all over and finally found a Buddhist-run "dorm" of sorts. She and I headed to Hawaii in August to claim her room, and, of course, gay dad was going to whoop it up with everything Target had. We got there the minute her room was available and made our list. Off we went.

We bought every bright fish item in the store: fish towels, fish sheets, fish posters, fish rug. You get the picture. Her room looked like we had found Nemo. The temps were really hot, so Corianna stayed with me at the hotel that night. We returned the next day to find that her roommate had just skated in under the deadline to move in and, lo and behold, was not into fish or color. Her entire side of the room was black and adorned with skulls. Corianna spent that night with me too!

The Buddhist part of the equation was also not what I had envisioned—quiet, meditation, humming. Oh, no, it was not Buddhist at all. They just owned the building. The one thing that turned out to be Buddhist was their leaving the "children" completely alone to find themselves: college freshman thousands of miles from home with no cellphones, just a payphone in the hall.

After getting her registered and sort of settled in, it was time for me to leave. Standing in the parking lot of the dorm, we hugged. I bawled as I sent her back to her fish dungeon. I drove to the airport and cried all the way home. Between ages nine and eighteen, Corianna and I had developed into best friends. She shared everything with me. And now our only connection was a payphone in the hall used for pizza delivery and pot connections. Dear God, what had I done?

At Christmas she came home, up about thirty pounds (thank you, Spam). She did not want to go back for spring semester. We had made a deal with her. If we allowed her to go all the way to Hawaii, she had to stay one year. She was so pissed and went to see a therapist friend and yelled at her a bit. At the end of Christmas break, she was on her way back to Hawaii. Good news came in the spring. Enough students had dropped out that she got a room on campus. That was better.

She had good reasons for not wanting to stay. She'd attended a pretty spectacular high school in Houston, and the University of Hawaii was a step back. There didn't seem to be a huge urge to excel—on the part of school or herself. The library kept some pretty sketchy hours when the surf was up (or so I was told). She didn't learn to train dolphins. After one year she came home.

She found Texas A&M Corpus Christi, which was right on the water. Off the bat she lost her Spam weight and was the belle of the Corpus ball. She had lots of friends, had a blast, created a few legendary Corianna stories in local bars with a fake ID, and improved her grades a great deal.

She was blossoming. But being a smart one, it just wasn't challenging enough either. Then four things in her life came together to guide her choice of the next university.

1. She had grown up as one of the most empathetic people I ever met. It was demonstrated by her deep love for misfits in school. Even more, she loved pets the most and had everything from dogs and cats to a duck and three hamsters (Fluffy, Muffy, and Buffy), one of which ate the other two. It was a sad day when we let the survivor go in a field, figuring he had skills and might just make it.

2. She joined the swim team. She loved everything about it, so much that she wanted to be enveloped by the smell at home, so she left her wet swim attire and towels in the floor in the middle of her room until management arrived, thinking some animal may had died there. Butterfly was her favorite. Then she injured her shoulder, and the first inkling of physical therapy crossed her brain—fleetingly.

3. She had spent much of teen life, from nine to eighteen, watching her dad's friends (and, by proxy, her friends) die of AIDS. They were our best friends. She visited them, loved them, and grieved their passing. She understood the uselessness of the whole thing and committed to do something significant with her life.

4. She really wanted to live close to her dad.

She decided to go to Texas Women's University, first in physical therapy, and then the excellent nursing program in Denton, only thirty miles from where Dad and her 200 guncles (gay uncles) were. After her basics she moved to Dallas for the remainder of her coursework and all those things you do to figure out where you fit. She lived in the guesthouse behind our house.

During her rotation she was focused on terminal illness (from her AIDS experience). Then she hit the pediatric oncology floor, and the rest of her professional life was set. It was her mission. She loved those kids, helped some of them get well, and even more of them die with nurse Corianna's smile in their memory. She did this to the detriment of her own body.

She was one of a kind—and the apple of my eye.

Chapter 39

The Experience

Erhard Seminars Training took the country by storm from 1971 to 1984. It consisted of sixty hours of intense training over two weekends. Celebrities jumped on board. Those who had gone through it felt enlightened and separated from those who had not. Some called it a cult (not unusual in the 1970s and 1980s). While most who took it were devotees, it had its detractors too. There was much written about the psychiatric damage done to many of those who took the course.

As with most things, the gays wanted one too. They wanted all the good stuff, but in less time! The gay offshoot was called *The Experience*. It had several parts. The introduction was twenty-four hours over one weekend. Then there was an advanced weekend. For those who did not feel abused enough, there was a weeklong intensive.

John Thomas really wanted me and my partner to do this. He swore by it. He had done the whole thing. We liked therapy—the gay kind, not the Baptist kind. We liked John. We thought, "A weekend away, what can go wrong?"

There were very strict rules:

- No watches
- No phones
- No talking unless called upon
- No talking to people around you
- No asking questions
- No eating or leaving your seats to go to the bathroom except during breaks
- No alcoholic beverages for the entire time—at home or at a restaurant
- No drugs

These rigorous agreements provided a setting whereby people's ordinary ways to escape confronting themselves would be removed. You were literally a prisoner in your own chair, until released. Now, why did we pay a large sum of money for this? Because of John. We would have done anything for him.

There was a large component of "helping" people come out. Everyone was required to write a letter to the person they feared the most to tell. Unbeknownst to us, people were then required to come to the stage and read their letter.

It resulted in plenteous tears, broken hearts, fetal positions, and, on Sunday evening, "Thanks for coming."

I stayed angry most of the time. I'd done my stint with controlling "cults." But then there was John. He was excited for all of us to "experience it" together. I won't tell you everything that happened—it's a big secret. But I learned two things (out of our entire weekend) that changed my life, my career, and the hierarchy of my life.

First: Complain Only to Someone Who Can Make a Difference.

We gathered in the hotel ballroom in fairly tight rows at 6:30 p.m. In the first thirty minutes they went over the layout for the weekend and the rules. They were serious about the rules, as we were about to find out.

I do believe the first lesson could have been taught in a much less bitchy, confrontational way, but who knows. It sure stuck. At 7:00, the guru, Rob Epstein, was introduced. Everyone applauded, because at that point we still liked him. That would quickly change.

He started his spiel about the weekend coming up and how he, single-handedly, would change our lives. The room was really warm. Since it was summer, everyone assumed the air conditioning would kick in. He kept talking. The room got warmer, until it was unbearable. But we had the rules right in front of us: No asking questions. No talking to our neighbors—not even to say, "Does it feel warm to you?" VERBOTEN!

It got downright hot. We were literally sweating. Finally, one brave rule-breaker raised his hand and politely said, "Could we do something about the heat? It's really hot." Everyone gasped, thinking his chair might be on a trap door and he would just disappear. There was a moment's pause when Leader Rob stared at this poor guy. Then, in the most sarcastic tone ever—even better than some of mine—he said, "Do I look like an air-conditioner repairman? Or the hotel maintenance man? I am not the person you should be addressing that question to. You'll need to wait until break and go find someone who can make a difference."

Stunned and sweating, we all looked at our rules and the schedule: thirty more minutes until break. Did they turn off the heat (obviously on full blast in the middle of the summer)? No, they did not. One would have thought they would after the brave man who broke the rules and asked the question—on behalf of EVERYONE—got thoroughly schooled and shamed. Nope, the room got hotter and hotter. None of us had signed up for a sweat lodge.

We made it through to break. The brave man sought out the hotel manager, who contacted the maintenance man. Of course, they were all in on this because they had been instructed to make the ballroom as hot as they could until 8:30 p.m., when someone would complain (to the right person) and they could then reverse the heat and turn on the air conditioning.

The room cooled off quickly. Rob, whose face had a horrible smirk, let us know what had happened: Change came only when someone complained to someone who could actually make a difference. Lesson learned! The attendees were put on alert. Follow the damn rules—all of them!

I went home and created a productivity tool (to which everyone in the chorus has access). It incorporates the lesson, not the shame. Simple.

Name

Who is your comment or complaint addressed to?

What is your comment or complaint?

What is your solution?

Who are those who agree with you?

I also call it my Kwitcherbitchin' Form. Chorus members don't go to the executive director with musical questions. They don't come to me with budget questions. Best of all, they can't say, "All of the altos hate this song." Nope, you've got to say which altos.

- Productivity Tool. Complain only to someone who can make a difference.
- Adulting. We do not heat the room like we're boiling a lobster to sweat it out of people!

Second: Time Is All We Have.

So we already hated Rob Epstein. What could get worse? Here we go. "Look around the room. In your mind rank each participant 1 to 4."

1. I had a conversation with you and loved it. I would very much like to get to know you better.
2. I haven't had a conversation with you, but I've heard you speak or just seen the way you move in the crowd. I'd like to know more.
3. I haven't had any specific interaction with you, but you seem okay. I would not be upset to find myself in a group with you.

4. I've seen you. I've heard you. I really never need to interact with you
   beyond the workshop.

Well, that's uncomfortable. "Now stand. Please get in two long lines facing
each other. On the count of three, give the person standing across from you one
of the four numbers."

Seriously? He counted down, and we ranked them. "Now each line step to
your right. Count down. Rank."

It was worse than "We're going to send you to hell to check out the temperature so you can go find the devil, who is the only one who can make a difference,
and ask him to cool it."

Everyone got angrier as the line dance with no music progressed. When
finished, we sat back in our chairs. I hated it but had learned another life lesson.

First question from Guru Rob: "How many of you gave everyone across
from you a 1?" Lots of hands went up. Then Rob said, "You can't give everyone
in your life a 1. You are a people-pleaser and willing to lie to make people happy
and feel good about themselves."

"How many of you gave a 4?" Only a few brave souls raised their hands.
"But it is reality. It is the truth. You don't want to hurt their feelings by telling
the truth?"

It took me a long time to apply this. When I did, the earth dropped from
underneath me. My heart broke a little as I realized this is what I had done to
Corianna and Judson. I worked and worked and worked. I gave my students 1s.
I gave my choirs 1s. I gave every aspect of my overachieving career 1.

I thought that was the way to get ahead. I had no 1s left for Corianna and
Judson. NONE. I pretended that taking them to a rehearsal was Daddy giving
them a 1 to be near him.

I thought of every aspect of my life. Every single person would be happy
with a 2. Hundreds in a choir would appreciate a 3. There were absolutely
people along the way who deserved a 4, but because we are supposed to "minister" to the least of these, we waste 1s, sprinkling them along the way on people
who don't care and are 1-suckers.

Whenever I give this life lesson to a group of music educators, there are tears
all around. We're the worst. Music educators work harder than anyone. There is
time spent in school classes. But there is before-school choir, after-school choir,
show choir, etc., and most singers have evening rehearsals or contest preparation
and the like. Where are the 1s for family supposed to fit in?

For choir directors, a handful of singers are always standing at your podium within minutes of the rehearsal's end. They are tugging on your sleeve. "See me! See me!" Some people either leave immediately or hang around the back of the room. They would never ask for a 1. Do they need a 1? Yes, they do. The problem in breaking through the 1-demanders is to seek out those who have self-selected 3 or 4.

I was giving this lesson to a statewide convention of music educators in Idaho. When I finished, a band director asked if he could tell a story. His voice showed him to be moved by the lesson. He had a large (200-person) band. He wanted to talk about his own experience with someone who assumed he was a 4: The mother of one of his tuba players had died. (Remember, tuba players sit in the back of the band.) He took a week off school.

When he came back, the band director passed him in the hall and stopped for a moment and said, "Tommy, I am so very sorry about your mother." Tommy stared at him for a moment, then burst into tears. When he had regained his composure, the teacher repeated something about how hard this must be. Tommy looked up at him and said. "My tears are not about my mother. I've shed those. I was just surprised, because I didn't know you knew my name."

The Tommys are out there in our lives. Because it is hard to look over or past the 1-demanders, we completely miss them. It's "the least of these" who need our 1s. Those clamoring folks can do with a 2 from time to time.

My children deserved all the 1s they wanted. Period. No lame excuses of "I'm too busy." I wish I had time to fix this. Perhaps you do.

Chapter 40

Sing for the Cure

Of all the wonderful things I have been allowed to do, it is commissioning large choral works that has been an amazing opportunity. It began in 1991 with *When We No Longer Touch* and has continued to the current commission in 2020.

In fall 1999 several things happened at once that led to the creation of a work about breast cancer. I was invited to lunch by Susan G. Komen Breast Cancer Foundation founder, Nancy Brinker, and the director of development, Peter Anderson. Nancy was well aware of the TCC and specifically the creation of *When We No Longer Touch* and the PBS documentary *After Goodbye: An AIDS Story*.

It was Nancy's dream to have a major choral work created from the stories of breast cancer survivors and the families and friends of those who did not live to tell their stories. She had a huge vision: a huge chorus and symphony. She laid out her dream and then said, "And we have no money for this. One hundred percent of our money goes to research and education."

The other thing that happened during the same period was the loss of Jerri Lynne, the first singing member of TWCD to die of breast cancer. This gave everyone the impetus to move forward with the project. There was only one fly in the ointment: no money.

As one would expect (it was a project coordinated by two GALA choruses, after all), the first task was to form a committee. The core of that committee included Peter Anderson, Gary Rifkin, and Eve Campbell. We created a pretend budget. We did not include the performance of the work, just its creation. We guessed $70,000 to get us started.

We needed a libretto. We selected Pam Martin Tomlinson to create one. Pam had survived her own brush with death from a brain tumor, extended time in a coma, and an extended rehabilitation. She had relearned almost everything, including her occupation as a poet and lyricist. Pam spent three days at the Komen Foundation interviewing survivors and family members and then began to write. The result was ten poems from different perspectives, with narration tying them together. Because we still had no money, she did it on faith that we would come up with some.

The next task was to find a composer. When Pam came up with ten poems, we decided to have ten different composers. The individuals we chose were more than happy to compose with no money up front. One of the committee members, realizing we were going to need supplies such as paper, paper clips, and postage, wrote a check for $5,000—seed money.

We needed a narrator, an orchestra, and a venue. Still with no money in the bank, we secured the Dallas Symphony Orchestra and the Meyerson Symphony Center for June 1, 2001. One day Peter called and said, "We need a narrator, right?" Trying not to be sarcastic, I replied, "Yes, we do." He responded, "How would you like it to be Maya Angelou?" I don't need to tell you they heard my jubilant response in a five-state area.

Gary Rifkin was acquainted with a company in Dallas that had experienced the breast cancer diagnosis of several of its members. He got me an appointment with the president, who happened to be in town. He was meeting with his team from around the country. I told them the entire story, including quoting one of the poems, "Groundless Ground." At the end of my pitch, he said, "Son, I don't think I have ever met anyone on more groundless ground than you!"

He asked how much money we needed to pay deposits and get started. I sheepishly said $70,000. He was too quiet as he thought. Finally, he said, "I have only $40,000 for things such as this." Then he looked at his regional team and asked if each of them would help. They said, "Absolutely!" We walked out with the whole $70,000. The librettist and composers would get paid.

With the text in hand, the music on its way, and a hall, an orchestra, and Maya Angelou lined up, others began to join in support of the project.

The world premiere was an experience we will never forget. A full orchestra and over 300 singers gathered for dress rehearsal. When Dr. Angelou walked on stage, there was a long, long ovation, and we began the rehearsal. Her sister had just recovered from her own bout with cancer, and as she began to read the first narration, her voice broke. She began to weep and simply put her head down on the podium. This was the moment we will all remember.

The two choruses joined hands and hearts, and at that event we changed our separate red and pink ribbons to one ribbon that combined our efforts for both devastating diseases. This was another moment we will all remember.

From that world premiere, the work has traveled across the United States and Canada. It has been performed hundreds of times, by GALA choruses and non-GALA choruses. It has been performed twice at Carnegie Hall, to overwhelming response. Many more performances are already in the works for the future. We did not know we were helping create a work that would ultimately have such a huge impact. We were just doing our best to make Nancy Brinker's vision come true. God bless Nancy, who singlehandedly has completely changed the fight against this disease.

If you have not heard the piece, find it. It also allowed me to sing live (with a really good sound system) for the biggest audience of my career—100,000 people—at the opening ceremony of the national Race for the Cure in Washington, D.C.

One of my greatest joys has been to commission large works that have been performed around the world:

> *When We No Longer Touch*, benefiting AmfAR (American Foundation for AIDS research), composed by Kris Anthony on a text by Peter McWilliams;
>
> *The Wisdom of Old Turtle*, benefiting St. Jude Hospital; Marlo Thomas, narrator; composed by Joseph Martin; book by Douglas Wood;
>
> *Tyler's Suite*, lyrics: Pamela Martin Tomlinson, Stephen Schwartz, Stephen Flaherty, John Corigliano, Ann Hampton Callaway, Jake Heggie, Craig Carnahan, Lance Horne, John Bucchino;
>
> *Sing for the Cure*, lyrics: Pamela Martin Tomlinson, Joseph Martin, Michael Cox, Alice Gomez, Rosephanye Powell, Robert Seeley, Jill Gallina, Patti Drennan, Stefania de Kennesse, David Friedman, W. T. Greer III;
>
> *Testimony*, based on the It Gets Better Project; Stephen Schwartz, composer;
>
> *Twitterlieder*, birth-to-death story of a gay man; James Eakin, composer; Charles Anthony Silvestri, librettist;
>
> *I Am Harvey Milk*, an oratorio; Andrew Lippa, composer;
>
> Unbreakable, 100 years of LGBT stories; Andrew Lippa, composer;
>
> *@QueerZ*, the voices of LGBTQ youth from Generation Z; Julian Hornik, composer.

They are my children. But I'll have to say that *Sing for the Cure*, with Dr. Maya Angelou narrating, was the biggest thrill of all!

Chapter 41

In the Kitchen with Maya

Maya Angelou and I first met in late spring 2000. I had no idea that I would be privileged to share significant time with her six times: twice in her home, once each at a press conference, a photo shoot, performances, recording, and her eightieth birthday

She Is the Real Deal

Once it was set that we would indeed have the one and only Dr. Maya Angelou as the narrator for the world premiere of *Sing for the Cure*, things began to unfold quickly. We found out that Dr. Angelou would be speaking at a luncheon in Dallas to a gathering of over 2,000 women. We immediately asked her "people" if she could possibly do a press conference for *Sing for the Cure* after her speech. Dr. Angelou was not in good health, so she said, "Have Dr. Seelig meet me as I come off the dais. If he can take me directly to the press conference, I can speak for ten minutes."

I stood at the side of the ballroom as she wowed the audience. When she had finished, her handler brought her down the steps and over to me. We had mapped a route through the kitchen as the easiest way not to have to brave the masses of beautifully dressed Dallas women. We ducked into the hot, steamy bowels of the kitchen and halls that facilitate feeding of the 5,000.

It was slow going, not because Dr. Angelou was feeble. No, the kitchen staff realized she was coming through and all stopped what they were doing. I tried to push her along, and she shrugged me off with an arm. As she walked through the maze, she literally touched the hand or arm of every single worker, red and yellow, black and others. I was stunned at this simple act. They would all go home and tell their families and friends, "A saint touched me today."

When we finally made it to the press conference, Dr. Angelou took the podium and began to tell about her sister's cancer diagnosis and the many close calls of other family and friends. Then, out of the blue, she began to sing, slow and sweet and low, "Sometimes I Feel Like a Motherless Child." There was not a dry eye—even among the press. She did not speak for ten minutes. She spoke and sang for twenty-five minutes, closing by encouraging everyone to do everything they could to support *Sing for the Cure* and she would be back soon. We were stunned!

For me, the best was yet to come. I took her arm, and we exited to where her limo was waiting, away from the throng. It was a very hot day in Dallas. She had given not one but two speeches. As we got to the back door (which the driver had opened), you could feel the conditioned air leaking out. Just as she turned to get in the car, a female voice rang out: "Dr. Angelou!"

I wanted to shove her in the limo to speed away, but Dr. Angelou turned to see a young woman with two adorable tow-headed children, probably ages four and six. Dr. Angelou leaned against the blazing-hot car. The woman went on, "Dr. Angelou, my children love you. Their favorite is "Life Doesn't Frighten You." They've drawn pictures for you."

In the sweetest voice Dr. Angelou said, "Well, bring them to me." They ran up to her, and each handed her a sketch. The older child had a picture of some humanlike characters and maybe a dog. Dr. Angelou told her it was beautiful. Then the younger child handed her a picture like so many us have received. It was completely indecipherable. Dr. Angelou bent down, opened the picture, and said, "Oh, this is beautiful. Tell me all about it."

The little boy was thrilled to be asked and had quite the description of his avant-garde artwork. Dr. Angelou told them to keep reading and keep creating art. She wished them well, and they gave her a lingering hug.

Photo Shoot

One of the big initiatives of the entire event was enlisting photographer Shawn Northcutt, my partner at the time, who was traveling around the country photographing breast cancer survivors. It was for use in a huge exhibit at the world premiere and also to be featured in the hoped-for CD. Several of the selected survivors lived in the Winston-Salem area. Why not "stop by" Maya's house for a photo shoot? She agreed. I went along. She asked us to arrive at 10:00 a.m.

Her house is exactly what you might imagine—a place of a grandmother and someone who very obviously is not concerned with things or, especially, the *latest* things. The living room had wonderful stuffed chairs and a sofa, none of which matched one another or the walls. Lots of pictures were everywhere, mostly of friends, not of Maya. She welcomed us in and chose to sit in one of her comfortable chairs. Shawn set up the lights.

She came in with a simple, flowing dress and a stunning, subtly patterned African turban. Shawn is a consummate professional. He would ask her to move her head this way or that. She was the consummate professional object of photographers. They immediately struck up a rapport, until he asked her to glance down.

She looked at him and said kindly, "That I will not do." You could hear the needle scratch across the vinyl. "When I was a little girl, my mother told me never to look down. It shows weakness and subservience."

Shawn, much the charmer, apologized profusely and said, "Dr. Angelou, perhaps it's time you let someone take your picture looking down. If you don't like it, you will be the only one who ever sees it." She looked at him warily and then turned her eyes toward her lap. (A week later, Shawn sent her the photo. She absolutely loved it—though I'm not sure she ever let anyone else take such a photo.)

"You boys come in, and let's have a drink and some cookies," she said. This was before she came to Dallas for the performances, so we had not seen the rider to her contract. As the three of us sat at her kitchen table, she called out to Mr. Miles, her assistant and driver. "Mr. Miles, can you bring up some vodka?" He brought it and fetched us some ice and orange juice. Maya poured hers first. I have to say, the orange juice might have had a spritzer added because the screwdriver was a pale yellow. We followed suit. We didn't want to hurt her feelings.

She then asked if we wanted to see her sculpture garden. Of course we did. She took us down to her backyard: some lawn furniture, a picnic table, and exquisite sculptures spread throughout. It was not a museum. It was her backyard. And she loved it. We went back upstairs and had a goodbye screwdriver. We parted as old friends. We would see her very soon in Dallas.

Recording

We found the recording studio and went in to get ready for Dr. Angelou. They had the requisite munchies (as outlined in her contract): cheese, crackers, fruit, a little something sweet, and, of course, her favorite wine, a lovely Chateau St. Michelle Chardonnay. They had brought crystal and china from someone's house (she records there fairly often and hates drinking wine out of Styrofoam, something else that sets us apart).

She entered shortly after 3:00, looking fabulous (admitting she thought she was doing a videotape). Dang! I wish we had known. When she came in, she introduced her sister, Dr. Dolly McPherson. Dr. McPherson (no one down here uses first names, period) is one of the two sisters battling breast cancer that Maya had mentioned. The other was the one for whom she had requested our thoughts and prayers on that Monday morning (she is doing great). Actually, Dr. McPherson is a five-year survivor. We gave her big hugs and congratulated her. Mr. Miles, Maya's driver of many years, drove her over.

The first thing she wanted to do was hear all about what had transpired with *Sing for the Cure* since she had left. She was totally focused on us and the mission. She bragged to Dr. McPherson about the choruses and told her how incredibly they all sang and how moved she was being right in the middle of that glorious sound. I couldn't have agreed more.

After about fifteen minutes and a nice glass of Chardonnay, she was ready to record. Talk about a pro—she did a sound level check, and off we went. She began the first narration about the test tubes. She read it rather quickly, fairly simply, and with wonderful inflection, especially compared to her live performance. It was great.

She began the second narration ("I'm sorry, the biopsy was malignant.") with increased intensity until the line "There is no escape from this nightmare, I am already awake." Her voice dropped to its bass range, leading us, mentally and absolutely perfectly, into the song "Borrowed Time."

She began the third: "My arms encircle her…I thought I could protect her from anything." With her sister, Dr. McPherson, sitting there, reading the text along with her, we began to get teary-eyed. At the end of that narration, Maya set down her wineglass napkin, buried her head in it, and wept. Dr. McPherson got up, went into the studio, and held her sister for a long time as they grieved, processed, and expressed their love for each other. Craig, Tim, and the engineer were wiping their tears away.

We continued. She LIVED OUT LOUD, kicking and screaming at the top of her lungs. Then the child's voice. At that point, Craig, Tim, and the engineer did not even dare to look at each other. Sister McPherson was on the couch just moaning her agreement with the sentiment, with an occasional "That's right" and an "Amen" or two. When Maya got to the end, she said in an absolute whisper, "I am still a motherless child." We were a wreck.

The humor on the tape is the funniest. She laughed out loud at the stories and at herself. It was infectious. Then her sister said, "Damn you, Pamela Martin! Our bond as sisters…I adored her; she nurtured me."

Then she was struck by the mirror, and the reality that she had almost lost her own sister. She made it through, just barely, then fell on her podium. Sister McPherson went back into the room and held her as they moved through these emotions together. I thought of John Thomas—how proud he would be and how I (and we) miss him.

She finished the last three, lifting us all to the heavens, once again, with her Sing! Sing! Sing!

One last time, Maya's sister went in and held Maya. We finished our weeping. She came out and sat down, absolutely drained. We shared a glass of wine as we experienced an intimate moment of working together toward this incredible goal.

As we sat there, Dr. Angelou said, "When do you all go back?" We told her we were returning to Charlotte that night and would leave in the morning. She asked what time our plane was scheduled to depart. I told her midmorning. Then she asked, "What are you doing tonight?"

"Nothing," we replied.

"You must come to the house for a cocktail," she offered.

I said that we would love to (Old Turtle and Craig smiled). She went on: "Well, I was going to ask you to spend the night with me, but I am leaving at 6:00 in the morning for vacation." (We just about fell over for just a moment, visualizing fighting with each other over who would get to wear Oprah's pajamas. It is legendary that Oprah kept a pair of pajamas in a dresser drawer at Maya's house for just such occasions.)

I asked when she wanted us to come over. She replied, "As soon as you are finished here."

When we arrived at her home, she had stopped at the local gourmet shop, and Mr. Miles had run in to gather some goodies: a hunk of pâté the size of a loaf of bread, assorted cheeses and crackers, olives, and on and on. Because Mrs. Thomas, the housekeeper, was otherwise occupied, Dr. McPherson was setting the goodies out on trays and onto the kitchen table.

Maya had us move from the table the stacks of books she was either reading or writing. We sat down, with a tremendous thunderstorm outside the window, and began to eat, drink lots of wine, and laugh and laugh. She and Dr. McPherson told stories of their past, bringing more laughter.

Dr. McPherson would retire this next year from the faculty of Wake Forest University, where she taught English literature for twenty-six years. She is incredibly bright, and they obviously adore each other. When our glasses were empty, Dr. Angelou would holler out for Mr. Miles to bring more wine. Mrs. Thomas arrived soon and from that point helped fill the glasses.

After about an hour and a half, we could tell Maya was fading. Since she was leaving early the next morning, we made nice and offered to leave. Maya said she had one favor to ask. I replied, "Of course!" She handed me a manila file folder and a pen. She said Dr. McPherson's arches had fallen and she was going to have special shoes made for her in New York City, but they needed a template to go by. In moments I was on my hands and knees on the kitchen floor, tracing Dr. McPherson's fallen arches onto the file folder. We bonded.

We hugged and kissed goodbye and left for our drive back to Charlotte. We felt so blessed to have had this opportunity. I told her as we sat there how honored we were to have been invited and how she must realize the feeling so many people had for her.

The whole scene was surreal. She was truly like a grandmother—A REALLY, REALLY FAMOUS GRANDMOTHER. Her Southern hospitality was in full force.

The 80th Birthday Celebration

After leaving the TCC, I had many jobs. One was as artistic director for Hope for Peace and Justice. We were thinking of having a big event at the Meyerson Symphony Hall sometime in spring. As we were sitting around, I just threw out, "Why don't we get Dr. Angelou to attend? It's right around her eightieth birthday." Everyone's jaw dropped.

I called her assistant and asked what Dr. Angelou was doing right around her birthday. Well, five days before her birthday, she would be giving a speech in San Francisco (where in the 1940s she had been the first black woman to drive a cable car). Then she would be getting on her bus and driving to Winston-Salem to be there on her birthday.

"Dallas would be the perfect halfway mark," I said. "Would you consider allowing us to throw a huge birthday party at the symphony hall where we performed *Sing for the Cure*?" She said she would ask. She got right back to us and said, "Dr. Angelou would love to be with you. It needs to be a matinee so that she can get on the bus and head on home."

She had but one requirement: By the time she boarded the bus heading home, she wanted ten pounds of the best barbeque in Dallas—for her bus driver and staff (wink, wink). We agreed to the terms! That was in addition to the other things required in her rider: wine, vodka, and champagne. We already knew those requirements.

We threw a sold-out humdinger: a chorus of over 200; a full orchestra; an enormous, stunning, Texas-sized layered birthday cake rolled out as 2,000 people and orchestra serenaded her. All of this to celebrate her! There was a lot of music (she loved it so much).

Then she took her place on a stool behind the podium. Her entire speech was "Behind Every Cloud, There's a Rainbow." She spoke of her life and sang bits and pieces inserted along the way. There were tears and laughter and chill bumps when she sang.

We bid her farewell at the bus. She smiled the biggest smile when we handed her the enormous to-go bags of barbecue, purchased by Gary Rifkin, and the wine, vodka, and champagne from her dressing room. We would not see her in person again. She made everyone feel loved and appreciated. But not many had the invitation to wear Oprah's pajamas!

Knowing her in this way has been one of the thrills of my life.

Chapter 42

Blue Tiles and Abortion

In summer 2018 all the talk was about Roe vs. Wade. Relatively few women who have had an abortion were speaking out. Corianna asked if she could co-write my article for the *Bay Times*. Of course, it meant her coming out to a lot of people. She and her husband, Clay, discussed it because the story absolutely affected him. His own colleagues would read it. He backed Corianna without hesitation. He was proud of her. He knew it was something she was passionate about.

> Pro-choice or pro-life? That's an odd question for a gay man to pose. It's not exactly a topic discussed at your local Castro bar or eatery. At first glance, this issue has only tangential impact on our community. Making babies, in our community, is most often intentional, purposeful and, in many cases, very expensive. "Choice" is an interesting word since we spend a great deal of time defending ourselves against the allegation that our orientation is a choice, a "preference." In this moment in time, we are hearing more and more about the pro-life vs. pro-choice controversy. Sides have been taken. Lines drawn. *Roe vs. Wade* appears to be in grave danger. But what does it mean to me? To us?
>
> As a teen, I just knew that occasionally someone I barely knew left school to spend some time "away." Most often it was at the local Buckner Baptist Home for Unwed Mothers. Later, as a straight (acting) adult and absorbed in the church every waking moment, it was not really discussed much. It was not a part of our lives at all. As far as we knew, no one in our church circle had any direct experience with this so-called pro-choice thing. Abortion didn't hold nearly as prominent a position as homosexuality did in the hierarchy of human sins. So, we didn't even talk about it with our children. Life was good. Choice also sounded good. What did any of that have to do with me?

In my mind, I would never have to face this issue head on. Never say never. I have a story to share. Well, actually my daughter, Corianna, has a story that she would like to tell, if you would indulge us. She's going to take the writer's pen at this point. It's a story she really wanted to tell herself. Here we go.

Corianna's Story

I was 21 years old, living in a garage apartment in Dallas. I was going to nursing school, working as a nursing assistant. I was fully living the life of a young person who had just retired my fake I.D. for a real one. One night, I met a great guy in a bar and we began dating. Trey was a stand-up kind of guy, a little older and stable. I was crazy and a bit wild. He accepted me for who I was and really wanted to settle down together. I was not ready to settle down, but he was so nice.

It was the holidays. His parents were out of town, so we had their McMansion in the burbs to ourselves. We had sex, upstairs... no protection. Of course, as a nursing student, I knew the risks, but was completely oblivious as to the real consequences. I took a test on New Year's Day, all by myself. I was pregnant.

The first person I told was my dad's partner. I knew he wouldn't judge and I needed help telling my dad. I just didn't know how he would react. Dad's partner called a few friends together for a drink at a gay bar after a rehearsal one night. I surprised him by being there. I thought it would be better with people around. I told him. He came around the table, and as he has always done said, "I love you. Now let's make a list of next steps!" I gratefully declined that help.

The next days and weeks I floated as if in a bad dream. I barely remember the details. I have glimpses of being at the bar, snapshots of people's faces. I felt ashamed and frightened. I told Trey last. He wanted to keep the baby, to be together. He worked out a plan. We went to look at places to live together. I remember standing in the bathroom of one of the beautiful houses, looking at the fish on the bathroom tile. I like fish and really liked the tile.

At that moment, having that beautiful bathroom tile was almost enough to make me consider having the baby.

I remember staring at the fish on that tile and thinking, "I can barely take care of myself. I can't pay my bills on time. I drink every night. I'm good at school, but that doesn't translate to having a baby." At that point, I had not one maternal bone in my body. I, myself, had not been mothered. At all. I had no idea what being a mother looked like. Dad was the closest thing I had to a mother. I was scared. I knew that I would be miserable. Trey would be miserable. The child would most certainly be miserable. At that point, I couldn't even take care of a fish or that f—ing tile.

I snapped. I didn't tell anyone what I had decided, but I knew. Several weeks went by before I built the courage to take the next steps. I made a phone call and an appointment. The clinic I chose was well-known because of picketers who had been outside for years. I had seen it on television news—never thinking I would need it. The news showed people screaming at everyone who entered…with pictures of mutilated babies and other unimaginable images. On the day of my appointment, the kinder, gentler protesters were on duty. I pushed through, ignoring them, and entered the most warm, welcoming place ever.

Two appointments were required. The first was to get an ultrasound and to have a counseling session that gives you all of the possible options. The next, if you chose to return, was for the procedure. I was worried about paying for it. I had no money. I couldn't ask Dad. Trey paid and didn't shame me at all, even though that was not his choice for how this would unfold.

At the first visit, I had the ultrasound and found out how far along I was. They told me how big the fetus might be and what it had developed. They didn't do it to make me feel bad but to be informed. I remember sitting very close to the counselor in a cozy room (like a therapist's office). I didn't cry. She offered me a picture of the ultrasound and I wanted it for some reason. She was lovely. I asked for a hug when I left and she seemed surprised, but obliged. It was a good hug…seemed like she meant it. Now, twenty years later, I'm crying as I write this!

I made an appointment for the procedure two days from then. I wanted to do it by myself, so Dad dropped me off and Trey picked me up. The procedure didn't last too long. They sedated me. There was a doctor and a nurse. I asked the nurse to hold my hand and she did, lovingly. I got the feeling that they really, really cared, and it made a huge impact on me. Trey picked me up and he was very sad. We didn't know what to say to each other. I puked on the way back to my apartment. He asked if I wanted him to stay and I didn't. I asked him to leave, and I'm sure that was the beginning of the end of our relationship.

On some level, I knew it was "wrong." I learned it in church, the media, movies, after-school specials. Abortion is different than drinking or even having premarital sex. For some people, abortion is that thing you just don't do. You don't do if you're a Christian. You don't do it if you're a good person, and you don't do it if you like kids…or value human life. But all of that really doesn't matter when you are faced with your own huge mistake and the lifelong repercussions of it. It's just you and your life and your choice in that room with you.

Had I gone through with having the baby, it would have crushed me. I would have loved the baby, I think, but I would have hated my life. Had I gone ahead with the pregnancy, that child would have entered the world with a child for a mother. I wouldn't have grown up. I may have never been a practicing nurse taking care of kids with cancer for the last 20 years. I would not have met and married my soulmate, who also spends his life in pediatric oncology. I may have never had a baby that I really, really wanted. I really, really want my little girl every second of every day.

Looking back these 20 years now, I don't have answers. I do know that I am so very grateful that I lived in a time and a country where it was my choice. I made a mistake. I owned up to that. I was able to make a choice that was best for everyone. What would I tell others in the same situation? Trust your gut.

If you have an abortion, you are not ruined. You will not be mangled. You may lose some friends. If you do, they weren't your friends. You can still carry a life and bear a beautiful child and you can heal. I would never tell anyone how to believe or what they should think. I do hope, however, that sharing this incredibly painful chapter of my life and the fact that two decades later I would have done the same thing, may give someone out there hope in the decision that they are making. I will also fight for every woman's right to make her own decision, should they find themselves as I found myself on that life-altering New Year's Day.

That's my girl—brave, courageous, vulnerable, and a healer. And she's an activist. She also ascribes to her dad's deeply held belief that it is only when we are willing to tell our stories—the good and the bad—that we are able to move the needle and change a little part of the world.

Of course, I knew my side of the story, but it was not until recently that I knew the details from Corianna's side. I wept when reading it. No parent wants their child to experience such pain. That brings me back to a quick recap of my own experience that fateful night when my views on abortion changed forever.

It was a Tuesday night—rehearsal night for my chorus. At the end of rehearsal, my partner said, "We're going to J. R.'s for a drink." (It was Dallas, after all.) That was unusual because it wasn't something we ever did, but I just guessed he had some reason, and a cocktail after a long rehearsal was a good thing. When we arrived, two of our best friends were there and—the big surprise—so was my daughter, Corianna. Had I missed a birthday? From their faces, it did not look like a party. We joined them at the table. They had already ordered us drinks.

We had been through a lot in our lives—coming out, divorce, bankruptcy, family drama galore. All of this had drawn us closer. Perhaps some of that helped us through this moment. In usual Corianna fashion, she did not beat around the bush. She said, "Dad, I'm pregnant." The earth did not open up or the sky fall. All I can remember thinking was how much I loved this girl of mine and wanted to protect her. I had somehow failed in that in this moment. But my next thought—and I hope actions showed—was: THERE IS NOTHING SHE COULD EVER DO THAT WOULD

MAKE ME REMOVE MY LOVE FROM HER. I think she knew—and knows—that.

I watched her go through her own steps of dealing with this—only standing guard from a distance and being willing to step in at any moment. But she really didn't need that. Whatever decision she made would change our lives forever. We all discussed the options and left with none chosen. She did that on her own.

I went through my own thoughts in the days that followed. Was I ready to be a grandfather? I thought I was, but I really wasn't. How would I feel should she decide to end the pregnancy? Would I be ashamed or embarrassed? I did a great deal of soul-searching myself.

I watch her now. I watch her be the most amazing woman and mother. I see a woman for whom every bone in her body just screams *Mom*! I see this beautiful woman who would not be the same had she not made this choice. Because of her courageous decision back then, I now have Clara!

We live in a world where women are standing up with courage on a daily basis. It was not that way twenty years ago when Corianna went through this trauma. She is my hero.

Am I pro-choice? Hell, yes! And I'm ready to continue helping in the fight to make sure other daughters have the same choice my little frightened girl had twenty years ago.

Chapter 43

HIV and Extortion

It was an exciting time. My son and I had reconciled. We had planned his proposal to Juliana. It was all taking place at our loft/studio. I had run by my doctor's office earlier in the week to do some routine lab work before my annual physical the morning of the big marriage proposal.

When I went to the appointment, I had already imagined the doctor's words: "Your cholesterol is high. If you don't drop some pounds, and soon, you will have to start taking a pill!" I was taking zero pills at that time.

My doctor came into the examination room and sat down. This is the conversation as I remember it (I am confident these are NOT the exact words).

Doctor: Tim, I so admire your work. You have been on the front lines as an AIDS activist for years. You've buried countless dear friends. Have you ever stopped to ponder how you would react if you found out you were HIV-positive?

Tim: Well, of course I have (not true).

Doctor: That's good, because you are.

I have no idea what he said after that. It wouldn't have mattered. The earth fell away. My T-cell count was less than the number of singers in my chorus. He recommended starting medication immediately. I just couldn't. I'd seen all of that. I needed to think. And besides, I needed to be the host with the most at my son's proposal to his fiancé.

The proposal went flawlessly. I was just overwhelmed that he allowed me to be a part. The youngsters left, and my partner and I went for sushi. Somewhere between the edamame and eel nigiri, I told him about the doctor visit. We had both been negative. He was tested on Monday—positive. We will, of course, never know who contracted the virus and brought it home.

I, too, was devastated. The shame I felt was indescribable. I knew better than to allow this to happen. I knew how to save myself from the plague. I had told countless others. I was a role model, after all. I had failed myself, my family, and my friends. I desperately wanted to "take to my bed," as all Southern women do when something bad happens. In the nineteenth century, women who took to their bed could order morphine or heroin from the Sears catalogue. I didn't take to my bed or order from Sears. I did what I had done several times in my life. I went back to music. I went back to my calling: waving my arms at singers! Before that, I was fighting and singing for *them*. Now, I was fighting and singing and waving for *us*. It was yet another huge paradigm shift.

I immediately thought back to the night John Thomas told us, in the depths of his anguish and shame, of his own seroconversion. He was my hero. He was my mentor. And he made a mistake. It cost him his life. I had made a mistake. Because of progress made in the fight against AIDS, it was not a death sentence for me. Survivor's guilt? Oh, yes.

The hardest thing was telling my daughter. It was a bright, sunny morning. We were at a Starbucks. Corianna was a nurse. She knew way too much about AIDS. She had walked with me through the massive losses. When I told her, she, in a very uncharacteristic emotional outburst, literally wailed, through tears, "No!" I held her. I had failed her—once again. My coming out—when she was nine and her brother seven—was apparently not enough devastating news to hear about Dad and their broken lives. Nope, there was more.

Extortion

Suddenly, I had to face another crisis point in my personal life. It was another "coming out," as it were. There were many times I just wanted to run and hide from shame. There were many times I just felt I could not go on, could not tell anyone or bear the stigma still attached firmly to those who are HIV-positive. I did not want to tell my son. I didn't want him to think less of me after all the struggles we had been through to get back to where we were.

Enter Corianna. During our regrets and remembrances session while she was in rehab, we shared our deepest thoughts. Corianna simply said, "Dad, you can't imagine how hard it was to admit my disease to the world. If we are going to be transparent as a family, you have to tell Judson—now."

I'm not sure why I was back at Starbucks for telling Judson, but I was. We met and talked about his sister for a bit, and then I just told him. He did not holler out as his sister had done. He got big tears in his eyes, stood up, and hugged me. That was that.

Fast forward. Corianna and Clay moved to San Francisco. She heard about the amazing AIDS Life/Cycle. This is a seven-day, 545-mile bike ride up and down the hills (mountains) from San Francisco to Los Angeles. It is grueling. Corianna had not ridden a bike since we finally took her training wheels off somewhere around twelve years old. She decided to go to the first "meet and greet" just to see what it was like. In her words, she walked in, was welcomed by a smiling face, and promptly fell into that person's arms, sobbing.

In her words—written on her fundraising page:

> *The truth is, I am scared. I am scared of the hard work. I am scared that I won't make it. I dread the sore legs (and sore other parts) and unavoidable ass-chafing.*
>
> *The day I walked into the first "meet and greet" for ride participants, I was met by warm, wonderful people who innocently remarked, "Oh, you are alone!" I realized I had been carrying all of these deep emotions alone. I started to cry and have cried off and on since then! Memories and stories and names and faces have flooded back. I have cried happy tears and sad tears on a regular basis since committing to this journey. I also just finished my first 30-mile ride!*
>
> *I am riding for my dad. I am riding for countless family members lost (Bob Stephens, Randy Rhea, John Thomas, and so many more) and so many others still living with HIV and AIDS. I am riding to challenge myself—and to challenge you never to forget. I am riding—and writing—to make sure we never relegate HIV and AIDS to some far-off country on another continent— because it is here, at home, in our own families! I plan to share all of this with you via Facebook. Please join me.*

When she stopped sobbing, the nice person said, "Do you cycle?"

Corianna, now laughing, "Uh, no."

"Do you own a bike?"

More nervous laughter. "No."

"Are there any other things that might hold you back from completing the ride?"

"Well, I have an eleven-month-old little girl."

I'm sure the nice person thought, "Why did I get this crazy woman?"

What she didn't know is this is exactly what always motivated her: the impossible or near impossible

The nice person told Corianna it was an expensive journey—including the purchase of a nice bicycle (without training wheels). That was fine; they had good jobs. Then the nice person asked the final question: "Can you raise at least $3,000?"

Thinking of her dad and his friends, Corianna replied, "Why, yes, I can!"

She wanted to ride in my honor. That was so sweet. "Oh, and I want to put your HIV-positive status on my fundraising page."

What? In my mind, this would go to the entire population of the planet. That was irrational, of course, but it would go to my entire family (Corianna would make sure of that) and my Turtle Creek and SFGMC families and more.

Well, I was used to big coming outs, but I wasn't ready. I said, "I need a little time."

She responded, "Go ahead and think, but I'm about to hit send, so hop to!"

Of course I said yes and started writing emails! It was the best extortion ever!

Chapter 44

Worst Cup of Coffee Ever

In order for this book to be as truthful as possible, Judson and I spoke recently about a meeting two decades ago. We have our own versions of the details. Yet neither of us wanted to make the schism deeper. Judson remembers me instigating a meeting in Houston, and I remember it to be at his request. Regardless, we met.

In the early days of Southwest Airlines, you could bop from Dallas to Houston for thirty-nine dollars. We set the following Sunday morning to meet at Houston Hobby Airport for coffee. We do remember the content of the meeting to be the same. Judson had told me he did not want me to come to his high school graduation in a few weeks. As I remember it, he also did not want a further relationship.

Vicki and I had agreed to share both kids' college education costs equally. I told Judson that if he did not want any more communication with me, it didn't seem fair that I would send a monthly check to a P.O. Box in Lubbock. He communicated that to be fine. His college education costs were covered. I did not know that Vicki's boyfriend, Tom, had helped her save the money to pay for it. It was a big mess. From that time on, Judson took care of his education costs with the money his Mom and Tom had saved, and I paid for Corianna, further deepening the divide.

I told him that I loved him (to be repeated when the BIG RUG got pulled later). I told him I would be at his high school graduation. It was in a 5,000-seat arena. I would not expect him to acknowledge my presence, which he did not. Corianna sat with me.

As I remember it, we ended the airport meeting by shaking hands, and he left. I boarded my plane back to Dallas. My therapist advised: Keep loving him.

The next six years were a bit of a blur where Judson was concerned. He stayed in contact with my parents from time to time. He stayed in contact with Corianna, but not regularly. I may have seen him at my parents' house a few times. He obviously needed space and got what he wanted, in spades.

He went on to get his MBA and became a CPA. He is nothing short of brilliant. Remember how sensitive he was and his "feelers"? They were still there, but he was trying his best not to show them—to anyone.

At the age of twenty-four, he was being recruited by the big accounting firms in Dallas. The possibility of moving to his "dad's town" was causing him a lot of stress and anxiety. Dad was a well-known LGBTQ leader and an activist. A BIG GAY. Judson was torn about how to make two things work: his need for independence and his need for distance from his biological father, realizing he would be living too close for comfort.

He called and asked to meet at my TCC office in Dallas. I was bowled over, feeling nervous and having no idea why he wanted to meet in person. I'll never forget his walking in. He was even more handsome than ever. He had filled out into a man. He carried himself with confidence. I was so proud that I almost burst into tears at the man in front of me. He had become this person on his own.

Once again, Judson was there to make an announcement that could not have been made in a vacuum. Again, I was not there for him as he was growing up, developing, deciding who to love and who not to love. I do know that he never doubted my love.

He sat down. Once again, his message was well thought out and delivered without emotion. Due to the incredible stress of his situation, he had decided to change his last name to avoid any connection to me. His message was clear: I do not want anyone to know you are my father.

I remember vividly looking across the desk, saying "I love you," just as I had done six years earlier when he walked away from the world's worst cup of coffee in the airport. I remember his saying to me, "That's not what I thought you would say." But I did say it. Judson Crawford walked out of my office.

It was a devastating blow, not just to me, but to the whole family. It is hard to imagine what forces and influences brought him to that final decision to sever himself from our entire side of the family tree. My parents were devastated. His uncle, aunt, and cousins were heartbroken. There could now be no Singing Seeligs!

Once Judson had moved to Dallas with a new name, he joined a large, contemporary megachurch. There, he was assigned a spiritual mentor. As Judson began to trust this person, he told him about his dad and the big gay thing. Their conversations continued, and eventually he felt he should ask my forgiveness. In Judson's words, "I knew that I couldn't be healed and continue to live with the pain I knew I had caused you. I also knew I needed you in my life; I just didn't know how."

Much later, Judson shared with me that his anger had many facets. In his words:

> *There was more than just the "gay" thing that angered me. Was I comfortable around all the gays at that time? No. I was comfortable around Louis and most of them one on one, but in large groups, I wasn't. Also, I have come to learn that there were two things that angered me most of all. 1) Okay, so Dad is gay. Why can't he just be a normal run of the mill gay instead of the "King of the gays" that often was in the newspaper, TV, etc. I couldn't comprehend until much later what you were leading these men through and what it meant. I just wanted a regular dad. 2) Here is the one that is going to be hard for you. What hurt the most is that I felt that you chose them over me. I know you needed a job but, to me, why not just take a job in Houston as a teacher or something. It felt in my adolescent mind that the gays were put before me.*

It wasn't long until Judson started seriously dating a wonderful young woman. She had a very different background than Judson's. She was not raised fundamentalist Baptist (praise the Lord!). She told Judson that in order to move to the next level, she wanted to meet his father in person. I told Judson that was great, but my partner would have to be included.

We hit it off famously. I'm not sure Judson was completely certain about double-dating with his dad, but we decided to do it again. I got to see Judson, the grown man, laughing, holding Juliana's hand, ordering wine! What?

I had known his fraternity had a reputation for drinking the most beer of any on the Texas Tech University campus. But here was my son, all grown up, doing something very non-Baptist right in front of me. He was ridiculously charming, self-assured, and amazing.

Some time later, Judson asked to meet me for breakfast. Still wary of hidden rugs, I met him at Cafe Brazil in Deep Ellum (Dallas's cool spot), where I lived. He opened his laptop to show me the engagement ring he had bought for Juliana. This old dad's heart soared. He said, "I need you and Shawn to help me with the proposal. Gay guys are so much more creative."

Well, we planned an incredible proposal at our rather enormous loft/photography studio. Judson invited his college friends over to hide in the bedroom. It was a huge deal. We had never met his friends. We set up the studio with a huge white chiffon pergola hanging in the middle of the room. There were literally hundreds of candles leading the way.

Juliana had no idea what was happening. She was just dropping by. When she got there, I said the package she came for was in the studio. When she opened the French doors, there was a path of candles leading to the pergola, where Judson was standing. I left (didn't want to!). Don't know what happened in there, but soon they came out to find all their friends there to congratulate them. It was amazing to be a part of that.

Juliana said she wanted us to help her with the wedding planning, as Dallas was not her home. We said, "Juliana, we would be happy to help, but we don't know any straight people." She responded, "Good. I don't want straight people doing my wedding." We followed through. I believe every single person who touched their wedding from location to caterer to photographer was gay.

Chapter 45

First Retirement from the Gays

Nearing the end of my nineteenth year with the TCC, we had commissioned Joe Sears and Jaston Williams of the *Greater Tuna* empire to write a complete musical. It was just delicious, with spoofs galore, including a sendup of Bush #2 titled "Baptist on the Roof."

For about four years, my most amazing therapist helped me get through much of the good and bad times. She knew I was just tired—but not at all of the chorale. I was tired of the shenanigans the board kept pulling. I would say, "Barbara, being the conductor of TCC is who I am." She would reply, "No, Tim, it's what you do."

I would say, "Barbara, you don't understand. It is who I am." She would patiently reply, "No, Tim, it's what you do!" But if I took that leap, what would I do? Who would I be?

One day in therapy I had a life-changing thought: Directing the TCC is what I do. Surely I can find other things to do. I literally went to my car, called the chairman of the board, drove to his office, and resigned effective the following June. After twenty years, it seemed right to give them a year.

It was really hard on the chorus members. Daddy was not leaving for another man—or woman. He was just leaving. I had no idea what was next. I just knew that it was time to take a leap, for my own good and that of the chorale as well.

It was certainly one of those times that reminded me of one of my favorite poems, "Faith":

> *When you come to the edge of all the light you have,*
> *and take that step into the unknown,*
> *faith is knowing that one of two things will happen:*
> *you will step on solid ground*
> *or you will be taught to fly.*

By Patrick Overton. Used by permission.

When I took that step, away from my family, which was the TCC, there was solid ground to be sure. I remembered the adage, "You can't die from jumping off a high dive." I jumped, came up out of the water, and would soon realize it's one of the best things I ever did.

Chapter 46

Final Choral Home

Remember how I described the first time a gay man walks into a gay men's chorus, and my feelings when I first conducted a big group of men just like me? Well, imagine walking into a big gay city—maybe the gayest in the world—and calling it home. I had visited San Francisco often, but always with a suitcase in hand and a return airline ticket. This time, I traded in my luggage for a U-Haul.

I had lived in Texas, where the gays were tolerated—as long as you didn't wave it in their face. Being tolerated, as if you had some kind of deformity, is exhausting. There were pockets of acceptance in the Lone Star State. Unfortunately, even our little enclave, Oak Lawn and Cedar Springs, had seen a dramatic rise in crime. I arrived in a place that left tolerance and acceptance in the dust decades ago.

In San Francisco it's full-on celebration of uniqueness. Hearkening back to the song I played my teenage children, "You can be anybody that you want to be. You can love whomever you will." Nowhere on earth is that more true than in San Francisco.

In 2007 I had wrapped up my long-term commitments to LGBTQ choruses. I was fine living in Dallas doing my thing: teaching, traveling, guest conducting, writing. But in spring 2009 the SFGMC invited me to guest conduct its spring concert. Every Monday brought me to the City by the Bay, where I could spend the night with Corianna and Clay. Then back home on Tuesday to teach at Southern Methodist University. It was perfect.

In late summer 2010 the chorus announced it was looking for a new artistic director. I was not looking for a long-term gig. But it was the SAN FRANCISCO GAY MEN'S CHORUS. It was the first chorus on the planet to proudly proclaim sexual orientation in its very name. It was the granddaddy of the entire LGBTQ choral movement. And it was in San Francisco!

Although I had conducted the chorus in two different concert sessions, and even though I thought I was done with conducting my gay chorus, I applied for the job. As the weeks wore on, the excitement of the possibility monopolized me. I took nothing for granted. I worked hard on my application packet and was thrilled be one of three finalists.

The next step was a conference call with the search committee. They had my C.V., recordings, past programs, books, and CDs. During the interview, the question was asked, "What are the three top things you bring to the job?" My answer threw them a bit. I think they were probably expecting me to tell them of my studies of musicology or vocal pedagogy. Instead, I told them the three things I felt were most salient to my candidacy:

- Empathy
- Sense of humor
- Musicality

I remember facing silence and some tapping on the microphone to see if they had somehow misheard what I had said. They asked, "Why would you choose those?" I was so happy they asked.

"I bring empathy. There is little your singers could have gone through that I have not experienced myself. I grew up in a very narrow religion. I was married with children. I had a difficult coming out. I have stood at the bedside of count-less friends as they died. And I am HIV-positive. I can put myself in their shoes or their seat or their place on the risers. It is the greatest thing I will bring.

"Second on my list is a sense of humor, something I am incredibly grateful not to have lost. Conducting a large gay chorus requires humor. It relieves a lot of tensions that arise. And audiences like humor.

"Finally, I bring musicality. That is different from musicianship, which is learned. I can improve my musicianship through hard work. Musicality is inborn. You either have it or you don't. It can't be learned. Musicality can be imitated but never authentically created. It requires risk-taking and a bit of courage. And a chorus that trusts you enough to follow."

I am certain they were shocked. That was my truth.

One of the most important things you can do in any audition, whether for singing or conducting, is to choose the right piece. It can certainly make or break you. The two who auditioned before me had not paid attention to that important point.

I chose a stunning piece based on "Eckhart Tolle" by Kevin Robison. The text is perfectly wedded to the music. It was composed for the Gay Men's Chorus of Los Angeles. I borrowed it.

In the Space of Now

In the space of now there is no shame.
For what has happened is only remembered.

In the space of now there is no fear.
For the future cannot be known.
In the space of now there is no judgment.
Of what has been, of all that is, of what will come.

Like music, this moment has no beginning
Like music, this moment will go on
Like music, this moment tells a truth
That you and I and all that is are one.
And so we sing in the space of now.

We sing because the music has no judgment
Of who we've been, of who we are, who we'll become.
Let us release our judgment of all that was and is to be.
Then, no longer prisoners of our thinking
In an instant, in this perfect moment
Through our song, we will have changed the world

Music: Kevin Robison; lyrics: Kevin Robison based on Eckhart Tolle. Used by permission.

The men sang it beautifully and with such commitment. Many tears were shed between the notes. That said it all.

The eight-month process of replacing an artistic director had been a difficult one. There was one person who guided the whole thing with incredible poise and calm. I certainly knew—and hoped—I could work with Michael Tate. The next week, Michael called to share the news. I had been selected as the next artistic director of the SFGMC.

I began work in January 2011. I was not a young man! But the challenge and the opportunity were just too incredible to pass up. Clara was born in late November 2010, so I arrived with my first grandchild being one month old. I also asked if we could move my first rehearsal back a day, to Sunday afternoon. They were amenable. Monday, the day of the actual first rehearsal, was my sixtieth birthday. I didn't want them to know my age!

It turned out to be a very good thing because we had to meet in a large church rather than the chorus's normal rehearsal space, which seated 125 comfortably. Two hundred seventy singers showed up for that rehearsal. On that morning, the staff of the chorus started desperately searching for new rehearsal space. Here I am almost a decade later, and the chorus remains at more than 275 singers.

The chorus began in October 1978. In its fourth week, city supervisor Harvey Milk and mayor George Moscone were assassinated. The chorus sang in public for the first time on the steps of San Francisco City Hall at the candle-light vigil to honor those two slain men. This began what is now a forty-year legacy of activism through music.

For obvious reasons Harvey Milk is the patron saint of the chorus. I have learned so much from this man, whom I never knew, about the joy of life and the message of hope. "You gotta give 'em hope." I've learned the importance of stepping out and being out. I've learned that normal, everyday people have potential and power. We commissioned Broadway composer Andrew Lippa to put those stories to music, resulting in an amazing oratorio, *I Am Harvey Milk*.

Back in 1981, the chorus took a national tour to encourage young choruses that had begun to crop up and to visit other cities without choruses, hoping to inspire them to start one. Both goals were achieved. The chorus performed in Dallas, Minneapolis, Lincoln, Detroit, New York City, Boston, Washington, Seattle, and the welcome-home triumphant performance at Davies Symphony Hall, where Mayor Dianne Feinstein awarded SFGMC the key to the city—the first time that honor had been bestowed on a gay organization. This began the chorus's presence on a national stage.

I would arrive exactly thirty years after that tour. Moving to gay Mecca and conducting the oldest gay men's chorus was the thrill of a lifetime. It was at once daunting and exhilarating. What could I do to help make a difference in the chorus's place in history? I jumped in with my usual drive, and we began to find out.

The creative activities had been going on at a furious pace for a long time. But arriving in San Francisco, sensing it was my last chapter, allowed me to settle in and look inward. There was and still is so much to learn. But I am finally in a place to welcome those lessons. San Francisco brought a new level of awareness and sensitivity and inclusion. It is truly one of the epicenters of all things LGBTQ. As such, we are called to stay ahead of the curve. It is a challenge and a thrill.

I had been in San Francisco only three weeks when the office received a call from Jon Stewart's *The Daily Show*. The *Advocate* had just come out with its list of the gayest cities in the United States. San Francisco had somehow landed in the eleventh spot. Minneapolis was in first place. What? The producers asked if someone from the chorus might agree to be interviewed about this outrageous revelation. The people in the office felt this would be a great way for their new artistic director to test the waters and earn his stripes.

I completely panicked. I had been a resident for only three weeks. I immediately called Tom Burtch, a singer in the chorus and our historian. Best of all, he is a docent at the GLBT Museum in the heart of the Castro. He arranged for me to come to the museum when it was closed for a crash course in San Francisco and its rightful place as the center of so many things gay—too many to count, actually.

The segment was done by the hilarious—and handsome—Jason Jones. I was a nervous wreck, fearful he would ask me a question about my new hometown that would ruin my cover. He did not. The piece is absolutely hilarious and, of course, proved that San Francisco is absolutely the gayest city in America. We've been "making San Francisco gay again" for decades.

Many of my friends from back home in Dallas have asked what it's like to conduct the SFGMC and live in San Francisco. Well, it has been simply out of this world. Previously, I'd been the right person in the wrong place at the wrong time. I'd also been the wrong person in the right place but at the wrong time (all of us have). This was the second time all three were "right" at the same time: Dallas in 1987 and San Francisco in 2011. Perfect bookends to the gay choral career I have been so lucky to have.

But this was the first time I have lived in a city that truly celebrates the whole alphabet of gays. That makes a huge difference in how you live your life and in how you lead a chorus. We model what we do on servant leadership, turning the pyramid of power point side down. We work on a reality of twins: music and mission. We must feed each of them every day. We do not have a favorite between them. They are equal in every way, in every plan, and in every long-range vision. Music is a means to the end—to change the world through our music, one heart or a thousand at a time!

If it seems trite to say SFGMC is a family, then let me be ridiculously trite. My friend Armistead Maupin divides the people in our lives into "biological family" and "logical family." We have an enormous family. We are messy people. We admit that. We try to be there when any of our family is in need. We do our very best to create a safe space where anyone who enters knows they have found a new family for themselves—nearly 300 siblings sharing a room at 170 Valencia St.—with not enough bathrooms or closet space.

In my sixth year conducting the chorus, we chose the title "Paradise" for the spring concert series. The repertoire included music about every possible thing people might consider paradise—from heaven to a beach in Hawaii to love. We had commissioned a large piece by our composer-in-residence, James Eakin, titled "Paradiso," based on John Milton's *Paradise Found*. It loosely followed the path of recovery and was quite powerful. Everyone in the chorus was excited about the concert because each person had a very favorite part, from the sublime to the ridiculous. Preparations began in January for the three concerts on March 31 and April 1.

Opening night is always exciting. "Will they like it?" "Will they like us?" "Will I remember my words and choreography?" "Do I have time to change from my tux to my aloha shirt during intermission for Act II?"

We gathered in the beautiful jewel box, 900-seat Herbst Theater in San Francisco for the 8:00 p.m. downbeat. The Hālau O Keikiali'I, one of the nation's finest halaus, were our guests. They also danced in the first half. Intermission came. Time to do the "quick" change from tuxes to our best "tourist visiting Honolulu" attire. It's always a mad scramble for 250 men in the always-too-small dressing rooms.

A few years earlier, what seemed to be a shy Hispanic man had showed up at auditions. In his own description, he was a big boy. He was extremely nervous. He did fine and was accepted. Later, he shared with us that he truly thought we would not accept him because of his size. Nothing could have been farther from the truth, but it was his truth. He jumped right in. Everyone began to fall in love with Ryan.

Choir rehearsals are an orderly thing. The conductor gives directions. The singers follow the instructions. Unless you are Ryan Nuñez. In that case, you feel that it is incumbent on you to keep a running commentary going from your seat in the lower baritone section. Sometimes the commentary was just for those around him—whom he kept in stitches—but often he provided his retorts loud enough for all 250-plus at any given rehearsal to hear. They were all timed perfectly to disrupt the flow of the rehearsal deliciously. Rehearsal became a "call and response" provided by none other than Ryan to "Doctor Teem," exaggerating his own Latin accent, which he loved to do.

It was not long until we found we needed Ryan's administrative and member services expertise in the office and he came to work for us. He kept to himself, did his work, and occasionally broke the office up with his retorts from his corner desk. It was this that brought him to the "Paradise" concerts.

On opening night, Ryan, being the "big guy," and being on the staff, had placed his clothing change outside the dressing room. He did it quickly and returned to the risers. As a tall guy, he was assigned to the ninth riser step, at the very top. Once he got there, he fainted—or so we thought. We have several medical professionals in the chorus who were summoned. I was brought to the stage, where they were doing CPR. We were ten minutes into the twenty-minute intermission. There was no response.

Our assortment of doctors and nurses were lined up to treat Ryan. The singers were held in the dressing/green room. I finally went out on stage to tell the audience we had a medical situation behind stage and it was being handled. I thought I would entertain them with stories of my life, my grandchildren. The hula troop actually came out and performed an extra piece.

Our executive director, Chris Verdugo, came out every ten minutes to whisper in my ear, "Keep going." One of our singers came out and did an impromptu solo. I kept talking. Finally, after maybe thirty minutes, standing in front of a sold-out audience, Chris did not whisper, "Keep going." Instead, he said, "He's gone."

I told the audience the situation backstage has turned dire and, unfortunately, we would not be able to proceed with the second half. We would be in touch with them as to a make-up concert or refund. Sensing we would not have done this without just cause, they filed out in silence.

I went backstage to see Ryan still lying on the top riser. I went up to say goodbye and then directly back to the holding room where the singers were gathered in complete shock. It was not a quiet scene, needless to say. Everyone loved Ryan. I climbed up on a table to address my boys.

I had spent twenty years standing in this very position, yet far from this position. I had spoken at countless memorial services for singers who died of AIDS. I had addressed the chorus about singers who had died. Thanks to my background in the church and my crash course in empathy, I always found the words. But those men were sick. Those men showed signs. There were warning signs—even if only for a few weeks or months.

There was obviously no warning. Here stood my family. And one of our brothers was still lying feet away on the risers where they were to have sung a second half. And, worse, the exact risers they would perform on for two concerts tomorrow—matinee and evening. Without Ryan.

I don't know what I said. All I know is I comforted them as a daddy would comfort a child. I spoke to them with a broken heart too. There is no cliché or pat set of words in that time. I offered none of those. I know I talked about love: the love Ryan had for every one of them and we all had for him. I talked about shock and anger. We were all there. Somehow, the positive lessons growing up in a faith environment came into my mouth. We took the time to hold each other.

Then I asked them if they could do something Herculean: sing the two performances the next day. Through massive waves of tears, they nodded. We decided to meet at noon, singers seated in the audience, and we would have a make-shift time of remembrance before the matinee at 2:30. And we did. And, miracle of all, Ryan's entire family showed up to bask in the warmth of his logical family. We tried to sing. That didn't go so well. We remembered all things Ryan—crazy, zany and heart-wrenching.

We gave those two performances. The chorus sang better than it ever had before. It was quite a tribute to Ryan and to what it is we do.

There is a rather tired cliché that you don't really appreciate something until it is gone. This was never truer than with our dear friend Ryan. Each of us had the feeling that he was "taking care" of just us. He did this with texts mostly, but also emails and phone calls of encouragement—all laced with a biting humor aimed mostly at telling us to get off our butts and get happy! What we didn't know was that he was doing this for everyone he knew. After his death, people started sharing their communication from Ryan. It was nothing short of astounding. Out of this tragedy Ryan's family continued to engage with the chorus.

On a personal note, Ryan and Corianna had a very special relationship. They were the same age—and had quite a text history. Each was more sassy than the other. They egged each other on. In the middle of the night, I called Corianna in Hawaii, where she and Clay and Clara were spending spring break. It was so difficult telling her. But she looked through her own shock and grief and comforted and encouraged her dad. She told me I could do this—when I wasn't sure. Corianna, my rock.

The event made national news. The shock of a singer dying on stage in the middle of a choral concert—and not being allowed to be moved for almost two hours—brought grief and condolences from across the world. Perhaps Ryan knew the hubbub. If he did, he would have been hiding behind his huge sunglasses, a boa around his neck, pursed lips, then a snap and a "YAAAAAASSSSS."

The whole section of the Castro grieved Ryan's loss. Our local Philz coffee was one of Ryan's favorite stops, where he would order a special drink concoction. After he passed, the Philz staff named the drink "the Ryan Nuñez."

We have a scholarship fund to help singers defray the costs of being in the chorus: dues, the purchase of a wardrobe tux, and out-of-town retreats. We call this special fund the Financial Assistance Network, or FAN. In any particular season we help twenty to twenty-five percent of the chorus needing some type of assistance. Running FAN was one of Ryan's responsibilities. After his death, we renamed it Ryan's Fund. Now we can tell every new member who walks through our doors the story of Ryan Nuñez.

Chapter 47

Bubbles

A number of things might pop into your head, maybe bubble bath or bubble-gum, specifically Bubbliscious. Maybe the word brings to mind champagne, or songs such as "I'm Forever Blowing Bubbles" or a favorite of everyone, "Bubble Butt."

Those are good answers, but this is about a man given the name "Bubbles," and the little girl who changed it. It's about this amazing bubble in which we live—seen through the eyes of a child.

When my daughter became "great with child," she decided I couldn't possibly be Papaw or Peepaw, or Meemaw for that matter. I would be called Bubbles! And Corianna got whatever she wanted from her dad.

As Clara grew into early toddlerhood, Bubbles just wasn't to be spoken. There was no way an eighteen-month-old could wrap her articulators around that word. She tried and tried. Corianna badgered her. She got there were two syllables. But "Bubbles," seriously? I am now proudly known as "Bop Bop." I dodged the "Bubbles" bullet. Because of the repetition, my husband became Dan-Dan to Clara.

Corianna took to motherhood as if she had been preparing for it her whole life. Well, she had. She had mothered everyone she ever met. She threw herself into mothering her own daughter. Lucky Clara! They began right off instilling their shared openness with Clara.

By that point, Corianna's dad was doing his thing—conducting the gays—in San Francisco! Talk about guncles! And those guncles adopted her from the very first concert she attended five months after Clara was born. Corianna and Clay took Clara to almost every SFGMC concert for the next seven years.

Instilling the sensibility of San Francisco into Clara was the greatest joy to them. They dragged her all over town to parks, festivals, ferries, and beaches. She marched in most every gay pride parade. Every Easter was marked by a picture with the Sisters of Perpetual Indulgence at the Easter egg hunt. Those pictures generated quite a stir when sent back home.

Clara marched in the women's rights marches. All because Corianna believed so strongly in raising a strong, independent, bright woman, unconsciously molding her in her own image. Corianna was plagued with health issues throughout her adult life. Every day, she dealt with chronic pain from a series of back injuries and surgeries. It never dimmed her bright smile or infectious charm.

Corianna had big plans for Clara: to make her the happiest child on the planet (aided by Clay, Bop Bop, and Dan-Dan), ballet lessons, piano lessons, martial arts, horse-riding camp, and the animal advocacy SPCA camp. Most of all, they gave her the gift of their time and love as they tromped around this beautiful city. While they lived in the Inner Sunset district, Golden Gate Park was her personal playground. She thought everyone had such a yard. Corianna also gave Clara the gift of passion for animals: dogs, cats, a bird, fish, and, briefly, a bearded dragon. The world was her magical menagerie—thanks to her mom and dad. She was now the princess.

In 2019 she started third grade in San Francisco. Those formative years were filled with wonder. Here is a brief list of highlights of Clara's San Francisco. It may be yours as well (at least the lessons therein).

- At seven months Clara attended her first San Francisco Gay Pride Parade. She began marching at age three.
- She has spent every Easter with the Sisters of Perpetual Indulgence and the Hunky Jesus Contest.
- Her favorite television star is not Dora the Explorer, but RuPaul.
- Christmas Eve is spent at church, of course. The church is better known as the Castro Theatre, where she listens to Bop Bop's choir.
- She was the flower girl at her granddads' wedding.
- She helped her father and granddads buy stilettos and makeup and stuff their bras with birdseed in order to raise money for the SFGMC scholarship fund. Her assistance was invaluable in the creation of the D'Lish Triplets. She learned it from watching RuPaul!
- Her favorite color is the rainbow flag. She insisted on dressing as a rainbow last Halloween.
- Her daycare was filled with children from every continent. She has no clue that they are not all the same. She is completely colorblind to the world.
- She looks at the homeless with compassion and empathy, not disdain.

Needless to say, none of that would have happened had her parents and Bop Bop stayed in Dallas. It wouldn't have happened had her dad, a brilliant physician and oncology researcher, and her mom, a pediatric oncology nurse, accepted the offers they have had in cities that provided more compensation (but less magic) for Clara.

What would life have been like for that same Clara Skye Seelig Gustafson in Dallas or Cincinnati or Atlanta? Fewer drag queens (including her father!), no Sisters, a different Easter Jesus, less green (more malls), less diversity, less gay pride, less gay chorus, less rainbow flag, less gay in general, and definitely less fabulosity!

However, Clara is a typical little girl in many ways. She loved *Frozen* more than life itself (Bop Bop is ready to "Let It Go"). She loves her pets and her family and understands that it extends far beyond her nuclear family. As our friend Armistead Maupin says, she loves both her biological and logical families.

What she did not learn is the narrowly defined existence foisted on many of us. She did not grow up with a sense of fear of "other" or "different." There will be no artificial, arbitrary boundaries because someone does not look like her, talk like her, pray like her, or have the luxuries of life she enjoys. She will continue to grow up without bigotry, religious constraints, or judgments.

She's just Clara—like Rice-a-Roni, a San Francisco treat (my little San Francisco treat)! We celebrated a recent birthday right back at "her" church (the Castro Theatre) with the sing-along *Little Mermaid* (lots of children and gays all dressed up). She will no doubt grow up to be a magnificent woman with the indelible imprint of this fabulous city and environment firmly stamped on her very soul.

Please join me in raising a glass of nonalcoholic bubbly in honor of our amazing city, all of its lucky children, and the lucky adults who share in it. May the lessons we learn from the children be ones that we carry throughout our lives. May we now honor and embrace those lessons, even if they took over sixty years to learn. May we walk through our streets with a smile on our faces, savoring our city and delighting in its eccentricities. There is no place on earth like this, especially as seen through eyes wide with wonder, the eyes of Clara Skye. Amen.

Chapter 48

Circle of Life

Sometimes we get all wrapped up in what we do professionally. But what we do does not define us. The most important thing in life is not what we do, but who we are. What I do is defined behind a baton or a curtain or a podium.

I have not managed a human relationship that has lasted "'til death do us part." There is one thing that has been and will be with me until I cross that rainbow bridge. The constant companions in my life, other than music and grandchildren, are dogs. I figure that of my sixty-nine years on this planet, I've had the companionship of a dog at least fifty-nine of them. I paused for college and graduate school. They frowned on dogs in the dorms and in my first set of tiny apartments.

In my early years I grew up with Honey Boy. He was a not-so-bright Cocker Spaniel. I later came to know that the designation "not so bright" is redundant for Cocker Spaniels, with the notable exception of the three Cockers who won the West Minster Kennel Club Dog Show in 1921, 1940, 1941 (same dog), and 1954. Then there was Schatze, the too-smart-for-her-own-good Schipperke. She was adorable and hyper. Both of those were outside dogs. After I left home, Mom and Dad got a Schnauzer and never strayed from that breed. They also moved indoors (the dogs, not my parents).

As soon as I married and had a place to call home, I started making sure we had pets. I always said it was for the kids. In reality, it was as much for me. Of course we had dogs, most notably Miss La De Da. Later, my daughter, Corianna, would laughingly say they should have known I was gay when I chose that name. We had a cat named Kitty, who wandered the southwest Houston neighborhoods. We had obligatory goldfish and betas. Their final swim was down the toilet upon their demise. Embarrassed to say we bought the kids those sad little turtles who had their shells painted. They were not a hearty lot. We "released" them in a local creek. The kids were certain they would thrive there and become Galapagos worthy in no time. There were birds and a lizard or two. (Much later, Corianna gifted her daughter, Clara, with a bearded dragon named Princess Shimmer, who went from eating crickets to frozen field mice as she grew. But I get ahead of myself.)

Then came the three hamsters: Muffy, Fluffy, and Buffy. Around Easter one morning the kids went in to see the trio, only to discover that one of them had killed the other two in a scene to rival *Game of Throne*'s red wedding. They were obviously traumatized. We released the survivor near the same creek as the turtle to fend for his murdering self. Feeling terrible about it, their grandparents, visiting from out of town, decided to replace the hamsters with something completely different—a duck—before leaving to go home. Duckie began life in the very hamster cage that was the scene of the previous murders. Ducks grow quickly. They basically eat and poop. Duckie grew into the laundry basket, the sides of which he soon could look over. He would sit in the front yard while we picked weeds. Then, one sad day, the neighbor dog, apparently having visions of Duck a L'Orange or some other poultry delicacy, ended Duckie's life abruptly.

Our children were very clear on the circle of life from an early age.

After our divorce, my ex-wife did not continue the pet menagerie, but I did. My first rescue occurred once I settled in Dallas with Louis. It also began the habit of changing the names they were given in the various shelters. She came to us as Brittany, which was not going to work for us. We changed her name to Miss Mona Pearl. Miss Mona for the part Dolly Parton played in *Best Little Whorehouse in Texas* and Pearl because her coloring was a little pearlish. She easily became my best friend. She was a beautiful fluffy white and gray mutt. When I started work at the Turtle Creek Chorale, we officed at the Sammons Center for the Arts. The executive director, Joanna St. Angelo, was a dog lover and met Mona the day I rescued her. After introducing her, I was about to leave when Joanna asked, "Where are you going?" I told her I was going to take Mona and leave her home. Joanna said, "You just rescued her from the SPCA; you can't abandon her at home. She's staying here."

And that began the next seventeen years of Mona's "Canine In Residency" program. She was the perfect office dog. She would go to the elevator, wait patiently for someone to come out or in, and ride to other floors—there were only four. She knew other workers had treats in their desks for her. Then, she would work her way back up to my office or someone would call, "Mona's on the first floor." Everyone loved her so much. When she was finally unable to function any longer due to health issues, she went on a weeklong goodbye tour of all the people who loved her, all over Dallas. We had a large gathering of family and friends gather after hours at the vet to hold her—and each other—as she left us. A friend of mine painted a huge portrait that still hangs in my home.

No dog could live up to Mona Pearl. Or so I thought. After Mona left us, my then-partner Shawn and I went down to the SPCA "just to look." There she was, in a little round enclosure like a play pen. She was quiet (most likely on drugs) and adorable. She was nothing like Mona. She was short-haired, more like a beagle but solid blonde. We took her into a little room, and she jumped up in our laps—it was so special (we are fully aware of rescue dog training: make sure to jump in every potential owner's lap, look lovingly into their eyes, and if they indicate they would like such a thing, give them a gentle kiss indicating they made the right choice and should not leave without you).

Well, she was great, but we didn't want to take the first dog they had obviously placed at the front door as a "resist this" temptation. We told the volunteer to put her back. We wanted to shop around to see if there might be something better. When we returned, she was not in her cage. We literally asked the attendant, "Where is *our* dog?" We'd spent all of a half hour with her, and all of a sudden, she was ours. Well, she was in a room with *other* people. We were sure she was not in their lap or giving longing looks and kisses. They made a big mistake; they put her back in the cage to go look around at other choices, just as we had done! Whew. We snatched her up and headed for the checkout stand! She was ours. Her shelter name was Carmel. We named her Carmella.

She made the trip to California with her "brothers" Big Daddy and Little Bear. When Shawn walked the three dogs in San Francisco, people asked for his card, assuming he was a dog walker. We were to learn that few people in San Francisco actually own three dogs. Carmella weathered the breakup of Tim and Shawn and left her brothers behind. It was just me and Carmella for almost a year and a half. She was the best partner in every way. When she met Dan, she pulled out her shelter training and with one jump in his lap and one longing look had him absolutely wrapped around his finger. He said to me, "Having grown up with cats, I never knew I was a dog person, but I am now." Dan ran to the pet store to do the things he thought would win her over. He purchased one of those plastic stick things that helps you propel the tennis ball across the dog park for your dog to fetch. It was awesome. Dan would fling the ball and then go fetch it himself. Carmella had absolutely no interest in "dog things" or exercise. Chip off this dad's block.

Years later, she had a sudden, virulent onset of pancreatitis. It took a week for the condition to turn dire. There was nothing to be done. We decided on a pet hospice company to come to our home, put her to sleep, and then carry her out in her favorite blanket. Dan and I simply could not face it. To our rescue came Corianna. We took our beloved Carmella to her house with a favorite blanket, said wailing goodbyes, and left her. Corianna snuggled her as she left this world we know. So brave, that daughter of mine. Pet hospice in-home euthanasia is such a warm, loving way to say goodbye.

Dan and I were inconsolable. I felt I needed at least six months to properly grieve before looking for another dog. In reality, that lasted about two weeks. I would sit at the end of the sofa, trying to hide my searches from Dan, who was doing the same thing at his end. We just didn't want the other to know. Finally, one day, Dan said, "Are you looking at puppy porn again?" I turned my laptop to show row after row of adorable dogs awaiting homes. From that time on, our puppy porn searches were done together in an open relationship.

Then we took the search out into the various shelters around the Bay Area. Of course, there is always a dog to fall in love with. I've been a consistent monthly donor to the SPCA for years. Corianna and I cried every single time the television ad came on with Sarah McLachlan singing "In the Arms of an Angel." At one of the shelters, a volunteer pulled us aside and told us about Copper's Dream Animal Rescue. It is a group of people who rescue dogs and put them in foster homes instead of shelters. You get to "interview" the foster parent about how the dog really is, rather than the hyperstressed environment of a shelter.

Our search didn't take long. We found the most adorable little girl. We did a meet and greet with her foster mom and fell in love. We named her Grace because she was such a gift to us after Carmella. She is a nine-pound Chihuahua mix. She never barks. Never! She is the cuddliest/laziest dog, and we say we have a stuffed animal that eats and poops. We seriously didn't even notice that she could have been Carmella's twin. Not only does she not bark; she doesn't fetch either. After an initial infection in her first month, she's been a healthy doggy, with one exception. Because she obviously had lived a hard life on the street with illness and malnutrition, our vet recommended a $3,500 procedure of basically painting on faux enamel. It would last one year before needing to repeat. We elected to go with soft food and treats. Happy Grace and happy daddies here.

Grace is now around six years old. The life expectancy of a mixed-breed Chihuahua is between fifteen and twenty years. With some luck, Grace will be with Dan and me for the rest of our lives, happily bouncing between homes. What a gift. When I retire, I will absolutely add to my doggy family.

Much has been written and many movies have been made about the relationship between humans and dogs. All I can say to all of them is a big "Amen" up in there. I have children and grandchildren. They are great, of course. You can't compare the love for them to the love for a dog. They are just different. I am so lucky to get to have both!

Hopefully, my travel log through puppydom has reminded you to do the same, remembering how pets have changed your journey. Life would not be the same without them. There is no unconditional love like it. I have held on to my dogs through my darkest days. They absolutely have a sixth sense and know when you are sick or hurting emotionally. There is nothing quite like having your dog sense your struggle and simply snuggle up next to you—or even put a paw or a nose on your leg as a reminder that they need nothing other than your love and are there for you.

There is a National Dog Day, a National Hug Your Dog Day, and a National Spoil Your Dog Day. I'm voting for all of those to happen every day!

Chapter 49

Heroes and Friends

This is an impossible task. I have made so many incredible friends, seen and unseen.

You Have More Friends Than You Know

We feel, we hear your pain, your fear.
But we're here to say who you are okay.
And you don't have to go through this on your own.
You're not alone.

You have more friends than you know
Some who surround you some you are destined to meet.
You have more love in your life
Don't let go, give it time, take it slow
Those who love you the most may need more time to grow
It's gonna be okay.
You have more friends than you know.

Be brave. Be strong. You are loved. You belong.
Someday soon you will see you are exactly who you're supposed to
be.
And you don't have to go through this on your own,
You're not alone.
You have more friends than you know.

Words and music by Mervyn Warren and Jeff Marx for the It Gets Better
Project. Used by permission.

Many whom I met in 1987 (and since) are still good, loyal friends. And I
certainly have friends who have passed.

When I started with the chorale in 1987, there were Gary Rifkin, Mike
Renquist, Peter Anderson, Craig Gregory, Eve Campbell. Antoine Spencer
and Anne Abritton were my accompanists and right hand, simultaneously, for
seventeen years with TCC.

At a Texas Choral Directors Association workshop in San Antonio in 1995, composer Joseph Martin previewed an incredible work, "The Awakening," the association had commissioned him to write for men's voices. It was incredible. After the session, I asked if he had thought of a mixed chorus version for men and women. "No, I haven't," he said. But recognizing the TCC on my nametag, he changed his tune.

An October concert was planned with the 225 members of the chorale, the 100 members of TWCD, and the 80-piece Southern Methodist University symphony orchestra. I asked if he might be able to get the SATB voicing ready. He said, "I believe I can." And our friend Brandt Adams jumped in to orchestrate it.

When October came, we were at the glorious Meyerson Symphony Center. The stage was packed with musicians. We began singing, and it was a wow! I had the thought, "We are never going to have this opportunity. I'm going to enjoy it." The piece received a huge ovation and has gone on to be one of the best-selling choral pieces ever. It is recorded and can be found at the TCC YouTube channel. Sometime later, Joseph decided to coin a new Italian musical term in honor of the experience. I had taken a piece he intended to come in at around six and a half minutes and made it last for almost nine.

So Mr. Joseph Martin introduces into our musical lexicon, "*Seligarndo.*" The translation is "Milk it for all it's worth." Thanks, Joseph. I do that at every turn!"

There are two friends who fit all three categories: composer, friend and hero.

Andrew Lippa

Friends would say, "You should get Andrew Lippa to write something for you." Jeez, people. I don't actually have him on speed dial—or any dial for that matter. But I kept hearing it. One day I got a call from my friend Emily Crocker at Hal Leonard Corporation. She was the head of music publishing. "Hey, Tim, I have a new TTBB (men's chorus) arrangement that has been submitted," she said. "Would you take a look and see if it is something you all might sing?"

"Sure, what is it?" I asked.

She said, "It's a song called 'Moving Toward the Darkness' from *The Addams Family.*"

"Catchy title," I said. "Who wrote it?"

She said "Andrew Lippa." I was one degree of separation. She shared his email address, saying Andrew is "the greatest guy." I felt like Barbra Streisand about to meet Nicky Arnstein.

I sent an email: "Dear sir, we at SFGMC are embarking on a project honoring Harvey Milk on the 35th anniversary of his death. We are planning to create a 60-minute piece. Each movement will be composed by a different composer. I know how very busy you are, but wonder if you might consider writing a piece for the larger work."

In barely enough time for him to read it, I got an email back: "Call me." He gave me his phone number. I fell out of my chair. I was about to talk to Nicky Arnstein.

When I called, Andrew said this is the piece he had been called to do for years. He said, "I'm a New York Jew and forty-eight. Harvey was a New York Jew and died when he was forty-eight. I have much more in common that I will share with you later. No, I will not write one piece for you. I will write the whole work."

And he did. It is a sixty-minute oratorio titled *I Am Harvey Milk*. And it is one of the most amazing works I have ever heard. Harvey's love song to San Francisco is a heart-stopper. As is the big disco number "Friday Night in the Castro." We had a hit on our hands.

Andrew and Laura Benanti sang the lead roles. It has been performed all over, including the Lincoln Center; the Kennedy Center, with Kristin Chenoweth singing the lead alongside Andrew; and at the GALA Festival in Denver, with 700 singers and full orchestra. It is a WOW!

We became friends as it traveled about and shared our deepest thoughts. When Dan and I got married, Andrew officiated—on a stage with Jake Heggie; Curt Branom, Lisa Vroman, Breanna Sinclairé (the first trans opera soprano); the James Graham dance troupe; and the SFGMC. At the wedding, Andrew played his own composition, "Dance with the Storm."

When we announced the Lavender Pen Tour, Andrew called. So thrilled and proud. "What can I do for you?"

Tim, without a pause: "Arrange 'Dance with the Storm' for us to sing on tour."

He did. We did. And now it opens our documentary, *Gay Chorus Deep South*.

Dance with the Storm

Now the quiet has returned.
Have I learned what I must learn?
Can I see the power around me?
But I've lost the strength to move.

I have struggled with the rain
Felt the sting of every pain
Do I take a step and follow?
Do I trust that all is well?

If I dance with the storm,
I'll be safe in your arms.
I can see past tomorrow
I can feel all your love.

I can run
I can rise
I can face all good-byes
If I dance with the storm

Now the sun has broken thru,
And I know what I must do
I must walk into the sunlight
I must brave the darkest night.

I can run
I can rise
I can face all good-byes
If I dance with the storm

Words and music by Andrew Lippa. Used by permission.

Later, we commissioned Andrew for another huge piece, *Unbreakable*. It tells mostly unknown stories of gay life for the last century. It is now traveling the country. In one of the most moving moments, the chorus sings "41." In 1981 the *New York Times* wrote the very first story of forty-one homosexuals diagnosed with cancer. In the song the chorus chants from one to forty-one, leaving not a dry eye in a five-mile radius.

We've loved each other through life changes. He is my friend and my hero.

Stephen Schwartz

In 2013 we did a concert with the amazing Stephen Schwartz. It was another Nicky Arnstein moment. I actually picked him up at SFO. He came down the escalator, smiled, and gave me a hug. We went to lunch at the gorgeous Palace Hotel and left as besties. I found out one of his besties is Andrew Lippa. Of course.

In the planning phase he mentioned that he had been so very moved by the courage demonstrated by the It Gets Better movement. I connected him with founder Dan Savage, and they worked together to create an incredible piece based on the stories of people who had been displaced. People who had found themselves on the street. The piece, "Testimony," can be found on YouTube and has been performed all over the world.

Perhaps the most shocking and wonderful moment of my life happened a few years ago when Stephen received the well-deserved Lifetime Achievement Award at the Tony's. In his speech he said he wanted to thank three people. I was one. Later, he said "Testimony" was the first real activist song he had ever written and it had opened the door to a new part of his consciousness and future work.

He went on to curate "Tyler's *Suite*" for us. It is based on Tyler Clementi, the young Rutgers student who took his life by jumping off the George Washington Bridge when he was outed online by his roommate.

The first part of "Testimony" uses the words of young people who have found themselves on the edge of life, considering taking the final step to ending it all. These are the words Dan Savage shared from the It Gets Better vaults and that Stephen set to music:

Testimony

I don't want to be like this
I don't want to be who I am
Every day that I don't change
I blame myself
I am not trying hard enough

When they find out
No one will love me
I'll lose my family
And all of my friends

I am impersonating the person I show as me
I'm an imposter
I am a spy behind enemy lines
I pack my feelings so deep inside me
They turn to concrete

Every night I ask God to end my life
(I am an abomination)

God take this away or take me away...
Today I'm going to hang myself, Today I'm going to slit my wrists,
*   Today I'm going to jump off my building...*
I'm trapped, I'm stuck, I'm trapped...
Take me away, take me away, take me away...

Hang in, hang on
Wait just a little longer
Hang in, hang on

I know it now, I know it now
If I had made myself not exist
There is so much that I would have missed...

I would have missed more wonders than I knew could be.
So many friends with jokes and laughter not to mention the joy of
*   living in authenticity.*
Sometimes I cry. Life can still be hard, but there is no part of me
*   still crying "Hide me."*
I have been brave. I grew and so did those around me.
Now look what a life I've earned.
It gets more than better. It gets amazing and astounding.

If I could reach my past, I'd tell him what I've learned.
I was more loved than I dared to know there were open arms I
*   could not see*
And when I die, and when it's my time to go,
I want to come back as me.

Words and music by Stephen Schwartz. Used by permission.

The chorus cries every time we sing this. It has taken half a lifetime for me to be able to embrace and believe those words for myself.

Looking back, there was no one burning bush by the side of the road telling me it would be okay. It was one step at a time. It was one person holding out a hand or speaking a kind word. It was the moment I could pay child support and look in the mirror with pride that I had lived to tell my story.

Every person who recovers from a devastating event looks back with surprise at the resiliency of the human spirit. That's hindsight. It never feels that way while you are in the middle of it. Just know that if you can find the strength to do one thing, take one step, ask for help, the light at the end of the tunnel will brighten until it shines like a spotlight on a fabulous actor at the end of a play. That would be you.

If you just read this and did not see your name, it was obviously my editor's red pen. Blame her!

Chapter 50

AIDS Memorial

When I arrived in San Francisco in 2011 to wave my arms at the gays, one of my first stops was the National AIDS Memorial Grove (NAMG). I was completely overwhelmed with its beauty and serenity. I looked for where the chorus's name was listed. It was nowhere to be found. It had been discussed many times but simply had not come to fruition. They were busy and didn't have the money.

From that point I was like a dog with a bone. I started thinking of having the chorus's name engraved in the Circle of Friends. While amazing, it just didn't seem right. I then considered an engraved boulder. Nope. Then I shifted my thinking to a bench. Getting warmer. Imagining something in the $25,000 range. All of this time we were working with the amazing folks at the NAMG to make sure everything would be just right when the chorus entered the grove.

On many trips to Hawaii, we would drive to the North Shore to visit the Valley of Temples. Our specific destination was the stunningly beautiful Byodo-In Buddhist Temple. On the gorgeous grounds stands a large pagoda-like structure with a huge gong. You would approach the structure, pull back the enormous gong, and, as the gong sounded, you would speak the name of someone you had lost. Their name would then be lofted into the world on the sound vibrations. It is one of the most beautiful experiences I have had. I have been there often and made a video recording of it.

In 2011 I first spoke to John Cunningham, executive director of the National AIDS Memorial, about my dream to include such an aural component to the memorial we would one day build. He said, "That's lovely. But the Golden Gate Park and the parks department would never allow that. We have no such thing in the Grove." John didn't know me well. He certainly didn't know I was already researching chimes from a foundry in the United Kingdom. One day in 2017, John called and said, "Bring your team over; we have something to show you." We went thinking it would be John and maybe one other. Nope, it was the whole Grove crew. They said, "Come with us."

They walked us up the path by the brook and up some stairs until we reached the top of the Grove and were looking at the DeYoung Museum. Surrounded by beautiful oak trees, it is directly opposite the Circle of Friends on the other end. We looked puzzled. We were hoping to find something down in the Grove, with a chime.

"This can be yours to build your own site," said John. "We would love this to be the chorus's memorial. And we would love it if you would then open it up to other arts groups who have had members die."

We were overwhelmed. It was more than we ever dreamed. Then John, never wanting to show his hand completely, said, "But there's more. Because of the location of the site (not being down in the Grove), the chime has been approved." It was more than I could take. My dream was going to come true.

However, there was only one potential obstacle: It would cost us $125,000 to excavate and build the memorial, not including the chime. I said, "Done deal," as I picked our staff members from off the ground.

On October 27, 2017, on the chorus's fortieth birthday weekend, we dedicated the memorial to the 300 singers we had lost. More than that, it is dedicated to all artists everywhere. We built a beautiful Artists Portal for all. And for the first time in Grove history, the memorial includes an eight-foot-long emperor chime. The tradition of striking a gong or a bell in meditation and memory has been a part of rituals across the globe and for centuries. Now it is at the NAMG.

So here we are, having come full circle. I learned of this horrible plague up close and personal from Jeff, sitting twenty feet in front of me, literally singing for his life. I learned about this plague from my sweet friend John. I learned about the stigma firsthand when I came out as HIV-positive. I am still learning what a community can do to make a difference in our world.

There is one more full-circle moment. The night before the memorial groundbreaking, the chorus performed *When We No Longer Touch* at St. Ignatius Catholic Church. In 1981 this church refused to allow SFGMC to perform there, in spite of a fully executed contract to rent the space. The chorus sued the Catholic diocese—and won. It was twenty-seven years after the world premiere of the requiem. Of course we sang at the memorial dedication too. It was the most beautiful music ever heard, except for the fact that weeping does horrible things to your voice. It didn't matter. We were surrounded by angels who filled in as needed.

The SFGMC's own Artists Portal will stand in memory of those we have lost as well as the warriors in the fight. There are more than eighty LGBTQ choruses from around the world already engraved in the stonework. It really belongs to everyone.

At the Artists Portal, these words are etched: "Take each moment as a gift and give it back again," from the song "Never Ever."

Never Ever

Never will there be a moment, ever.
When we all will be together, ever.
Never such a moment.
Never will we look around and see these faces, all these faces.
Never will we hear these voices. Never ever hear this sound.
No, never, will we have that first time, or this last time or just this
*   time*
Never get to live our lives all over. Never.
Oh! Life will take us where it will. New beginnings, ends.
Take each moment as a gift.
Give it back again.

Words and music by Robert Seeley. Used by permission.

Chapter 51

Lavender Pen Tour and Reverend Jim Dant

The 2016 election brought shock and horror. The chorus's fortieth anniversary was coming up. We were planning a big trip to China—the first gay men's chorus to visit. Two days after the election, Steve Huffines, our board chair at the time, called to say, "Why are we spending the money on a tour to China when we are needed at home? How about a tour of the U.S. South, where we can encourage our brothers and sisters and spread some love?"

Everyone loved the idea. We looked for the states that, at that point, had the most egregious discriminatory anti-everything laws on the books: Mississippi and North Carolina (Alabama recently joined that hall of shame).

We called the tour company: "Hi, we'd like to swap out Beijing for Birmingham, Alabama, and Shanghai for Charlotte." You could hear the phone hit the floor.

"In our sixty-four years of producing concert tours, we have never done a domestic tour, only international. Let me consult my staff."

The amazing owner of ACFEA Tour Consultants, Hugh Davies, called back within hours. "The staff voted to do it! They are 100 percent behind the mission, and all want to go!" We had a tour company to help with all the details: buses, hotels, meals, performance venues. We could not have done it without them and their meticulous planning.

The next task was to choose a name for the tour. Early on, my choice was "Priscilla Meets Dixie." I had the graphics ready: a big tour bus—full of the gays—with a huge stiletto-heel shoe on the top from which would fly two flags billowing in the wind—a Confederate flag and a rainbow flag. My idea was vetoed. Others were suggested that were way worse: "The Love Bus," "Movin' on Down...to the South."

One day as we were throwing out names, someone said, "The Lavender Pen Tour." It would honor our gay patron saint, Harvey Milk. In 1977 he presented San Francisco mayor George Moscone a lavender pen to sign the nation's strictest antidiscrimination bill. It was replicated all over the nation. The chorus's first public performance was for the tens of thousands of people gathered at the candlelight vigil for Harvey and George.

I am from what most people would consider the South. Many in the Deep South, however, do not include Texas in their little coven of states; it is considered its own country. In recent years we Texans are not all that sad to be left out of their ignominious clan. Nonetheless, my upbringing, taste in food, and accent after too many margaritas are all most definitely Southern. I WAS COMIN' HOME! Or close to home.

Off we went with just under 300 singers to the previously mentioned three states as well as to Tennessee and South Carolina. We were joined by the Oakland Interfaith Gospel Choir, under the direction of Terrence Kelly. We made twenty-five appearances in eight days. Six buses, a number of vans, and a security detail, including a police escort in many of the cities. It was for us gargantuan, ginormous, momentous, and life-changing (I'm running out of superlatives).

The preparation was incredible. The singers raised the money for their trip. The organization raised the money for all the things that make a gigantic tour like this work, including renting huge performance halls, marketing, and outreach. We did all of this so we could leave the $100,000 we raised in the five states where we sang.

When word got out that the SFGMC and the Oakland Interfaith Gospel Choir were heading to the South, we had a number of people approach us wanting to document it. We listened to their vision for the project and, of course, the specific story they wanted to tell. The production team we picked was a real gift, because they had the backing of our incredible San Francisco-based company Airbnb. Their mission aligned with ours, and it was a match made in heaven from the start.

Immediately upon announcing the tour, we had three film entities vying for the opportunity to document the tour. We selected a documentary team led by director David Charles and executive producer Bud Johnston (I still like "Priscilla Meets Dixie"—maybe we can create a sequel of bloopers and outtakes).

During the tour I was allowed to share some of my story. Soon, with the great help of ACFEA, we began firming up and renting the largest performance halls in each city in each of the five states. For each state we had a captain (an SFGMC singer raised in that state) to help with details on the ground and mostly to help connect with local groups we could aid along the way.

The captain for South Carolina was Erwin Barron, a Presbyterian minister who was very familiar with the landscape of the state. One day, he called, very excited, and said, "I've heard First Baptist Church in Greenville, South

Carolina, might host our concert there." I thought but did not say, "You have run upon some really great stuff at your local dispensary!"

"The pastor's name is Dr. Jim Dant," he said. "You should email him."

I thought, "Dear Lord, haven't I had enough rejection at the hands of the Baptists?" He did not answer. We're what one might call "estranged" at the moment.

I got Jim's email address and sent what must have been a completely strange note: "I've heard through the grapevine we might be able to sing at your church. This tour is really awesome, and we'll act real nice. I know how to do that." I offered a little of my own Baptist pedigree...blah, awkward, blah.

To my surprise he wrote back: "Why don't we visit on the phone?" Oh, dear. It looks like he wants to let us down over the phone rather than via an email. So I picked up the phone and dialed the number for a Baptist church, and they put me through to Pastor Dant.

We talked for a bit, and then he said, "I'll have to bring this to my deacons. It will probably take a few weeks before we can get back to you." Uh huh. Blame it on the deacons. I had!

That was a Friday. On Sunday afternoon Pastor Dant called and said he did not want to wait until the next deacons' meeting. So he called an emergency meeting immediately after Sunday morning worship (I'm sure this got the deacons' attention—that could only mean he was resigning). Well, he wanted me to know that the deacons voted unanimously to open their church and hearts to these wonderful people.

I still didn't believe it. I had to see it for myself. We would spend a day at the church on our advance tour in August. It is very hot in the South, but it was much hotter than the temperature indicated as we pulled up to this absolutely gorgeous church and sprawling campus.

We pulled up to the front of the church, and a man came out immediately. Dressed casually, he could have been a part of the maintenance team for all we knew. He stood in the middle doorway. With a smile as big as Dallas (okay, Greenville), he simply opened his arms and walked forward. He embraced every one of the fifteen travelers and invited us in as if it were his home and we were long-lost relatives (which we were—very long-lost relatives).

I sat with Jim. He was the real deal. Every person working in the church that day knew who we were there and what we were "up to." We were basically judging them as to whether or not we thought they were sincere. Every single person we met—staff or volunteer—greeted us with openness and love, not the judgment we brought in the door. It was incredible.

What happened at the concert is the thing of legends. The huge sanctuary was packed. We got a standing ovation just for walking in. They hadn't even heard us sing, but they wanted so badly for us to know how much they loved us. A whole bunch of gay prodigal sons were coming home.

We wept. They wept. I wept the most. It had been thirty-three years since I had stood on the podium of a Baptist church, leading a choir, and testifying! And there was Jim Dant, the real deal. The church had received scores of hate calls. There was a bomb threat, resulting in a bomb sweep while we, unknowing, ate the best fried chicken ever (we had had fried chicken at every stop!).

At the opening of the concert, Jim addressed his congregation that was overflowing the sanctuary. He said, "We've been getting a lot of calls at the church the last month or so." (Laughter.) "I just want to answer two questions: No, I am not gay." (More laughter as he stood there in a pink dress shirt.) "And the second one that many of the callers want to know is why? Why are you doing this?" And I simply say, "Because I am a follower of Christ." (Drop the mic.)

We sang our hearts out. Easy to do because we'd already put them on the floor with the first note.

Jim has become a friend of mine and of the chorus. The next thing they did was fly their youth choir to San Francisco to sing with us on World AIDS Day at the NAMG! Most importantly, Jim takes my calls. He answers my emails. He helped me through some very difficult relationship issues. Never once did he use Scripture, knowing that was not where I am. I consider Jim as a dear friend— and I have to say that Rev. Dr. Jim Dant has become my pastor.

When I got home, Clay jokingly asked if I had gotten saved in Greenville. He was afraid he had lost one of the members of the informal agnostic/atheist group we had formed. I assured him that my name that was written in the Lamb's Book of Life at the age of six and then surely erased sometime after 1986 has not been engraved there again. Not to worry.

I was invited to come back to First Baptist, Greenville, to do a choir workshop and direct them on Sunday morning in the big church. That all went swimmingly, so to speak. The service opened with baptism. Jim stepped into the baptismal font—the largest one I have ever seen. Six-year-old Corianna would have had a blast.

Following Jim was a handsome black man. This sent all kinds of alarms. I don't think I had ever seen a black man baptized—ever. I thought that was remarkable, and I was so happy. Then a man walked to the pulpit. This was extra strange. Jim was the only one who was supposed to speak. Everyone was focused on this man. He said simply, "It is with great joy that I stand here today sharing in the baptism of my HUSBAND."

I have no words, because I cry every time I recall that moment—Tim's ugly cry, from the podium! I didn't care.

Because it was September, next they invited all the children who were starting school to come forward with their parents to get a special blessing. Another blessing? They had already had the biggest blessing of all. They went to church on a normal, warm Sunday morning. And their "normal" was to see a beautiful black man baptized, with his husband standing alongside him.

First Baptist, Greenville, was one of the churches that helped to found the Southern Baptist Convention. It must be the end times.

Here's what I tell people: Let's say you have been estranged from your family for years. They do not accept you for who you are, so you do not go to their home, even for holidays to which you may or may not have been invited. One year, your momma reaches out and invites you specifically to Thanksgiving. You meet her halfway and accept. It's awkward, to say the least. Is all hell going to break loose? Is this an intervention? These were all things I thought when I walked into First Baptist, Greenville.

The door opens, and, like Jim Dant, your momma is standing there in her favorite apron, with arms thrown wide open welcoming you home! And Dad and the other family members are behind her, smiling. No judgment. No "Well, we haven't seen you in years."

You step through the door, still not trusting. And the smell of the turkey and pecan pie (no one can bake like momma) hits you like a ton of bricks. This brings up good memories, smells, tastes, and hugs. All of a sudden, you remember only the good things. The bad memories were dropped at the door.

That was my visit to First Baptist, Greenville. I remember the smell, the music, and the happy faces. I was completely comfortable. It felt like sinking into that tacky Snuggie someone gifted me last year. It was good. It flooded my soul.

Just like Thanksgiving, we delighted in the wonderful things from our memory. Were the disagreements and arguments still there at the front door? Of course. Did they still vote for Trump? Duh.

When I went to church, the good memories flooded back. It was healing. When I move back to my real life, will pain still be there? Of course. I mean, seriously, I wrote a book about it. But it is tempered by new experiences of old memories.

Often I've been asked how I have personally reconciled having been thoroughly indoctrinated into one of the most conservative of all religions and being a BOG (a Big Ole Gay). The most important response is that there is no magic remedy and not one answer fits all.

I really do appreciate churches that are willing to affirm our community and attempt to bring religion and gay together. Personally, I don't need religion and gay to merge. I am fine with the concept of "separation of church and Tim." But that is my own path.

Each of us has a responsibility to examine what place organized religion holds in our lives. As for the separation of church and gays, that is a personal decision. As for separation of church and state, that is not a choice. We must resist. We must fight to maintain that.

I have often said that recovery from growing up Southern Baptist (insert Mormon, Catholic, Pentecostal, etc.) is a twenty-four-step program (twelve steps are not enough). You must rinse and repeat often. Even then, I don't believe we are ever fully released from its grip. It comes back on you when you least expect it, often in debilitating ways. This all depends on how religion was delivered to you when you were growing up, as a required course or an elective.

There are many parts of the religion of our past that remind us of moments when we felt something so deeply that we weep: an organ playing, a choir, a prayer, the "smells and bells" (for you high-church folks), Mormon funeral potatoes, Lutheran one dish, Baptist green bean casserole, Pentecostal green Jell-O mold, and Catholic bratwurst and beer.

Sometimes, in moments of weakness, I think maybe it wasn't that bad. Then I am reminded that it was. At my brother's funeral, the pastor used the scripture "In my Father's house are many mansions. I go to prepare a place for you." Steve suffered debilitating and excruciating brain cancer for four years. It was supposed to be six months.

The explanation of this lengthy suffering was that his mansion just wasn't ready yet. I wanted to jump up and scream out, "Of course it wasn't ready. All the interior decorators are in hell. The three straight ones who made it to heaven are busy, busy."

Or "Are you kidding me? God wasn't able to get his mansion ready? Aren't there carpenters standing by (like your Son)? You allowed him and his family to suffer three and a half years while the pearly gates were polished?" Not a God with whom I need to cut deals. He's apparently really bad with deadlines.

As I said, Rev. Dant is now my pastor. There will be more phone calls, no doubt. I never thought I'd have a pastor after all the negative Christian counselors I had. When I question our relationship, I will always remember the "Why?" and his answer: "Because I am a follower of Christ. And he taught us to love, not hate" And, Jim Dant, because Christ put you in the right place at the right time to help your brother, this brother, in his time of need.

Chapter 52

The Death Train

Mom

By 2011 Mom's health continued to be an increasing challenge. She was eighty-eight. Dad was eighty-six and pretty much her full-time caregiver. It was wearing on him. He was no longer able to lift her.

Her doctor said, "You need a hospital bed in your house." She was adamant that she did not want that. I stepped in and told her, "Yes, that is what you must do. Dad cannot get you out of your normal queen-of-everything bed." She acquiesced because I was the one asking her. The schedule was set for delivery—the following Monday. On Saturday her friend Sue came over for a voice lesson. She had long stopped charging, but on Sue's way out, Mom hollered, "Just leave the check on the counter!" She was still laughing and making fun.

Monday morning, a hospital bed was moved into their home and her room. Mom was up and perky, sitting in her wheelchair watching all of this happen and listening. She had her hair gussied up, and she painted her fingernails bright red and put on a full "Texas" face of makeup. Finally, she put on jewelry that she loved. These things were all hugely important to her.

That afternoon, the home healthcare company suggested that they have a nurse stay overnight since it was the first night with the hospital bed. They had never had a healthcare person in the house overnight before. Dad said Mom, as usual, joked with the nurses and the handymen setting up the hospital bed.

Monday evening, he helped her get ready for bed. The nurse stayed with her. At 2:00 a.m., the nurse woke my dad and said he should come into the bedroom. Dad said a few minutes later she smiled and took her last breath. Because my family has a fabulous sense of humor, everyone delighted in teasing me that I had killed my mother by insisting she get the bed. Her final smile was to me: "I told you I wasn't going to sleep in a hospital bed and mess up my hair!"

The days that followed were difficult and complicated. You know, it's the South: a long visitation with an open casket, a funeral with an open casket at Mom and Dad's Baptist church, and a graveside service followed by lunch for family and friends.

The funeral was amazing. Hundreds of people traveled great distances to attend. The congregation was filled with preachers and ministers of music and singers and friends from the Sunday school class Dad taught for over thirty-five years. My brother and I were "in charge" of the service. We both spoke, and we sang in tribute to Mom. Five of her students also sang, as did the whole congregation.

We laughed a lot over the many stories of her great humor. It was truly amazing to hear the impact of her life on generations of musicians. The service ended with Mom singing "The Lord's Prayer" (from one of her recordings). She did not just teach voice; she taught life. The impact of her life is something wonderful to recognize and an inspiration to all of us.

Brother

In 2013 Steve was diagnosed with stage 4 glioma brain cancer. He had two surgeries back to back and an estimated life expectancy of six months. I went there for the first surgery. He was lucky to be at M. D. Anderson, one of the best cancer hospitals in the world.

The morning of the surgery, lots of church folks filled the waiting room. This was the first time in thirty years I had seen people from Houston's First Baptist and Second Baptist churches. It was awkward. I was sitting by Dad, who was in a wheelchair. They would come over to say hello to the elder Dr. Seelig and turn and walk off, having totally ignored the younger Dr. Seelig. After a handful of those, Dad looked at me and asked, "Has this been what it's like?" I replied, "Yes, sir." He was so shocked and angry that he scooted his wheelchair behind a partition to stop the one-sided reception line.

Our family was in the waiting area with others we didn't know—people in complete trauma because their loved one was in surgery for some kind of cancer. In marches one of the biggest, loudest Texas women I have ever seen—sporting big, platinum-blonde hair and wearing loud Texas clothes and big jewels. She was yelling so that all, including the entire waiting room of strangers, could hear her tale.

She said, "Listen, you all. We just need to pray for Steve" (never mind all the other people who may or may not need prayers for their loved one). "I was across the way with a friend who had a brain tumor just like Steve's, right in the middle of his head."

She pointed with huge animated gestures to the middle of the rat's nest that had been teased within an inch of its life. "They did an MRI to find her tumor right in the middle. We prayed for her, and by the time they wheeled her across the street and into surgery, that tumor had moved to the side for easier removal."

She paused—not to take a breath, but for her dramatic story to soak in. Then came the big finale, with each statement one dynamic louder: "You know, they tell me brain tumors are just like toothpaste." Jaws dropped. "Prayer can make it just like squirting a tube of toothpaste. It will squirt right over to the side of your head." Amen.

What do you say to that? We do wish it had been true. It was not. Steve fought and was funny to the end.

Bonita was his Florence Nightingale. She stood by his side during the worst of days. He lived almost four more years. There were 2,000 attendees at his funeral at Second Baptist Church., and it was live-streamed.

Dad

Two years before Mom died in September 2011, she and Dad had moved to a beautiful senior apartment complex in Fort Worth. Their apartment was on the third floor with a big window. Mom got to watch the sun set over her home—West Texas.

Dad stayed in the apartment, sleeping in his La-Z-Boy recliner. For the first time in his life, he was able to chew his tobacco out in the open! He could spit to his heart's content. Dad had been sleeping in his recliner for probably fifteen years. He never used the small daybed in "his" room. He had lots of Baptist friends at the same facility. Many were in his early bird Sunday school class. So when Mom passed, he still had plenty of friends around.

Dad became much more communicative and showed moments of humor we had not seen. On one of my trips to Fort Worth, he asked if we could go the cemetery and see Mom's grave and his plot next to hers in the Garden of Love. Dad was weak and using a cane. Once we got to the grave site, he had a fit. "That plot is not big enough for me." I said, "Dad, it was big enough for Mom." He was having none of it. In an instant he was lying on the ground on his plot with his tombstone above his head. I took pictures. We laughed until we cried. A rare moment.

Dad's health declined. He fell and fractured his hip. Surgery and six months of rehab at a place called Broadway Plaza. He actually called it hell. One day short of the six months that insurance covered, "Hell Home" sent Dad home. He wasn't physically ready, but he also didn't want to pay cold cash for one more day. Because of his fall, we moved him to a lovely apartment in assisted living. He did not like one thing about it—mostly the food, which was actually delicious.

While in hell, the staff had ignored the melanoma growing on the top of his head. When we visited from time to time, we would ask them about it. "Oh, it's just a sore. We just keep it moist with Vaseline." By the time he got his walking papers and an appointment with his plastic surgeon, it had grown to the size of a silver dollar and was obviously deep. He was rushed to two back-to-back Mohs surgeries to prepare for the big one. By this time the lesion was baseball-size. We thought the surgery would be his end. Nope. He had that thing removed. It had grown into his skull, but he bounced back. The surgeon had done an amazing job taking skin from his leg and moving it up to the top of his head where the hole was.

The bionic man recovered. The only lingering issue was that he looked like he had had a face lift. He looked at least fifteen years younger. But as the days went by, he fell into depression. He rarely got out of his chair. Every day, he asked God to take him home to be with Virginia. He prayed that prayer on the day God took Corianna instead.

Dad was a meticulous control-freak in every aspect of his life. He had been planning his funeral for probably twenty years. He kept changing out pallbearers as they died. He had seen a full-color, six-panel brochure he wanted distributed at his funeral. He actually copied the pictures he chose and taped them on a trifold piece of paper so we would know exactly the way he wanted the six panels to be laid out.

I got a graphic designer friend, Alejandro, to do the layout just as Dad had wanted it. I gave it to him in the envelope Dad had given me. In a day or two, Alejandro said he needed to drop by the office. Alejandro showed me what he had done. He said, "I think there is something you should know. Your dad has a lovely cover. He has two pages of his work: pics with Billy Graham and so on. He has two pages of his horses and one of his wife and him. He has the text written for each block describing the pictures."

I said, "This is lovely."

Alejandro looked at me, puzzled, "Tim, there is no mention of his family or his children or grandchildren."

I was not surprised. I shared that news with Dad. He had no retort. He took one of the work pages and filled it in with one panel covering two sons and their spouses, eight grandchildren, and two great-grandchildren. All on *one* panel. Thanks, Alejandro, for the save.

Dad's world began to shrink. We did the best to be near him. I called him every day for the seven years following Mom's death. But he was lonely. In his mind the hours between someone calling or checking in grew longer every day.

He had an infection on his foot that he told no one about until an attendant downstairs noticed blood coming out of his shoe. He was rushed to the hospital, where they began large doses of antibiotics. He did not get better. He jokingly said, "I didn't think God was going to take me home over a bunion!"

Because I held his advance medical directive, the doctor in Fort Worth called: "We've ordered the helicopter to fly your dad downtown, where we have better facilities for infections and can intubate him before he goes." I relayed only a bit about Dad's asking every day to "go home," not in a helicopter. He was ready for his bunion to take him. I asked them to cancel the intubation and the helicopter ride and to keep Dad comfortable. He passed within an hour.

Dad had a Seelig funeral: a big church affair with lots of music and preachers. Dan, my husband, came to Dallas. One of the best moments for us was walking down the aisle and back up the aisle holding hands. I think Dad would have been proud.

One more story: When my brother died, Dad wanted to purchase burial plots near his and Mom's. The funeral home sent a salesperson to go through the papers and get the money. In Dad's words, she was a lovely Hispanic woman. She asked if he had any other children.

Dad said, "Yes, a son." She asked what he did, to which Dad replied, "He conducts the San Francisco Gay Men's Chorus," just as proud as one could be. The woman paused a moment and started crying. When she regained her composure, she said, "I have a daughter who has just told me she is a lesbian, and I have no one to talk to. We are very religious. What do I do?" Dad took her hand, looked her in the eyes, and said, "Just don't build walls."

Dad didn't join PFLAG, but I know there were many moments like these when he ministered to friends and strangers and never told me. I wish he had.

Chapter 53

Someone Told Her She Was Broken, and It Stuck

Strong Enough

So be careful the doors that you open
With the words that you speak
Or the people who will hold them
Cause long ago, someone told me I was broken
And it stuck
I've tried to pull the words away
But my hands are never strong enough

Have you ever read a shadow sentence
That filled your spirit with shame
People can call you by so many things
That aren't your true name
And yes, we all get angry
And yes, we all get tired
But just remember what leaves your heart
Can fuel or fade someone else's fire
So be careful...

Now when a hurting soul hurts you
They're only passing their pain
They probably don't know your story
And they don't know your true name
That you are loved and forgiven
That you are good at your core
That you are stronger now because of
The shadowlands you walked through before
So be careful...

Oh, just takes a second to feel it
But oh, it can take a lifetime to heal it

Oh, just takes a second to feel
But oh, it can take a lifetime to heal

And long ago someone told me I was broken
And it stuck
I've tried to pull the words away
But my hands are never strong enough
But I know my true name, I know my true name
Long ago, someone told me I was broken
But I know my true name...

Words and music by Bobby Jo Valentine. Used by permission.

Bobby Jo Valentine's lyric says it all: "Someone told me I was broken and it stuck." Some people report being told they can't sing, so they never try. Some are told they're not artistic, and they put away all dreams of painting or even drawing.

That was not what Corianna heard. Somewhere along her childhood path, she was made to feel fat. We come from a long line of hearty stock. But it was not just being "hearty" that pierced her heart early and tortured her the rest of her life. The wound delivered when she was young would never heal.

When she visited Dallas as a preteen and teen, she felt beautiful. There were no scales, no judging eyes, no watching what she ate. She felt suspended—and weightless—around her guncles.

Her weight fluctuated a lot when she was a teenager. This is not unusual, of course. But it was something she thought about every day. She thought she was just never thin enough. Being overweight somehow showed a deficit in her upbringing. She suffered the barbs out loud and those delivered silently with just a disapproving look. When she did lose weight, she was constantly met with, "Oh, you look so good" (meaning *thin*).

Once she got her nursing degree, she was immediately on top of the world. She was also thin. When she had lost a lot of weight after college, her breasts lost a proportionate amount of weight. We coinvested in a new set of breasts, and she was a knockout. Whatever would make her feel good about herself, I was in.

It wasn't long until she got the wanderlust again. She applied to a traveling nurse company and told them she wanted to be assigned to Hawaii. They laughed until she told them she was a pediatric oncology nurse. She was pretty much on the next flight to Honolulu. She did her six-month contract and then another.

After that, she was ready to come home. She didn't stay long before she was off again to one of the best hospitals around, Cincinnati Children's. Then she came home again. We thought it a little strange that she couldn't sit still. She had an amazing job at Dallas Children's Hospital whenever she was in Dallas.

I had just landed in Hawaii for a Christmas trip when I got a phone call from Corianna. She told me she had just checked herself into rehab for an eating disorder. Of course I wanted to get on the next plane, but there was no reason to come home because she was checked in for at least twenty-eight days. Patients were not allowed visitors for the first week or so. We cried on the phone. It broke my heart. I went to Barnes & Noble and bought every book I could find on eating disorders.

She was bulimic. As much as she could remember, she had purged every day for the last nine years. No one knew. Her demons were torturing her every single day.

I got home in time for the "regrets and remembrance" family counseling session. Her mom was not there. Corianna shared from the bottom of her soul. She let out the anger and despair she had felt when I left. She had felt betrayed. It felt like I had ripped the support rug out from under her. There was no substitution for that. In her mind she had been left alone and defenseless. It broke my heart. But when it was over, we were loving each other unconditionally.

We started planning her wedding. She and Clay chose San Francisco. We checked out the Cliff House, then the Red and White fleet for a cruise under the Golden Gate Bridge. Then we started trying to work out the seating chart. They eloped to St. Lucia. We were left to throw the biggest luau in Dallas!

Then Clay got a job in what he considered utopia. That's when I accepted an interim conducting gig with the SFGMC, so I got to spend every Monday night with them for five months.

Then they were pregnant, and I was applying for the full-time position at SFGMC. Clara was born in November; I started my job in January! We were together again—with an extra Seelig! Clay was incredible accepting that Corianna's dad was her best friend and they would talk or text every day (or more often).

Corianna's health suffered. Her back was ruined by years of taking care of—and picking up—the children she served, who were up to eighteen years old. And she also had to catch parents when they fainted bedside.

The medical recommendation was anterior and posterior spinal fusion. She had gained weight. She had to have gastric bypass before she could qualify for the surgery. It was brutal. But even more brutal was the spinal fusion. The pain-management folks did their best. She was addicted. It took her almost a year to wean herself from the pain medications.

Even Clay and Corianna, both healthcare professionals, were caught off-guard by the severity of the effects. She couldn't do her beloved nursing, saving the children as best she could. She was depressed and distraught about this and about how her illnesses—physical and emotional—were affecting Clara. She just couldn't do the things she thought a mom should do. She obviously couldn't lift Clara, but there were so many other activities in and out of school that she was simply unable to do. This really wore on her emotionally.

She went through some truly dark, frightening periods, but she assured all of us that she would not harm herself. She would never leave Clara (or us). We loved her every minute. Clara loved her every minute. She took care of her mommy and loved her just the way she was. She had seven years to make Clara know she was loved beyond words and that she was beautiful just as she was.

Chapter 54

Death Comes Knocking Again

Despite what seemed a lifetime of loss and natural disasters, the grim reaper was not quite finished with me yet. On October 18, 2018, Clay, Clara, and Corianna went to a school function. Everything seemed fine. When they got home, Corianna said her back was hurting. She went downstairs to lie down.

Clay and Clara watched a movie. When Clay went downstairs, Corianna was unresponsive. He called 911 and then me and Dan. We were only ten minutes away. We rushed over. Clay and I sat on the bed in their bedroom as seven paramedics attempted every way possible to revive her, continuing CPR for an entire hour. They were committed to bringing back to life this beautiful young mother who lay before us.

Dan was upstairs trying to keep seven-year-old Clara occupied playing games and reading, as far away as possible from what was happening downstairs. Corianna had a very faint pulse, which gave us a tiny specter of hope. They put her in an ambulance as Clay and I stood in the dark street, holding each other. Clay went in the ambulance with her to the hospital. Dan and I took Clara to our house to get her settled in. Then I went to the hospital. Corianna had been pronounced dead by the time I got there. I did not know that when I arrived.

I was met by the ER trauma doctor, a nurse, and a social worker. They led me to a room where we all sat down. But I just wanted to see Clay and Corianna. First, the doctor spoke: "I just want you to know we tried everything we possibly could to save Corianna." I stared at him as if he was confused.

The social worker said, "We are here to help you in any way we can." Then stupid Tim kicked in, the large-and-in-charge leader/minister Tim, "Big Tim" some call him. I actually said, "I'm gay. I am the conductor of the San Francisco Gay Men's Chorus. I have buried countless friends through the years. I am not unfamiliar with grief."

All three looked at me like I had a horn growing out of my head. I looked back at them, not understanding why that hadn't fixed it. They let it sit for a moment, professionals to the core. Then the social worker leaned forward, knees almost touching knees, and in the most loving but firm way looked right in my eyes and said simply, "But they weren't your daughter."

A house fell on my heart. All hope was smashed. That final verdict pulled every rug I had weaved out from under me. Every layer of protection I had built around my own pain over the years was ripped away, all at once. There is no describing the pain. I needed to see Clay and Corianna. They felt that and took me to where they had put her.

My façade shattered. Clay held me. We cried really loud. The nurse asked us to move inside the room. We were in the ER. There were living patients in the rooms experiencing their own trauma. We were not helping them.

There she was, as beautiful as she had ever been, breathtakingly beautiful. They allowed us to stay for a bit and then asked us to go outside while they made some preparations. Clay and I went out to the plaza. We began calling family and close friends. "Corianna just died." "What happened?" "We don't know." It would be seven months until a final toxicology report.

When we returned to the ER, they had wrapped her like that baby in swaddling clothes and placed a rose on her chest. She looked so beautiful. Clay stood on one side and I on the other. We said stupid stuff about what we were supposed to do next. Then we would cry.

Then we talked about getting Clara to school in a few hours and getting her lunch made at home and her backpack. Then we cried about her lunch. The strawberries at home were too ripe.

The nurse said we could stay as long as we wanted. We did. I have no idea how long that was, but I know very clearly that I couldn't leave her, my beautiful, troubled, pained little girl.

Clay went home to clean the tornado of needles, packages of medication, clothes that had been ripped off of her for access during CPR. I went home to get Clara. We dropped by Corianna's house (what had been Corianna's house) to get Clara some school clothes, lunch, and her backpack. She never asked a single question about what had happened. I took her to school, smiling, and allowed her to have whatever the hell she wanted for breakfast on the way. Kid's hot chocolate and madeleines from Starbucks. Who needed to think about protein at that moment?

The day floated by. Clay's sister had taken the first flight from Dallas, and his dad flew in from Florida. We had the worst lunch ever. I'm pretty sure it was pizza, but robots were eating it. Clay had called the child psychologist at the hospital where he and Corianna both worked in the pediatric oncology area. He had said, "Ask Clara what she remembered from the night before.

Then ask her if she remembered when their dog Bosco died." He gave us a few other questions to help her get in touch with her feelings and to get her to open up.

I brought Clara home from school and, surprise, there were Clay, Clay's sister, and Clay's dad. Clay said to Clara, "Peanut, let's go to your room for a minute." She followed silently. Clay asked the first question. Clara's answer, "Did Mommy pass?" Clay was shocked. Not knowing what to do, he asked the second question. With more insistence that she get an answer to her question, Clara simply looked at Clay and asked again, "Did Mommy pass?"

When he said yes, the dam broke. From the living room, all sitting in silence staring at the floor, we heard a little heart break. Oh, that sound. Two hearts breaking together. There would never be a mommy or a wife. Nor would there be a daughter or a sister for Judson.

She left us that night. She had been in such physical and emotional pain. She wanted to be the best mother ever. And she was. But it was not the way television shows portray it. She couldn't do the physical activities with Clara she wanted desperately to do. Clara couldn't have cared less. She and her mommy watched every episode of *RuPaul's Drag Race*. What mommy does that?

Ultimately, the toxicology report revealed her death was caused by a mix of prescription drugs she had been taking to try to ease the pain, physical and emotional, we knew was there, though not to what extent.

The funeral home had to set up cremation. We requested, against their usual practice, to see her one more time. They suggested bringing a quilt since she would be on a gurney with just a sheet. Judson went to her favorite store, Target, and got one in her favorite color: ocean blue. They took it first and covered her with it.

When she was ready, they led us down the stairs. She never looked more beautiful. Her face was calm, with a slight smile as if she had just told us a stupid joke or shocked us by adding the F-word. The five of us (Clay, Judson, her beloved cousin John Mark, Dan, and me) wept and wept and held each other. And we kissed her. Then we laughed. It came out of us just like it did every time Corianna was around. We told some stories and laughed until we cried some more. This was male bonding at its best. She would be happy at that.

I left for rehearsal; it was a Monday, for heaven's sake! Five days later, I conducted the SFGMC in its fortieth anniversary concert, a requiem based on the stages of grief. It was live-streamed across the world. The concert was dedicated to Corianna.

Judson, who had stopped coming to my rehearsals in his mid-teens, came to rehearsal that night with all 250 men singing their hearts out. Midway through, he walked up to me at the podium and asked if he could say something. He had never said a word to any chorus I'd led since he was eight.

Now thirty-nine, he took the mic comfortably and confidently and spoke for four minutes: "Thank you for being my dad's family all these years. I haven't always understood. But I do now. I know you will do your best to take care of him and Clara. Thank you. I feel like family now too."

Two weeks after Corianna died, we rented a big theater where SFGMC gives most of it concerts. We made it Hawaiian themed. "All attendees must wear aloha wear. Anyone wearing black will be denied admittance," read the invitation.

The stage was set with blowup palm trees and flowers. Guests were met by drag queens—lots of them—giving out cheap leis. This was the way Clay and Corianna's wedding luau had started. We knew she would have loved it. We had some beautiful video from that luau only ten years before. Friends took over the management of the event, adding a stunning video of the last ten years. Because Clara had literally grown up with the Sisters of Perpetual Indulgence, they were there en masse to bring a spiritual quality to the event.

There were approximately 1,000 in attendance. Corianna was so loved and respected. There were speakers from the hospital—doctors and nurses. The other speakers were Judson, John Mark, Clay, and myself. It was totally irreverent and bawdy—as Corianna would have wanted. Clara sat with us in the front row. She smiled and laughed at her mommy and her antics and at herself as a baby.

Then SFGMC surrounded the audience and sang "I Shall Miss Loving You" from *When We No Longer Touch*. Once again, as we have experienced throughout our lives, the music hit its mark. Clara fell apart. She crawled over to her daddy's lap, and they lost it together. They would spend the months ahead trying to find it, trying to put together all the pieces of the puzzle that had blown apart.

We call "Gameboard God" the idea that some uncaring being is sitting in front of a gameboard with all of us on it as his little pawns (or queens). And on October 18, "Gameboard God" thought, "Today, I'll take Corianna, forty-one years old, mother and wife, and knock her off the board. I'll pass up John Seelig, who is ninety-three and has been asking me to take him off the board every single day for the last four-plus years. Let's leave him. That will be fun." This concept is not something we acknowledge as a possibility.

In memory of Corianna Seelig Gustafson

Great Flowing River

Whenever the shadows grow too long
And the day fades into night,
When voices can no longer join the song—
We need only remember their light.

Whether they lived to wise and old,
Or taken far too soon,
Their light lingers on in sun's warm gold,
In the soft, silver glow of the moon.

Hold on to the joy,
Hold on to the laughter,
Hold on to the spirit of youth!
Come and step into
The great flowing river
Of love, of forever, of truth!

The river continues its journey far;
Each spirit joins the flow,
Each one born in the heart of a star,
With power far more than we know.

Those we have lost—they linger still,
So set aside all pain;
For the river surrounds, enfolds, until
We mingle with starlight again!

Hold on to the joy,
Hold on to the laughter,
Hold on to the spirit of youth!
Come and step into
The great flowing river
Of love, of forever, of truth!

Music by James Eakin. Lyrics by Charles Anthony Silvestri. Used by permission.

Chapter 55

Happy Thanksgiving... Corianna's in Hell

I tell the following not to disrespect Dad, but to give a small window into the religion in which many others and I were raised. It falls into the "You can't make this stuff up" category.

Corianna died on October 18, 2018. We were heading into the holiday season. For sixty years when I would call home, Dad would immediately say, "Here's your mother," assuming I did not want to talk to him. He was correct. Mom and I had everything in common and loved our girl talk. After Mom died, I began calling Dad almost every single day for six years. You know what it's like if you start that and then miss a day.

In the weeks following Corianna's death, I apparently had some kind of brain seizure and thought for a moment, "Dad's a minister. He has preached and taught Sunday school for over sixty years. Perhaps he would have a word of help or encouragement for his son."

One morning, I was feeling especially down. I called Dad and told him I was having a hard time discerning the line between grief and self-pity. I felt it was my task to make everyone else feel better about the horrific situation we found ourselves in. I told him how wonderful my chorus had been and the hundreds and hundreds of encouraging responses on Facebook.

Apparently, that was what set his heart racing. He launched into a tirade about my sharing my grief with others. His first sentence was, "You're a big boy now." He actually used those words. I was sixty-eight!

He told me I was to bear my grief alone. If you have to tell someone, tell Dan, but no one else. "You don't need to be putting that on Facebook. This is for you to work through on your own with the Lord's help."

Thanks, Dad. Too late on the Facebook part, or my monthly column in the local gay paper, or the fact that the SFGMC concert nine days after her death was dedicated to her and live-streamed literally around the world. Oopsie-daisy.

It saddened me that keeping up appearances and the Seelig brand was more important than his son's mental health. Apparently, "You're a minister, you don't get to be human" was still his mantra at ninety-three.

I was truly taken aback at his words. They brought up every possible emotion about a loveless relationship with him. I waited about a week before calling him again. I was missing Corianna so badly. His "comforting" words for me were, "You need to stop this crying and be happy that Corianna is now in heaven with your mother and brother and that they are all pain free with glorified bodies." My head exploded.

I told him as gently as I could that Corianna had a different belief about where she would be when she passed. She and I had talked about it often. I told him that Clay shared our belief as well. He was a bit taken aback, though he should not have been. I guess he wanted to go over the answers to the quiz yet again.

In a pretty accusatory voice he said, "Well, where did she think she would be?" I gently repeated what I had just told him. We all believe that we are scattered into the universe. We believe that we are a part of those who have come before and will live on in many ways. I continued to say that I absolutely knew that Corianna was in the water and waves she adored so much. She was in the beauty of Northern California, where she truly felt at home.

He could take it no more. He interrupted with, "So you don't believe in heaven?"

"No, Dad. And you've known since I was a teenager that I could not reconcile the existence of a hell with my best friend, Alan Hamill."

"So you don't believe in God?" he asked.

"Not as you define him. Definitely not. I told you and Mom that around 1990, when you backed me up against the refrigerator and asked these very same questions."

He seemed speechless. We ended the call worlds apart in our belief systems.

Why is it always Thanksgiving? The big family gathering took place at my niece's house outside Dallas. I did not attend. Dad was the guest of honor, as most of the eighteen attendees were somehow related to him or friends of the limbs on his family tree. Judson, Juliana, and Eden represented my progeny. The others were all kids, grandkids, and friends on my brother's side.

This recounting was delivered by my son, with seventeen other witnesses scattered throughout the house. At one point Dad raised his voice and said, "Everyone come in here. I have an announcement to make." He waited until all were there—including the little ones bringing up the rear. Everyone was a little excited. Perhaps Dad had decided to give each of us a twenty-dollar bill.

Maybe he had an announcement about his retirement fund (perhaps most of it was not going to the Baptists after all). Maybe he had a new girlfriend.

Everyone listened to the patriarch. As best as I can piece it together, it wasn't a long announcement, but it was succinct: "There is someone who is not with us this year (stating the obvious). I just need to tell you that Corianna is in hell. She didn't believe in God, and neither does Clay or Tim."

Apparently, several in the congregation started softly crying. He went on: "None of you have taken care of me. Alfredo (the van driver at the old folks' home) has treated me better than any of you."

More tears from the attendees, and some shock. By this time anyone not related by blood had fled to the comfort of football on the large-screen television—turning up the sound!

Then came, "Pass the gravy."

I have no comment.

Chapter 56

Gay Chorus Deep South

When the chorus made the decision to go on tour to the South, we chose a film company with the backing of Airbnb to go along. The film crew was everywhere, filming everything. They were up in our grill for eight days. When we came home, they kept filming!

Almost a year later, they hired one of the best editors anywhere, Jeff Gilbert. In January 2018 they handed him approximately 300 hours of film and basically said, "Call us when you have watched it all!" He watched and called back, blown away by what he experienced.

The hard work began. By August they were testing it with private screenings for people in Los Angeles who didn't know anything about the chorus or the tour. They helped David hone in on some stories, asked for more of some, less of others. Bottom line, they all loved it.

They finished the film, and finally showed it to our executive director, Chris Verdugo, and me. We were blown away. On the plane back to San Francisco, Chris and I wrote a few notes for the production team, just small, helpful things. We sent them. The message came back like when you text your deepest love to someone, finally opening your heart.

They responded, "K. Thanks." That's what we got, along with the knowledge that "they've got this." Some might say I am a controlling person (yes, I "hear" those unison eyes rolling), but I'll just say that turning over the complete creative process to others is not my favorite thing to do. But it paid off this time, aided by the fact that I had no choice. We did have one moment of input.

Thus began the process of entering the film into film festivals. It had its world premiere at the Tribeca Film Festival in New York City. We took eighty singers, who performed following the credits and again the next day at the Stonewall Inn. It won the Audience Favorite Documentary award—a really big deal.

A week later it won Audience Favorite Documentary in Zurich, with a two-minute standing ovation by the normally stoic Swiss. To round out a trio, it won Audience Favorite in Edmonton, Canada. Three countries! It went on to a total of about 100 film festivals. I had the very difficult task of representing the chorus at the festivals in Honolulu and Vancouver, B.C. (am I hearing those eye rolls again?).

"What now?" you ask. Well, we will all see. It has been purchased by MTV—amazing! The message of love, hope, and reconciliation is touching countless people in places we never imagined.

Chapter 57

The Mormons and Me

In 2018 we received an email in the office from a person named Arthur: "The Mormon Tabernacle Choir (MoTab) is coming to the Bay Area on tour. They'll be in Mountain View on Monday, June 25. Sometimes they invite members of local choruses to join them for their afternoon rehearsal. Wouldn't it be great if they invited the gay men's chorus?"

We thought for sure we were being punked. But he gave his full name and a phone number. It was too outrageous not to give him a call. He knew someone who knew someone. Not to distrust Arthur, but we needed to hear from someone in the MoTab ranks officially.

The invitation was indeed real from both the publicist and the general manager. My laptop did not burst into flames. That's when the real discussion began internally. It included our members who had left the Mormon religion—mostly not of their own accord. They are former Mormons (FoMos).

We were puzzled by the invitation coming from one of the most anti-gay religions anywhere. While the Mormons have not been physically abusive as some religions are, they have been guilty of emotional and psychological abuse, resulting in countless broken hearts and lives. It was not lost on us that in a week when families were being forcibly separated at our borders, the same has happened to thousands of families at the hand of the Mormon Church.

What should we do with this invitation? We went directly to our own mission statement for the answer. It says we build community, inspire activism, and foster compassion through music. The answer was clear: All three of these pillars would be served by accepting the invitation.

We had three requirements:
1. We would be introduced as the San Francisco GAY Men's Chorus.
2. We would wear SFGMC t-shirts: bright purple with a rainbow swoop and the words "Love Can Build a Bridge" (designed by a FoMo).
3. We would bring our own photographer (also a FoMo).

The answer was yes to all, and there were no caveats or contingencies placed on us in return. The t-shirt we wore said it all. Building bridges is an interesting thing. In the best case, it begins on both sides of the chasm. In this case, regardless of their motivation, they had laid the first brick on their side. We responded by laying the first brick on our side.

We were clear from the outset that the bridge would not be completed anytime soon, but how could we not do our part? We felt that we were doing this for all of our LGBTQ brothers and sisters for whom this might give just a glimmer of hope.

They allowed us to bring twenty-five singers. Nine of those were FoMos. There are more who couldn't make the Monday afternoon event. By the way, recovering Baptists are greatly outnumbered by FoMos in the chorus. The remaining slots were filled on a first-come, first-served basis.

On Saturday morning, June 23, as I was getting ready for two shows, the phone rang. It was Scott, the MoTab general manager. I was fully expecting, "We're so sorry. It's not going to work out for Monday." Rather, his message stopped me in my tracks: "We are excited about having your singers. We also wondered if you would be our guest conductor for the encore?"

I said, "You mean at the rehearsal?"

He said, "No, at the performance."

Lordy, Lordy. I picked myself up off the floor as he told me I would conduct "This Land Is Your Land, This Land Is My Land." Could it get any better? They would also present me with a special commemorative baton.

On Monday our little gaggle o' gays arrived at the enormous Shoreline Amphitheater. The massive Mormon chorus and orchestra were already on stage. Within five minutes I was approached by three large men in dark suits and ties (even though it was a very sunny, warm day in the South Bay). I was a little frightened, but they were smiling and introduced themselves as elders, shook my hand, and told me how delighted they were that we were there. Seriously, they seemed delighted.

As the rehearsal began, our singers joined MoTab on stage. They stood out in their bright purple/rainbow swoop, colored hair, and beards. I thought they were going to sing one song, but they stayed as much as an hour. One of our singers was actually placed by his cousin who sings in MoTab. You can't make this up. The MoTab singers were absolutely gracious. Of course they were; they are Mormons. But everyone sensed that it was not just "Mormon nice," but something deeper.

Toward the end of the rehearsal, I was escorted to the stage. I wasn't invited to say anything, but that has never stopped me. I called out the big rainbow elephant in the room. I thanked them for putting aside our differences long enough to make music together. It was a moment I will never forget. I can't, since it was filmed!

After rehearsal and before the concert, Dan and I were invited to a VIP reception, where we were introduced to many of the Mormon elders. We introduced ourselves as husbands to everyone we met. That was fun!

Then the concert began. The chorus of 300 and the 60-piece orchestra performed flawlessly. Not a note or a hair or a pearl necklace out of place (only the women donned pearls—another difference from SFGMC).

During intermission, Dan and I visited with one of the elders. We asked how the decision had been made to make this happen. Apparently, it had been discussed among the MoTab folks first. They were coming to the Bay Area. It was Pride month. They knew of SFGMC's reputation, and I am an acquaintance of their conductor. They decided to send the idea up the hierarchical flagpole.

They did not expect a yes. It finally landed in the Quorum of the Twelve Apostles. To everyone's surprise, they said agreed. That explained some of the overt friendliness. They had been given their blessing by the highest body of the Latter-day Saints (LDS) church. The gays and the church had found a small plot of land where we could coexist—a land called music.

Then it was time. The announcer told the audience, "Tonight's guest conductor is the artistic director of the San Francisco Gay Men's Chorus." An immediate cheer went up from the audience and continued as I made my way to the podium and took a bow. (Film of this is also on our Facebook page.)

Everyone knew something significant was happening. The song went well. I got my baton. The ovation from the audience—and the choir and orchestra—was overwhelming.

The choir then sang their traditional blessing that they always end with, a cappella. The powers that be asked that I turn and allow the choir to sing it to me and to the audience. "God be with you 'til we meet again." There were many tears among the choir members (okay, and a few from me).

Not everyone thinks it's a good idea to have taken this foray into "enemy" territory. Some think it is folly—or worse—for us to have accepted the invitation. I have explained our reasons: It's about building bridges. It's what we do. We have accepted an invitation from Baptists. We've accepted an invitation from Catholics. These kinds of things are the only way we are going to continue to keep the rights for which we have all fought so hard.

We are not foolish. The current use, by some, of "religious freedom" is a thinly veiled attempt to limit our rights and to disavow our very existence. We will sing on, wherever invited.

As a group, we are far from being Christian. But there is irony in that the gay men's chorus actually demonstrates biblical truths, such as forgiveness and loving your neighbor. It was the right thing for us. We hope it was the right thing for them.

Chapter 58

107 Valencia. National LGBTQ Center for the Arts

Most residents of San Francisco hail from somewhere else. Since its founding, the Bay Area has been a landing spot for people from all over the world. It is one of the things that makes our city great. Almost nine years ago, I joined the incoming throngs.

I arrived in San Francisco ready to start a new job, in a new city, in a new state. I soon encountered the biggest challenge to everyone who moves here: housing. I moved here with a partner and three dogs. We relocated from a 4,000-square-foot loft/studio in Texas to an 800-square-foot apartment with a roommate. Then there was the challenge of getting a residential parking sticker!

The second shock was the real estate needs of my new employer, the SFGMC. The chorus has struggled for its entire existence to find suitable rehearsal, office, performance, and storage spaces. Although 1978 was an exciting year for the chorus to launch, it was also the beginning of forty years of wandering in the real estate wilderness of the Bay Area. In my nine years, the chorus rehearsed at multiple venues: the Kanbar Center at 44 Page, First Unitarian Church, Mission High School, First Congregational Church, Everett Middle School, Bahai Center at 170 Valencia St., Academy of Art at Union Square, Laguna Honda Hospital, among others.

The chorus had experienced the same itinerant status over the decades prior to my arrival. Singers, not having read the fine print, consistently showed up at the wrong place for rehearsals. The only permanent address was our U-Haul storage unit.

Office space was no better. The chorus has had offices from people's homes to over the "Sit and Spin" laundromat, to what is now the current Soul Cycle place at Castro and 18th Street. When I arrived, the administrative offices were at the LGBTQ Center, and the artistic offices were across from Costco on Harrison Street. We eventually moved into the Harrison St. space before being evicted to make room for a startup. We landed in a fabulous spot in the Castro above Wasabi Bistro.

We travel the entire Bay Area for our approximate sixty appearances a year. The trek through the forty-year wilderness continued. As gays, many of us have experienced displacement in our own lives. This may have been the result of coming out or the searching for a logical family and a place that felt like home. Or it may have come from people moving from place to place just to locate affordable housing—or a new set of roommates. Regardless, it leaves a mark. There is an insecurity that comes with not putting down roots, not knowing exactly where you might live next or how soon that might come. That is how it has been with SFGMC. It has had no place to call home for all of these years.

The Bahai Center fit our needs like a glove, but three years into our happy rehearsal life, the owners put it on the market. We knew we couldn't afford such a building, even though it was perfect for us. Interestingly enough, the Bahai folks really wanted us to have it. We shared a core value in our mission.

We began to dream of what it would be like to be in one place. Executive director Chris Verdugo and I first visited with the realtor and then our board. As the months went by, we kept dreaming and talking. One of our founding members, Terry Chan, who had been present at the very first rehearsal and had followed the chorus to every venue, knew firsthand the impact a permanent home would have. Six months into doing our due diligence, Terry and his partner, Ed, made an anchor donation toward the project. With their generous gift, there was no turning back.

After another seven months of contracts, inspections, appraisals, insurance, zoning, and more, on the night of January 14, 2018, board chair Keith Pepper stood before the chorus—in the rehearsal hall at the Bahai Center—and announced that the chorus had "bought the building you are sitting in." You would have thought the 49ers had just won the Super Bowl. Our dream was coming true! It was as if forty years of pent-up angst was suddenly released and 300 bottles of champagne popped all at once. There were cheers and tears and hugs.

Terry was there to share the story of his grandfather coming to this country as an immigrant and building a life for his family. He spoke of how his family had taught him the importance of hard work and of giving. And he spoke of the day he remembers too well in 1978 when, as a young gay man, he saw a flyer for a new gay chorus on a telephone pole in the Castro. He joined. He was there at the chorus's first public appearance at the candlelight vigil for George Moscone and Harvey Milk. And he was there every step of the way since.

As the thirteen months of planning progressed, the chorus completed a five-year strategic plan. We were encouraged to dream big and to look at the impact of the chorus not just locally, but nationally and internationally. Our thoughts turned to what we could do with the magnificent resource that would make a larger impact on the world outside of the Bay Area.

Following months of preparation, study, and planning, we announced the formation of the National Center for LGBTQ Performing Arts—also to be housed at 170 Valencia Street. We are beginning this with five major initiatives to make the dream a reality. The center will be a "national home for arts and activism."

We are thrilled to dream of what will be, and grateful to every person who has had a part in supporting the chorus across the years. We stand on the shoulders of those who have gone before and who no longer have a voice to join in our song.

Our permanent address has changed from U-Haul storage to 170 Valencia Street. We have found our promised land. And we are moving in!

Chapter 59

Four Grand Girls

If we only knew then what we know now.

About ten years ago, Corianna and I were having dinner, as we often did. We were more the people who believed giving a random gift because it's Tuesday, or because the sun was shining, than a special occasion.

It was "the night before Christmas." Though not needing to buy anything, we went to Dallas's posh Northpark Mall just to watch the crazy, desperate people grab last-minute gifts the receiver would absolutely not need or appreciate. Men mostly chose the path of least resistance, meaning the first thing on sale at the entrance of every store: perfume.

When the stores closed, we then treated ourselves to dinner at the Italian eatery, Maggiano's. We always shared a huge Italian chopped salad, spaghetti and meatballs, and cheesy garlic bread. During our conversation, which was always colorful and hilarious and irreverent, she tossed out a totally random question: "If I ever get married, or even if I don't, do you think I should have children?"

I was unprepared for that and answered too quickly and rather emphatically, "No, I don't." Her face told me everything I needed to know about how very wrong my answer was.

My answer was based on three things:

1. She was an independent thing. I wasn't sure she would ever settle down or anyone could put up with her idiosyncrasies.
2. The state of the world was on a slippery slope with war and guns and Bushes.
3. I knew all too well the pain parents can rain on their children—unwittingly for the most part.

I shared my three reasons. Her face told me those didn't matter. She didn't really want to know what I felt other than to take joy in the fact she was even thinking about such a step. She had met Clay. Things were different. I was shocked she was even talking children because she hadn't been too warm to the idea before. After all, she spent her days and sometimes nights taking care of children. Wasn't that enough?

There was no real reason for me saying she shouldn't have children. Maybe I didn't want to share her with anyone else. Thank goodness Clay was thrilled Corianna had a BFF in the shape of her dad. But that was one of the bigger mistakes I made with my kids. And she never let me live it down. We would be out doing something amazing with Clara, and she would look at me mischievously and say, "Hey Dad, remember that Christmas Eve?" We would die laughing and revel even more in the miracle that was/is Clara.

Clay and Corianna got married, moved to San Francisco, and started their jobs. And I guess they were doing that thing that results in children (the one topic Corianna and I did not discuss). When she became pregnant, it was a thrill. She was married to a hell of a guy. She was settled and felt in her soul she had the love and resources to bring a child into the world.

I was over the moon. I was going to have a grandchild. Corianna also loved being pregnant, even though her body rebelled. Within an hour of Clara Skye launching out into the world, I was there. Since both parents worked at UCSF, they were given a penthouse suite with two sides of enormous windows looking out over Golden Gate Park and Bridge. There were a few bumps, but "knowing what we know now," the birth went swimmingly.

After two days in the penthouse, the hospital needed it for a paying customer. Corianna and Clara had to stay a little longer. It was like going from upstairs to downstairs at Downton Abbey.

Clara retained the coveted position of only grandchild for five years. Then Judson and Juliana got pregnant. Eden Mae arrived, and Bop Bop had two apples—one for each eye. She was, just like Clara, gorgeous. And the two could not be more different.

Obviously, I got to see Clara more than Eden since I lived only fifteen minutes from Clara and Eden was in Dallas. Life just ticked along as they grew. Then the unthinkable happened, and all of our lives changed forever.

In the midst of our shared grief following Corianna's death in spring 2019, some incredible news came. Judson and Juliana had been doing fertility work. It was to be their last attempt; they had two viable eggs—yep, twins!

Nothing is ever easy for this clan. The babies were due January 2, 2020. In August, Juliana's water broke, and she was confined to the hospital to keep the buns in the oven as long as possible. She was a trooper. The girls—yes, both girls—were born October 10, 2019, at twenty-eight weeks. They were each in the two-pound range. Of course, in the first days, it was touch and go.

I can't imagine what Judson and Juliana were going through those days. I can tell you that the entire family was divided into two camps. The Baptist camp was praying hard. As we say, the babies needed the prayers, and they needed the practice. The other camp was praying too, just different prayers. And we were also doing a little threatening and yelling at God, if she exists, that this was too much! Just the specter of the worst happening was too much to embrace.

The days trudged by, with each bringing a small victory. The girls were covered in tubes, needles in appendages, and bandages. We didn't have much idea what they even looked like. One by one, the intrusive yet life-giving tubes and needles were removed. Little people began emerging. Of course, Judson and Juliana were spending countless hours at the hospital standing watch and guard, putting their hands to the incubator so the babies could at least feel their touch. Family was in to help Eden, who had to wonder what was up and why her babies weren't coming home.

The first days, the babies did not have a name. They were Baby A and Baby B. On day four, armed with a little more security and better news around the girls' future, Judson and Juliana decided it was time they no longer carried those monikers. They gathered themselves up, armed with a smartphone, and made a video to each of them.

Baby A was the stronger one. They actually took her out of her incubator and placed her on Judson's chest. The top of her head and eyes were covered with a lovely white toque that would have been very fashionable on the slopes. Her face was covered with medical accoutrements. Judson looked down at the tiny, two-pound baby and spoke to her heart: *"Baby girl, your name is Ivy Hope. Ivy is a plant that grows from a little tiny thing and grows into a strong plant that takes over everything around it. Hope because you already bring your mommy and me such hope and joy."*

Then Judson kneeled and spoke to Baby B through the round opening on the side of the incubator. Baby B was having the harder time. But Judson and Juliana wanted to give them both their names. He said: *"Baby girl, we are ready to tell you your name. Your name is Cora Rose. Cora is after your Aunt Corianna. It's half of her name. I know that she would pick you because she was always one to choose the underdog to take care of. Rose is because it is a beautiful flower, but also prickly, and you are a little fighter. And your great-grandmother's name is Rose. We love you Cora Rose."*

On my very short trip to Dallas in November, I had planned to look through a window and see the girls for the first time. However, they had prepared a

"Bop Bop special pass." Instead of a window, they walked me right into the NICU room. I said, "I can't hold them," as they prepped me to do just that.

I sat down and was handed Cora Rose. I fell in love immediately. Yet my heart broke into pieces as it struck me that the best pediatric nurse in the world, Corianna, would never meet her namesake. I gathered myself a little, and, Lord, if they didn't hand me another one! Ivy Hope. Cue the waterworks. The girls are so precious, but I wanted Corianna to be there to push me out of the way and tell the nurses how they were doing everything wrong. I held them for more than an hour.

I was telling Ivy Hope the story about how her aunt tried to name me Bubbles, but had to settle for Bop Bop because Clara couldn't say Bubbles. In the middle of the story, Ivy gave me a huge yawn and fell asleep, which was followed by a little sharing about Bop Bop's stories and she would need to learn to stay awake for those.

Judson was not there for the visit (thank goodness), but later the nurses in NICU said, "Having now met your Dad, we know why you cry all the time!" Then it was home to see Eden Mae, who thrills my soul.

I immediately planned a trip to see them all again on the day after Christmas. On Christmas morning Judson and Juliana went to see their girls at the hospital and were met by excited nurses who said, "Merry Christmas! You can take Ivy home today!"

She was in the hospital seventy-five days. Cora "got" to stay a little longer. There are, indeed, Christmas miracles. Eden loves Ivy, as do the dogs.

Clara and Clay visited as well, so we had four beautifully grand girls in one city. We didn't get them all together in one place, because Cora was still in the hospital. There is little joy such as this. To think I could have somehow messed the whole thing up had Corianna taken my advice that night over spaghetti.

As a parent who has now lost a child, I look back and think, "If I knew then what I know now." How different would my answer have been to Corianna? Would I still say, "You don't want to bring a child into this world because of the possible pain?" Hell no. I think of the joy Corianna brought me for forty-one years. Oh, there was pain, but mostly extravagant joy.

We all know to make sure that Corianna remains alive in their minds and hearts. We will tell the four precious ones about a woman who loved more deeply than anyone I have ever known. We would be so lucky if we could instill some of that in the four grand girls. Each will grow in their own space and time.

They will be as different as one star from another. We can just hope that they all shine like their Aunt Corianna.

I just hope they look at Bop Bop and see a man full of love, who wouldn't sing karaoke with them—not *Frozen* or *Frozen 2*. As Eden says, "Bop Bop, you're silly!"

Maybe I wish I were still called Corianna's first choice of a name for me: Bubbles.

Chapter 60

My Conclusions

Looking back over my life, it is hard to imagine actually riding the roller coaster named Tim. I think some refunds might be in order. In hindsight it was filled with more thrills and chills than any one human should have. Exhilaration. Laughter. Pain.

I get to look back as if the roller coaster had a rearview mirror and take such pride and joy in all the twists and turns. Even the scary ones. When all is said and done, it has been a life of joy.

I got all strapped in for the ride on January 10, 1951, and the journey began. It chugged uphill, passing all the things you have read about. Often, it dropped in a death-defying plunge. Some did not defy death and fell out along the way.

But the roller coaster continued. Up and down. Round and round. A couple times it did a loop-de-loop that keeps the stomach unsettled. As the coaster slowed, the ups and downs were supposed to get smaller. Oops. But it does eventually slow down and give time to reflect on why the hell you ever got on it in the first place.

We don't choose our own parents, who strap us in at the beginning of the ride. As exciting as it was, this is one ride I would not rush to do over.

I don't have any secrets of how to face loss in your life—whether 22,000 fellow church members or Mom, Dad, brother, and daughter—and still survive, much less thrive. I have no magic pills, potions, or platitudes that would soothe. All I know is what I know.

Each time I have faced loss, disappointment, or failure, I have been emptied out. I have had nothing.

I have been at the edge. I have imagined the world would be a better place without me in it. I had one of those moments less than a year ago as I stood at the edge of a massive cliff in Bodega Bay with crashing waves on the rocks below.

It was a cliff where, one year earlier, I had stood with Corianna, arms around each other as we shared the awe of looking at the mighty power of the ocean she loved so much. This time, there was no Corianna to hold.

I looked down and saw her in the waves, on the rocks and the surf. I wanted desperately to join her—wherever that might be. It would have been so easy. Had I been there alone, it may have come to pass. But I wasn't. There was someone there to walk up and put his arms around me as I wept. Thank you, Bobby Jo.

Then, much like the cemetery scene in *Steel Magnolias*, tears dissolved into laughter as I realized snot had run down into my mustache and beard and not a tissue to be found. Corianna would have loved it. She and Judson had a thing for snot, boogers, and other body oddities.

How does one move from empty to full? When I was thirty-five, I learned there was no one there but me. Alone in a motel room. Cut off from the life and people I had known. I learned that the words so many had used before were no longer soothing or encouraging.

I had hurt before, but I had always been surrounded by people and lots of advice on what I should hang on to. This was my first time to be on empty. No one to even get me to the next station. Nope, just me, a vibrating bed, a pay-as-you-go television, and a few quarters.

I slept well. For the first time, the heavy millstone of living a lie had been lifted from my shoulders.

Then I got up. Although emotionally bankrupt, I was hungry! I went to the Luby's Cafeteria next to the Motel 6. Right there before my eyes was the answer to my empty stomach at least. Watch out cafeteria ladies with your fetching hairnets, here I come! In previous visits, when the first helper said, "Salad for you?" I asked for my usual lime Jell-O with crushed pineapple and cottage cheese. Next came the entrees. Chicken fried steak with cream gravy, please. Then the sides: black-eyed peas and collard greens. I'd have the jalapeno cornbread to sop up the potlikker from the greens. Finally, I'd top it off with the lemon meringue pie.

Today, rather than all of those Southern delicacies at Luby's, I was going through the Cafeteria Line of Life. My tray was completely empty. I could choose anything I wanted. It had been cleared off. No one was there to tell me what to eat or how to eat it or what blessing I should say before the first bite. No one was there to criticize me for choices during previous visits. I was truly free. The truth had done that—set me free.

The things I put on my tray that day were music, empathy, humor, and truth. The approval I had been seeking all my live was given freely. It was in a simple word from a cashier at the cafeteria of life.

She was standing there in her little waitress outfit (okay, it wasn't little at all). It was well used from years of wear and tear—stained by beets and collard greens. She wasn't special or beautiful in the world's eyes. Truth be told, her eyeliner and shadow were a little excessive for my taste (jealous).

She was not there to judge what was on my tray. She was just there to observe each person as they passed by. She didn't look at me with pity for my losses. She had lived a hard life herself. She didn't need anything from me. She didn't have anything particular she "needed" to say.

I pulled out my Apple Pay, and she said, "Oh, honey, you've already paid for these! There's no charge. And you chose well. Those are my favorites too. I'm just tickled pink. God bless."

But I needed one more thing. I needed to know it all the way from my bald head to my toes and from the bottom of my heart to my befuddled brain. I needed to know that all I needed or would ever need was right there inside me. It wasn't in a book—even the "Good book." It wasn't in the clichés repeated so many times in my youth that they became a part of me. I believed them simply from repetition and because they came from those I trusted. Some call that indoctrination. Others, brainwashing.

No, I needed to know I was enough!

Lo and behold, the cashier at the cafeteria gave it to me with a smile. She said my choices were great, and she blessed me.

Maybe that beautiful, life-worn, hard-working woman who gave me life's riches at no charge was actually God. She wanted nothing, required nothing, and didn't judge my tray. Who knew you could find her at Luby's?

Remember the "I chose my own clothes" button I wanted for Judson? Well, I need a button that reads, "I chose my own life." We do have choices, of course. I am not judging your cafeteria choices if they work for you. But this is my trip through the "line of life."

It is fascinating how when you have nothing left emotionally and you look at your life and the hard lessons learned, you will see grace. In this empty space, you can find faith. You can find hope. And you find love. The Bible does say love is the greatest of all. I am a believer!

It's more than okay to love yourself. And if love is the greatest gift of all, then we will love the least among us. And when we love them, we find ourselves fighting for them, bringing them along, lifting them up as we sing and dance.

Before we know it, we are full again and ready to face the storms—and even dance with them, as Andrew Lippa wrote.

As I close the book (not my life), I don't know where the time went.

It was obviously time to look back and take stock.

I hope I have been a "good and faithful servant" to myself, my family and friends, and to my art.

I don't know if it was "a job well done," but it wasn't for lack of trying!

One burning question: Did I throw the baby out with the dirty bathwater? Certainly the dirty water went. That dirty includes organized religion. It includes the cruelty based on fear and insecurity propagated. Every once in a while, it laps back up around the edges, but it is no longer the core of who I am.

If the baby is a deep sense of the spiritual, then the baby is alive and well. I know I am to find it in myself, in those around me, in the beauty of the world, and in those who have passed who have chosen to surround me with their love. Every day, I wake up, look at the sunrise, and know I have another day to live and wonder how I can make it a great day and make a difference. Perhaps my epitaph will read:

He found himself and gave himself away.
He lived through music and loved beyond measure.

I simply must close with this: You may not remember what you read, but I hope you never forget how it made you feel!

Biography

Tim Seelig is conductor, singer, teacher, and motivational speaker. He is the Artistic Director of both the San Francisco Gay Men's Chorus as well as the National LGBTQ Center for the Arts. Dr. Seelig holds four degrees and has authored seven books and DVDs on choral technique.

His most recent documentary, *Gay Chorus Deep South*, has garnered 35 audience-favorite awards, including the Tribeca Film Festival in NYC where the film debuted. He conducted the Guinness Book of World Record's Longest Choral Concert (20 hours) and carried the Olympic torch as a Community Hero and AIDS activist. He hasn't run since.

Known for his enthusiasm and sense of humor, *Grammy Magazine* noted, "Dr. Seelig takes eclecticism to new heights." He is the proud grandfather of four grand girls: Clara Skye, Eden Mae, Ivy Hope, and Cora Rose.

CPSIA information can be obtained
at www.ICGtesting.com
Printed in the USA
FSHW010324230620
71429FS

9 781635 281064